500 DECLARED

SCYLD BERRY

500 DECLARED

THE JOYS OF COVERING 500 CRICKET TESTS

BLOOMSBURY SPORT
LONDON · OXFORD · NEW YORK · NEW DELHI · SYDNEY

BLOOMSBURY SPORT
Bloomsbury Publishing Plc
50 Bedford Square, London, WC1B 3DP, UK
Bloomsbury Publishing Ireland Limited
29 Earlsfort Terrace, Dublin 2, D02 AY28, Ireland

BLOOMSBURY, BLOOMSBURY SPORT and the Diana logo are trademarks of
Bloomsbury Publishing Plc

First published in Great Britain 2025

Copyright © Scyld Berry, 2025

Scyld Berry has asserted his right under the Copyright, Designs and Patents Act, 1988, to be
identified as Author of this work

For legal purposes the Acknowledgements on p. 259 constitute an extension of this
copyright page

Extract on pp. 248–251 courtesy of Scyld Berry/Telegraph Media Group Holdings 2024

All rights reserved. No part of this publication may be: i) reproduced or transmitted in any form,
electronic or mechanical, including photocopying, recording or by means of any information
storage or retrieval system without prior permission in writing from the publishers; or ii) used
or reproduced in any way for the training, development or operation of artificial intelligence
(AI) technologies, including generative AI technologies. The rights holders expressly reserve this
publication from the text and data mining exception as per Article 4(3) of the Digital Single
Market Directive (EU) 2019/790

Bloomsbury Publishing Plc does not have any control over, or responsibility for, any third-party
websites referred to or in this book. All internet addresses given in this book were correct at the
time of going to press. The author and publisher regret any inconvenience caused if addresses
have changed or sites have ceased to exist, but can accept no responsibility for any such changes

Every reasonable effort has been made to trace copyright holders of material reproduced
in this book, but if any have been inadvertently overlooked the publishers would be glad to
hear from them.

A catalogue record for this book is available from the British Library

Library of Congress Cataloguing-in-Publication data has been applied for

ISBN: HB: 978-1-3994-2586-5; eBook: 978-1-3994-2590-2; ePDF: 978-1-3994-2589-6

2 4 6 8 10 9 7 5 3 1

All interior images courtesy of Getty Images

Typeset in Bembo Std by Deanta Global Publishing Services, Chennai, India
Printed and bound in Great Britain by Clays Ltd, Elcograf S.p.A.

To find out more about our authors and books visit www.bloomsbury.com
and sign up for our newsletters
For product safety related questions contact productsafety@bloomsbury.com

To neighbours
For being such good friends

Looking back, I appreciate what fun England cricket tours were: many an unprintable quip, which stayed on tour. But please note how diligently the notebook is kept. Taken on a flight out of St Vincent on England's 1980–81 tour of the West Indies.

Contents

Foreword   viii

1970s   1
1980s   51
1990s   111
2000s   151
2010s   195
2020s   223

Acknowledgements   259

Foreword

It is hard to believe that any way of life could be happier. Starting in the 1970s, when a champagne lunch could be claimed on expenses in Fleet Street, every day of cricket journalism has been different, and almost every day warm, not only in temperature (except in New Zealand's South Island), but in being packed with comradeship and laughter.

Blessed with this economic foundation, I have watched more than 500 men's Test matches live, in person. That is more than 2000 days, or about six years, trying to convey to readers some of the fun and fascination in watching elite cricketers.

Richie Benaud, late and great, was the first to this landmark. Early in 2003 he calculated, for *Wisden Cricketers' Almanack*, that he had seen 486 Tests. He covered a couple of summers more for Channel Four, and more again for Channel Nine in Australia, and even a few more Tests in England for the *News of the World:* he would slip surreptitiously into a press box with a case in one hand and a sandwich box in the other, so he had no hand free to sign autographs – enduring fame always exposed him to requests. He had, of course, played in 63 of the Tests he had seen.

A photograph taken in 1959, a famously hot summer, shows a scrawny boy sitting in a garden reading the back page of the *Sheffield Telegraph*. From what I can see, Yorkshire were playing a three-day game against the Indians at Bramall Lane, a mile away, so I could hear the roars of the crowd. Yorkshire won the County Championship that summer, and seven times in ten years. What else for first love?

FOREWORD

In the summer of 2025 I became the first to reach the landmark of covering 500 England Tests live. I watched the odd day of Test cricket as a boy, at Headingley in 1969, and Sir Garfield Sobers's last hundred at Lord's in 1973, but I am tightening the definition from 'seeing' to 'covering' or 'attending in a professional capacity'. John Woodcock of *The Times* told me a few years before he died that he had covered the most England Tests, about 400, and another 20 played by other countries, and his judgment I would not question.

In the half-century since my career began, Test cricket has changed enormously. It can still look the same as ever if a spinner is bowling to batsmen trying to defend, but many are the differences, and I will explore them in these pages. As a way of life, cricket journalism has changed, too: it has not quite gone the way of lighthouse-keepers or steam-engine drivers, but the number of full-time cricket journalists working for British newspapers is down to two handfuls. Websites employ a few more, intermittently and often working remotely. This way of life in front of a screen is not quite the same as living out of a suitcase on the road, and on planes and trains. Colombo to Kandy has been my favourite train journey, through rainforest so luxuriant it promises to come through the window at 5 mph on hairpin bends. I will not romanticise though in these pages: one train journey in Pakistan was made memorable by dinner being cooked on an open charcoal stove in a corner of the carriage, before ending up on Lahore Platform 4.

It is a less stable world half a century on. War is no longer Cold, unemployment is high, jobs are for months not life. Here is my justification of this way of life: the need for escapism has increased amid this uncertainty. And what can offer escape like a Test match that lasts all day, and up to five days, and a series that lasts the best part of two months if it is the drama that is the Ashes? My ambition is to share with the reader this joy.

The best choreography in cricket: Dennis Lillee makes an almost irresistible appeal to Dickie Bird during the fourth Test at the Oval in 1975, backed by Rod Marsh, Ian and Greg Chappell. England's Barry Wood somehow escaped.

1970s

Test No. 1
Trent Bridge, June 1973

My debut Test in a professional capacity came when, aged 19, I entered the press box for the first time. It was an afternoon of heat in Nottingham for the opening match between England and New Zealand in a three-match series. Ted Heath was prime minister; television channels numbered three; olives and aubergines did not exist in Britain, definitely not in Sheffield where I was born. Tony Lewis had captained England in India and Pakistan during the previous winter, but Raymond Illingworth had just regained the leadership, as would Harold Wilson the following year: a northern breeze, if not wind.

Although windows were open in the press box, a fug prevailed. An inner sanctum is customarily full of smoke, but this was not incense: almost every journalist smoked cigarettes during or even throughout the day, while a few switched to pipes when deadline approached.

No woman was permitted in this inner sanctum, unless it was for some menial task, like sweeping the floor or trimming the lamps.

No screen, either, of any kind. No television, no replays, no slow motion, no computers, no data, no scorer until Wendy Wimbush was hired for the benefit of the press by the first sponsors of England's Test team in 1978. The essence of a cricket correspondent's job was to watch every single ball.

The high priest of this inner sanctum arose in the front row. He turned towards the novice. I was summoned to approach.

'Come!' E.W. Swanton boomed, softly, for a sanctum must normally be silent. 'You might as well start at the top.'

I walked down the steps of the press box past several rows of journalists. Almost uniformly they were wearing a blue shirt, tweed jacket, tie and dark blue trousers. (As a first-year student, I had a tie for every day of the year that I wore one: none.) I followed behind Mr Swanton along the front row towards the right-hand corner.

'Hello, dear boy.' If John Woodcock did not greet me thus at our first meeting, in a rather high-pitched voice, he would do so in following decades. He was sitting in the far right-hand corner because he could only hear through his left ear, and because there he could stretch out his right leg which had hobbled him since septic arthritis in childhood.

This introduction sounded like self-deprecation on the part of E.W.S.: here was John Woodcock, of *The Times*, at the top. In hindsight I see that E.W.S., whose seat was next to Wooders, expected this inference to be drawn: 'the top' consisted of a duopoly, *The Times* and *The Daily Telegraph*, equally eminent.

England were already batting in their second innings. A hail of wickets had fallen on the opening day and second morning. On the second afternoon, after 24 wickets had gone down, a partnership was growing between Dennis Amiss and Tony Greig, both wearing their England caps. Trent Bridge was flattening out, as it had done since Victorian times, into one of the friendliest featherbeds: the Gunn family had scored more than 80,000 first-class runs for Nottinghamshire, using the bats they made in the city with Moore.

Dismissed, I returned to the back row, to await orders. My job was to be E.W. Swanton's 'amanuensis'. Not his 'secretary' – no, goodness me, nothing so vulgar as that. A secretary was what Don Mosey would parade when trying to keep up with the Old Etonians of *Test Match Special*, Brian Johnston and Henry Blofeld: 'The Alderman', based at BBC Manchester, would announce that he would be bringing 'his secretary' to the Headingley Test. No, I was to be the 'amanuensis' of E.W.S., the latest in a long line which included Peter West and Daphne, Mrs Benaud-to-be. A suspiciously long line, I should have realised, but I was young, naive, and ready to give anything in cricket a go.

Seated at the back of the press box, I scanned the rows for John Arlott. He and Brian Johnston were as Len Hutton and

Denis Compton had been: friendlyish rivals to be number one in the nation's affection. When I wrote in *The Observer* about Arlott's retirement in 1980, after shadowing him for a day at Lord's, I likened him to Beethoven; Johnston, lighter and fizzier, to Mozart. Arlott had stolen a march during this Test against New Zealand. Richard Hadlee, to become the highest Test wicket-taker and duly knighted, was making his second Test appearance in England, and prompted one of Arlott's immortal phrases. On *TMS* commentary, deep-throated, he had said that Hadlee started his run-up 'like Groucho Marx chasing a waitress.'

When the great broadcaster entered, he sat down at his desk, beside the aisle, not in the front row. He breathed heavily; with a handkerchief he mopped his brow. A bottle of wine, though not his typewriter, had been opened. I craned and strained: a red but the label was not visible. A Châteauneuf du Pape 1947 or possibly '48? It proved, on closer inspection, to be a new brand sold by supermarkets, called Nicholas, at 99p a bottle.

In tune with post-war practice, this Test had started on a Thursday, but I could not arrive until the second afternoon. I had to take the last of my first-year exams on the Friday morning, before catching the next train from Cambridge to Nottingham. At least I was still in time to perform the two most sacred duties of the amanuensis once deadline approached.

This is the Faustus moment. All day the press box indulges in food and drink, wit and repartee. Eventually 5 p.m. approaches, then 6, and lo, Mephistopheles comes to claim your soul. The sheets of paper remain stubbornly blank, no word written, except the journalist's name and his venue. The deadline for first editions is 7 p.m., as every letter must be set in metal, if not stone. Do not look into the void, Dr Faust: that way lies writer's block, if you think of a hole in the newspaper, the blank half-page where the report of this Test match should be. Mephistopheles will seize your soul if you do not write a thousand words in the next hour.

The previous winter E.W. Swanton – 'Jim' only to his equals, whom he deemed to be few – had addressed the Cambridge University Cricket Society. In the bar afterwards I had dared to ask what he thought about Kenneth Weekes of West Indies. Asking about the Barbadian Everton Weekes would have been the straightforward question: Sir Everton, as he was to become, had played for E.W. Swanton's own XI in the West Indies, in those off-seasons when a journalist would raise a touring team, rather than an Indian industrialist intent on his own T20 franchise.

I had asked about Kenneth Weekes, a left-handed batsman, no relation, far more obscure; yet he had played an innings which would today be termed 'an outlier'. In the Oval Test of 1939, Weekes's 137 in 135 minutes (balls were often not recorded in those days) had been, in my reading, the first outstanding example of West Indian hitting on the international stage (George Headley had never felt free to attack, Learie Constantine never came off in Tests). Or even, perhaps, of uncoached batting since Weekes, a black Jamaican, had not grown up like the batsmen of England, Australia and South Africa. When England took the second new ball, Weekes hit England's opening bowler Reg Perks for four consecutive fours. In the first four overs of the second ball it was mainly Weekes who hit 43 runs. One caveat: this was the only season, 1939, when English cricket used the eight-ball over. Still, here was a run-rate that Test cricket was not to behold again for half a century or more, and this was only Weekes's second Test and, because of the war, his last. I thought of him working as a nurse in Brooklyn in his years after cricket, before he died in New York in 1998, no Indian Premier League contract to enrich him.

'Aaah, "Bam-Bam" Weekes!' E.W.S. boomed at the bar. I liked the onomatopoeia of this nickname: Bam-Bam, on song, must have played a shot a ball. No further recollection of Weekes was forthcoming. Everyone in the Oval press box in August 1939 must have been distracted, I suppose, or should have been.

A letter arrived a couple of weeks later from Delf House, Sandwich. Would I care to take up the post of amanuensis in the coming summer? *The Daily Telegraph* would provide my hotel room, while E.W.S. himself would drive me to most matches and pay £50 per week for the various duties, like answering his readers' letters.

Time for the first of the two sacred duties had arrived: to phone in E.W.S.'s match report to the *Telegraph*'s copytakers in London. Nothing smacked of manual labour like a typewriter on his desk: he and Wooders wrote their reports in longhand. Wooders stooped to dictate his own copy, using the hired telephone on his desk, to *The Times*. I was to withdraw to one of the phone booths at the back of the press box, dial 0 for the operator, transfer the charges to the *Telegraph* switchboard, and dictate to a copytaker word by word. At the end of each paragraph I was to say 'point, par'. In the *Telegraph*'s house style it was all but mandatory for a paragraph to consist of no more than one sentence.

The first page of holy writ was dictated down the phone line without incident. England – in the early summer of 1973 – had never lost a cricket match against New Zealand. The control of professionals over amateurs had been reasserted in the course of day two: England, thanks to Alan Knott, converted their overnight 216 for nine into 250, then dismissed New Zealand for 97. By the close of this second day, after England had lost four wickets for 24 at the start of their second innings, Dennis Amiss and Tony Greig were embarked upon centuries.

On the second page we came to the incident, during England's second-innings stumble, when Geoffrey Boycott did not run a partner out but was, himself, run out. On the radio E.W.S. did not pronounce his surname as others did: he said 'Boycutt', as he had been wont to say Denis 'Cumpton'. (Freud would have called it 'the narcissism of small difference'.) Boycott, going for a single, had been sent back by Amiss, belatedly. In Swanton's summation, this was 'a case of the biter bit.'

Or was this highly relevant word, written in longhand, actually 'biter'? I stared in the booth's gloom. Should I ask the copytaker to hang on, put down the phone and check with E.W.S., or would that be a first fatal sign of weakness? Furthermore, should it not be 'a case of the biter bitten' rather than bit? Should I, on the day of my initiation, go and tell the high priest that his scripture was ungrammatical? Or was the word something else, rhyming with biter, which several Southern amateurs might have used of a Northern pro like Boycott?

I ploughed on, though it might have been my grave. First lesson of journalism: if you do not like the heat, stay out of the kitchen. (Mistakes in my university exams would be noticed by a single person, to be discussed quietly after a long vacation.)

After 20 or so minutes of dictation, I returned the sheaf to E.W.S. Six o'clock was fast approaching: time for the second major task. I had to find sufficient ice to put into his hip flask that it would not melt in his whisky before his summary of the day's play on *TMS*. This was the communion wine.

Water by the bottle and flask has become the staple drink of press boxes around the cricket world. Not then. A press box at a Test ground in England had its own bar reserved for journalists. They did not eat much during the day, a sandwich or two, but they smoked and drank pints of bitter, often graduating to spirits in the search for inspiration. This press-box bar at Trent Bridge did not have any ice! A bar on the ground floor of another stand saved me. Woe betide the Test-match venue which did not provide ice.

We walked around the ground from the Radcliffe Road End to the pavilion side, and climbed steps and scaffolding. Test matches in the era before professionalisation – before Kerry Packer's World Series Cricket – would wind down in the final hour of a day. Tired bowlers, unmonitored by speed guns, would conserve lingering energies for the morrow. Batsmen would play for stumps; the nightwatchman who ventured a shot let his whole side down. Match reports could therefore be composed and filed before the close without much risk of a rewrite, or anything more than the insertion of the close-of-play score.

E.W.S. could compose his thoughts, drink and gargle, before listeners to Radio Three heard the close-of-play summary on *Test Match Special*, delivered in tones not far behind Churchill's for gravitas.

'It has been an absorbing day's play and I shall start by reading the card. Boycutt, run out...'

A1, June 1973

Was E.W. Swanton too insensitive, or I too sensitive? He was driving south towards Sandwich, while I sat in the front passenger seat, after the Trent Bridge Test. He asked me about my mother, who had died suddenly six years before. England, emotionally, was still Victorian and stiff upper lip. I had not talked about this subject to a single person since, and never did, until I trusted a girlfriend sufficiently.

Paternalistic and pompous, even in the eyes of his friends, E.W.S. never had children himself. He might have been trying to be kind when he asked about my mother, but the scars were too raw. He said something on stiff-upper-lip lines: never mind – that might even have been his actual phrase – and carry on. I was incensed. As soon as I got home I wrote a letter of resignation. He wrote back, demanding the return of readers' letters which had yet to be answered and signed.

Bam, bam. After eight days as E.W. Swanton's 'amanuensis', I was gone.

Test No. 2

Lord's, June 1977

My second Test in a professional capacity, as a journalist in my own right, came four years after the false start. This interim saw the beginning of the biggest change in the history of cricket since the legalisation of over-arm bowling in 1835, bigger even than the later advances in technology for umpires.

Ironically, as we can see in retrospect, it was an unintended consequence.

Mike Brearley had experienced, at first hand (or head), West Indian fast bowling on their tour of England in 1976. Four shocks have convulsed English cricket, each time upon realising that it has fallen behind the pace. White Australia's first visit in 1878 unleashed the Demon Spofforth; in 1921, England faced – or flinched from – two fast bowlers working as a pair for the first time, Jack Gregory and Ted McDonald; the third shock was the post-war rockets of Ray Lindwall and Keith Miller; and the fourth was delivered by Andy Roberts and Michael Holding. Brearley, after playing in the first two Tests of 1976, talked to Tony Greig and visited a company in Nottingham which manufactured skull protectors for children suffering from epilepsy who were in danger of damaging their heads during a fit. (Greig suffered from epilepsy; in those days, before social media, the press had agreed not to touch the story when he had a fit on tour.)

A previous attempt at protecting a batsman's head had been made by the wife of another Middlesex and England player, Elias or 'Patsy' Hendren, in the 1930s when Bodyline sprang up. Mrs Hendren sewed some towelling into the cap of her compulsive hooker of a husband. A similar skull protector fitted inside Brearley's cap. 'I wore the little skull cap against Australia in 1977 and thought they would be scornful,' Brearley recalled in an email for this book. 'But they weren't, and merely thought the helmet had to be more substantial. Within a few months everyone except Viv [Richards] was wearing one.'

Helmets were designed to protect heads against fast bowling. The unintended consequence, as we can now see, was that it made batsmen fearless when facing all sorts of bowling, and especially spin. My interpretation of the written and anecdotal evidence before helmets is that just as many injuries occurred when the ball flew off the top edge of bats as from direct hits to the head. This fear of a top edge into the teeth was what stopped batsmen sweeping balls that were not heading down leg side – until the arrival of helmets equipped with grilles or visors. The survival instinct will simply not allow an unprotected head to get behind the line of a hard ball and keep the eyes open while sweeping or reverse-sweeping, ramping or reverse-ramping, scooping (my definition of a scoop is a ramp with some follow-through) or reverse-scooping.

Gradually from 1977, rapidly after T20 was introduced in 2003, batsmen tried all manner of shots with a bat at any angle they wished. Ryan Campbell of Western Australia and Tillakaratne Dilshan of Sri Lanka were pioneers who had millions of imitators, like a boy in the nets at King's College Taunton; Jos Buttler had grown up wielding a tennis racket from the age of two while his mother was playing at her club in Wedmore.

In that Trent Bridge Test of 1973, New Zealand had been set 479 to win. They fell short by 38 runs. England's two spinners, Ray Illingworth and Norman Gifford, bowled 38 overs for only 66 runs, which allowed the three pace bowlers a long breather between spells. Had the New Zealand batsmen worn helmets and felt emboldened to sweep balls that pitched straight or outside off stump (not simply going down leg side), they might have got closer to their target and won – or else they might have been caught off mishits and top edges and fallen shorter. For certain, the result would have come more quickly than the fifth afternoon, and New Zealand would not have batted for all of 188.1 overs – of which 51 were maidens – to score 440.

In the entire five-Test Ashes series of 2023 in England, Australia bowled 34 maiden overs. Of those, their spinners bowled four. Such was the impact of the helmet.

I climbed back on the bicycle slowly, making sure the bike was mine. I wrote a few articles for cricket magazines, paid and unpaid, sufficient to assemble a few cuttings. In the spring of 1976, with a view to the perfect vacation job after finals, I wrote to The Observer and asked if I could write about cricket for them. A brief, formal letter of reply said no. The one requirement to become a journalist is the desire to become a journalist, and The Observer was still the home of the finest writing in journalism: Hugh McIlvanney on boxing and football, Clive James on television, Neal Ascherson on eastern Europe, Eric Newby on travel, Anthony Burgess on newly published books, all masters of their subject, or Michael Davie – Journalist of the Year – on anything in his Notebook. I wrote a second time, saying that when Australia toured the next summer I would stand in a net facing Dennis Lillee without a box if they didn't give me an opportunity. Invited to the Observer offices, I could afford the train fare but decided to save on the underground: on a Tube map Blackfriars did not look far from Liverpool Street. The sports editor, Geoffrey Nicholson, took pity on a late, sweaty, dishevelled student and took him to the pub next door. A week later a letter arrived, asking if I would report on Saturday's game between Cambridge University and the county champions Leicestershire – and would I also care to write a feature? Yes I would, never mind finals next month. Alastair Hignell, England's rugby full-back, had just returned from Cambridge's rugby tour of Japan and had switched with seamless success to batting at Fenner's. For the headline Geoffrey, bless him, echoed Christopher Isherwood's novel Mr Norris Changes Trains with Mr Hignell Changes Boots. A witty headline always makes the piece seem better. This was the start of a pleasant vacation job; essentially it still is.

Harrogate, August 1977
I was bowling to Ian Chappell. He had retired a few months earlier as Australia's Test captain, but had been brought back by Kerry Packer to head up Australia's World Series Cricket team. Now here he was, at a press match in Harrogate in the middle of the 1977 Ashes series, chipping a return catch straight back to me.

This was the time when international cricket was rent asunder, as never before and as never since, because the Indian Premier League and its T20 imitators have taken over the calendar gradually, not overnight as Packer did. The Headingley Test was staged in the vortex of these events; and on its rest day, the Sunday, a media game between England and Australia was played. The Australian media XI featured not only journalists but Ian Chappell, who was keeping his hand in, and Packer himself, built like an elephant though less mobile in the field (I suppose he qualified for selection, owning half of Australia's newspapers). Another non-journalist in their ranks was David Lord, the agent of Jeff Thomson, who alone of Australia's best cricketers had not – yet – joined WSC.

Test cricket was therefore on the verge of being reduced to Second XIs representing Australia and West Indies, and much-weakened teams representing England and Pakistan. Nobody cared much about New Zealand, South Africa were banned, Sri Lanka and Zimbabwe yet to be given Test status, which left only India intact as their players were controlled by their board. At this stage in the summer of 1977, there was no certainty that both sides – the official boards and Packer's WSC – would ever climb back into bed together (it took two years for the Australian board to concede). With the champagne barely dry on the lips of those who had celebrated the Centenary Test in Melbourne five months earlier, Test cricket was splitting apart.

Battle lines were clearing. The Old School hated Packer as the serpent in Eden: cricketers should feel honoured to represent their country and grateful for any money they were given (not earned). The New School thought: 'Elite athletes are entitled to monetise their talent – nobody is going to look after them in their old age.' I noticed that the major critics of cricketers taking World Series money were, themselves, affluent.

Chappelli (being Chappell I.M.) had meanwhile played one amazing shot off my bowling, even though he had scored no more than seven not out. I haven't seen it more than half-a-dozen times since. A filthy leg-break was heading down the leg side when he caught up with it and, with an almost vertical bat, paddled it to the vacant fine-leg boundary. One of my teammates said: 'Compo used to play that shot.' Modern batsmen, helmeted, would have slog-swept it for six.

I tried again, a straighter leg-break. Harrogate had a slow, soggy pitch. A decade earlier Yorkshire had clinched the Championship there, a couple of times, with their finger-spinners. And when Chappelli chipped it straight back at me, waist height, I dropped it. For all eternity, the scorebook should have read: I.M. Chappell c and b Berry 7.

Well, how could I be expected to watch the ball when the batsman was one of Australia's finest and certainly Australia's bravest in the pre-helmet era? (Chappelli hooked everything until Packer ordered him to wear a helmet, as he did not want his captain in hospital.) Besides, the umpire at my end was Jack Fingleton, not only Australia's finest cricket writer to that point but the scorer of four centuries in consecutive Tests: try handing your sweater to him to hold without being distracted. Wearing an old-fashioned white umpire's coat, Fingo was actually as good as gold. Later on that tour he was talking about visiting Cairns when I asked him cheekily if that was where the international film festival was held. His reply reflected his salty, not peppery, nature. Then, at the end of my spell of 7–0–53–1 (my only wicket was Lord, top-edging a pull and caught by Henry Blofeld at midwicket), any feather would have knocked me over when Fingo said my bowling action – a windmillish delivery off a longish run-up – reminded him of Bill O'Reilly.

Chappelli was to become cricket's Elder Statesman. When *The Sunday Telegraph* signed him as a columnist, at the same time as Mike Atherton and Nasser Hussain, my job was to bring them together over dinner and ask them questions about the ongoing or just-concluded series. What was probably the first round table in cricket if not sports journalism – I am fairly sure it had not been tried before – occurred in 1980, when

I submitted written questions to Sir Leonard Hutton, Jack Fingleton and Bobby Simpson, who were *Observer* columnists, about cricket issues of the day. *The Sunday Telegraph*, having more resources, could bring their columnists together to exchange views over a meal. Chappelli would set all patriotism aside and, after England had been wiped out yet again by Australia, he would put one metaphorical arm around Atherton and his other around Nasser, and urge them not to be beaten before the start, to forget their scarring and attack the world Test champions as if they were human. Specifically, in Australia, this meant preparing for an Ashes series by playing against and beating State sides, not only to acclimatise but to cause doubt in home ranks. This is what Andrew Strauss succeeded in doing in 2010–11. England have never undertaken that form of preparation since; and, before 2024–25, did not win another Test match in Australia.

Cricket's eternal verities, the fundamentals, Chappelli told them to you straight. No fear nor favour, never one-eyed. The first job of cricket's administrators? To maintain the balance between bat and ball, he said. Secondly, learn how to bat on bouncy pitches, then you can always adjust to lower ones, never the other way round. (See Pakistan's litany of batting failures in Australia, and England's too for that matter.) Of English cricketers, Chappelli respected Yorkshiremen most. On their 1968 tour of England, he said, the Australians viewed their game against Yorkshire at Bramall Lane as the sixth Test. They drew the Test series 1–1, and lost to Yorkshire by an innings.

After a round table dinner in Adelaide, we were reeling back through city centre streets. I could see why Chappelli had left his native Adelaide: it is the stuffiest of Australian cities (John Woodcock used to say the Adelaide Club refused to stock Australian wine until the 1950s). An indigenous man, sitting on the pavement, probably more sober than we were but down and out, hailed Chappelli. Like the Ancient Mariner, he probably accosted us all, not 'one in three'; but Chappelli was the one who stopped, listened, and talked to, or rather with, him.

Rawalpindi, November 1977

On my first England tour, to Pakistan in 1977–78, in the context of the times, it was not strange that I should umpire an England game, bowl in their nets, and be detailed by the England captain to entertain his wife.

One agency, George Wareham Travel, booked players and journalists alike on the same domestic flights, on the same bus to the airport (though fortunately not the same early bus to the ground on match-day mornings), and in the same hotels wherever possible. It was not possible in Lyallpur, the Manchester of Pakistan, or Faisalabad as it had just been renamed. Players were lucky to be accommodated in a basic company guest house, journalists were billeted in Ray's Hotel. 'Ray's a laugh,' one of us said (punning is one of our finest attributes). But the one telephone in the crumbling concrete pile seldom worked; the one shower offered a mix of brown water and rodents; and every driver celebrated his dawn departure from Faisalabad – and I can understand why he wanted to celebrate – by playing on his horn some high-pitched tunes outside our dust-encrusted windows.

England had arrived in Pakistan after winning the 1977 Ashes 3–0. Brearley had selected five bowlers and always had the Australians on a leash: in the first four Tests their highest total was 309. In Pakistan he asked me to help entertain his then wife, Ginger, an American who had flown in from Berkeley, California, a graduate of philosophy, not interested in cricket. Who was I to say no? A diplomatic AND journalistic assignment on my first England tour: a very diplomatic one.

I arrived ten days in advance of England's touring party, in order to travel to places which we would not otherwise visit, including one which must remain forever unique. I checked into what was to be the team hotel, the Pearl Continental in Rawalpindi, and went to the nearby airport to buy a ticket to Chitral. It could only be an open ticket: at dawn every morning the PIA crew had to weigh up whether it was safe to fly their Fokker Friendship into the Karakoram range.

Next morning, no luck. Flight cancelled. I returned to the Pearl. Ahead of England's arrival, security men were guarding every entrance: sallow men who lived in shadow, always unsmiling and moustached. The hotel had, and still has, a sort of honeycomb in front of every bedroom window to keep out direct sunlight. Corridors were dark – power cuts were so frequent the hotel needed its own generator – and dank, as if the carpets had not been fully dried after shampooing. The air-conditioning unit in your room rattled. The hotel's PA system played tapes of lute or sitar music too slowly, as if there was not enough electricity. That vile invention, the chicken sausage, stared balefully back at you at breakfast. A swimming pool was too cold in November; and, of course, under the rule of General Zia ul-Haq, there was no bar. I had spent a year in Kuwait, and another in North Yemen, so I knew what Islam felt like, but this was different. Religion did not rule Pakistan, the army did. Frequent roadblocks are a government's official admission of not being in control of its people.

I walked half a mile down the Grand Trunk Road to the cricket ground where England were to play their opening warm-up game. On the other side of the GTR stood the Raj's hotel for civilians in town, Flashman's, and the steepled St Paul's, where the Church of Scotland ministered unto many Scots soldiers. The half-mile between the Pearl hotel and the 'Pindi club ground was occupied by the Pakistan army headquarters, barricaded behind barbed wire, which the British had built for their Northern Command. In 1947 their successors had moved in and carried on seamlessly: it was the only institution in Pakistan that fully functioned, not least because the army and Inter-Services Intelligence appropriated over half the country's entire budget for themselves. (When England toured Pakistan in the 1950s and 1960s, they were flown to fixtures in military aircraft.) Most of the pittance left for health and secular education went into ministers' pockets, hence the need for Abdul Sattar Edhi, hailed as the greatest humanitarian of the 20th century, whose charity still runs all Pakistan's ambulances.

On taking control of India, Jawaharlal Nehru had broken the power of the big landowners so they did not dominate politics. He sent the army back to barracks, to be placated with pensions, and he used American aid to build Institutes of Technology in the main cities, founts of learning which, in return, have produced the majority of CEOs in Silicon Valley. Pakistan made none of these reforms (Muhammad Ali Jinnah, the country's first leader, was too sick, even if he had wanted to). The Americans, instead, built air bases in Pakistan and used the country as an ally against India, Russia and China. Thus it remains, as Imran Khan was to find out when he became prime minister – seeking to normalise relations with Pakistan's neighbours landed him in prison.

Pakistan was the country I first toured: it is, therefore, like a first love. But it makes you feel as though there is a ceiling which, whatever your height, is six inches lower than your head. It inhibits personal growth and private enterprise. Unless you emigrate, the army will keep you under control: if you do not obey, watch your family disappear. It is a sterile society wherein men spend their time with men, women with women, without cross-fertilisation. A former long-term *Times* correspondent in Pakistan, Anatol Lieven, wrote in his book *Pakistan: A Hard Country* about 'the same strategy that all the rulers of Pakistan have sooner or later adopted: a combination of reliance on the state bureaucracy, army and police with handing out state patronage to the rural and urban elites in order to win their support.'

Next morning, the flight to Chitral allowed me to escape to the hills. I was one of about a dozen, all male, passengers: some wore Chitrali caps made of yak wool, which can be rolled down to protect your whole head from icy blasts, a cap-cum-snood. I sat on the wooden verandah of the Chitral Inn (50p per night) and drank the scenery in until drunk: the Chitral river, no longer swollen by spring's snowmelt, leaping like salmon down towards the five rivers of Punjab, dark scree slopes crowned by pure white peaks, the background of an ever-speckless sky.

Colonel Durand had built Chitral fort in the 1890s, but the hand of colonisation had not stifled local life. Almost nobody spoke English; if one did, he was liable to say 'we are a simple people.' And so they were, then. This was close to Shangri-La (in the Hunza Valley I went to a village in 2006 where a woman was said to remember Durand, in which case she was over 110). The Soviet Union had not invaded Afghanistan, so the drug trade from there to Karachi via police roadblocks had yet to corrupt Pakistan. To the left, from my verandah, a valley led to the Kafir Kalash. I am a sucker for green eyes, like theirs, but this was November, the snows were coming, passes would be cut off and flights cease. As it was my first tour, I thought it wiser not to try and reach the supposed descendants of Alexander's army. Not a good career move to have to send a telegram to *The Observer*: 'Sorry, cut off by snow for winter in Karakoram. Will file April.'

To return to the plains, I bought a seat in the back of an open four-wheel drive which left Chitral at dawn to cross the Lowari Pass at 10,000 feet: except that a 'seat' was about one square foot of space, so while the hill-men squatted and huddled, I stood hanging on to the rail at the back. The shadows of the peak were freezing until the sun, rising above the snow-line, coaxed the temperature up to zero: no gloves, but at least I had bought a Chitrali cap. We stopped in a dismal roadside town called Dir – bottles of fizz, old tyres, rubbish – but by evening I had made it to Swat, and a wood fire in my bedroom, where I tried in vain to recall the Raj's limerick about the ruler: 'There was a young Akand of Swat.' Like Kashmir, Swat could have become one of the world's prime tourist destinations: ski slopes in winter, Alpine walking/running/climbing in summer.

I carried on into the plains by car, train and plane to Dera Ismail Khan in Punjab. In their inaugural first-class match in 1964, DI Khan (as it was abbreviated) were not simply defeated by Railways: after declaring at 910 for six, Railways dismissed DI Khan for 32 and, in their less successful second innings, 27. For losing by an innings and 851 runs, and bringing shame on the game, DI Khan had their first-class status suspended for many years by the Pakistan board. I visited 13 years later, to the week, after their defeat (you could not even say they had come second). I checked into the Dak bungalow, built for postmen to stay overnight, and in a nearby village tracked down DI Khan's opening bowler, Inayatullah. It was difficult to tell – he did not speak English or Urdu but the local language of Saraiki and we communicated through an interpreter – but I think he was still embarrassed. He had kept going for 59 overs, as DI Khan had only three main bowlers, and taken one wicket for 279. He smiled only at the memory of his opening partner, an army man, walking back to his mark in Lahore, who then kept on walking until he hid behind the sightscreen, pretending to run away. I asked for Inayatullah's autograph, the only one I have requested for myself. On the day-long train journey back to Rawalpindi, I wrote up this story, and was later told a copy of *The Observer* made its way into England's dressing-room during the tour-opener and was deemed amusing.

When players and press alike were invited to the British High Commission in Islamabad for a reception at the start of the tour, England manager Ken Barrington headed the queue of guests to be presented to the High Commissioner, followed by the England captain Mike Brearley. *The Times* and *Telegraph* correspondents followed, then other ranks of cricketers and journalists.

Everything that happened on tour stayed exactly there; names were never to be named, no source revealed. The horse's mouth could tell you, in confidence, that a teammate was carrying an injury, or that a pitch was two-paced: binoculars could tell you it looked patchy, but only the players themselves know if it is two-paced and impedes strokeplay.

This High Commission party was attended by several female secretaries, British subjects flown to Islamabad on assignment from the UK, not local staff. Bottles were drained in the knowledge that dry evenings lay ahead; and not every secretary was obsessed with sportsmen.

One player was so smitten he took a day out from the tour, without permission, to fly from Peshawar to Islamabad and back again, when supposed to be acting as 12th man. He told me of his adventure while we sat at the back of the bus to an airport, in complete confidence. I was allowed to bowl in the nets at Hyderabad on the rest day of the second Test: half the ground was covered in sand, not grass, so the nets allowed my leg-breaks to grip for once. I was bowling against tailenders and squad members not involved in the Test, but still. And as it happened on tour, I cannot name the batsman I effectively dismissed twice in three balls. This is the way it was. It was one party.

One long party.

Short of match practice, England squeezed in a game against a club side in Lahore. Not any old side: Lahore Gymkhana, the most pukka club in the country. They owned the Gymkhana ground built by the Raj in Lawrence Gardens, modelled on the Parks at Oxford, including the pavilion, but warmer, leafier, more luxuriant. Here Pakistan had played their first Test in Lahore, before their board could afford a concrete stadium.

I walked to the ground at lunchtime from Lahore's Pearl Continental. No, I had not been idle that morning: over coffee in the hotel I had been trying to explain to Ginger the difference between Sunnis, the majority sect in Pakistan, and Shi'is. Captain's orders! To be obeyed. On arriving at the Bagh-i-Jinnah (or Jinnah Gardens as it has been renamed), the pavilion was in uproar. In what was intended to be a practice game, Geoffrey Boycott had batted through most of, if not the entire, innings to score a hundred. Younger batsmen desperate for a hit, like Mike Gatting, Graham Roope and Brian Rose, did not get the practice they needed. So far as Boycott was concerned, what England needed most was for him to be in form for the Tests. Any other concerns were secondary.

For some reason, one of the two local umpires had seen enough and left. I volunteered for the vacancy. Qualifications? Well, I'd stood for a bit in a few club games. John Lever was now handing me his MCC sweater (this was the first England tour when their official title was England, but they still wore MCC colours); he was running in to bowl against Lahore Gymkhana's right-handed opener, the new ball swung in and pinned his half-forward front pad right in front. The England fielders appealed, and I was about to raise my finger when J.K. spun round and shook his head while walking back to his mark. He was not appealing; he was being chivalrous, although this Gymkhana batsman was soon at home once the ball stopped swinging and smacked 30 or 40.

First-change bowler at the Pavilion (my) End was Phil Edmonds. He asked me to stand back so he could run between umpire and stumps. I wondered if Wilfred Rhodes or Hedley Verity was any better equipped, physically, to bowl left-arm orthodox? Edmonds had the strength, height, action and spin, but he could get bored and send down a wrist-spinner, which would infuriate Brearley when it was pulled for four. Of Edmonds's successors, only Monty Panesar at his best was lither or whippier or had more bounce. Edmonds did not entirely fulfil his talent after taking five for 28 against Australia on his Test debut in 1975, although his economy was a key to England winning the 1984–85 series in India and the 1986–87 Ashes. His figures would have improved if he had mopped up naive batsmen in Australia's second XI in 1978–79, but Brearley preferred to blend Geoff Miller's all-round steadiness with John Emburey.

The original relationship between England's touring cricketers and the written press (no other media representatives until radio commentators began to tour after the Second World War) appears to have been cordial, if guarded. A letter home by the England captain of the 1882–83 tour to Australia, the Honourable Ivo Bligh, refers to the only journalist accompanying his party, Martin Cobbett of the *Sportsman*, as 'a good specimen for the class luckily for us.' Feelings were reciprocated. In his memoirs, *Sporting Notions*, Cobbett referred to Bligh, who became Lord Darnley, as 'a model cricketer, game to do any mortal thing to make sport and play any part – high, middling, or humble.' Cobbett was given a game when Bligh's team were one short in Tasmania.

I had interviewed Brearley before my first Test series. Jack Fingleton said he had happily written for newspapers in Scotland, so I went to the grand Edinburgh offices of *The Scotsman* in September 1976, with a gradually expanding cuttings book and the hope of covering the 1977 Ashes when not required by *The Observer*, for whom Tony Pawson was the chief cricket correspondent. As Middlesex were about to be crowned county champions, the sports editor Ian Wood challenged me to secure an interview with their captain Mike Brearley and write it up.

The scene at Lord's was a preview of the film the *Full Monty*, where the unemployed manager is trying to focus on the people interviewing him for a new job while a mate makes faces through the window behind them. Brearley sat in state in the home dressing-room, I at his feet, while one of his fast bowlers was standing behind him and slowly turning the pages of a porn magazine. Anything Brearley said, however, would have made a decent feature.

We were to have some witty exchanges on tour, and Brears came to my wedding – and ultimately we were able to compare notes on having Indian wives. Once some England players were waiting in a Melbourne hotel lobby when a group of Thai Airways hostesses checked in and fluttered towards the lifts. 'Have you ever been tongue-tied?' I asked Brears. If only for a few moments, he was.

Ever since, while on tour, I have tried to live in the country where I am. If I switch on the television in my room, I watch the local news. I do not follow what is happening in Britain unless a story makes international news in the country where I am. Living in the present, and the actual place, makes compartmentalising easier. I try not to think of home until I speak to my family on the phone. This is the hardest part of the job, if you can call it so.

Pakistan, December 1977
It was so long ago that Test cricket in Pakistan consisted of eight-ball overs, while England's one-day internationals consisted of

35 eight-ball overs per side. Eight balls in an over is too many, in my view, just as five is too few.

England won their inaugural Test in Pakistan in 1961–62, and no other there in the rest of the 20th century. Hours of daylight in winter in Pakistan are almost as short as in England; sunlight in cities is dulled by the smoke of cooking fires. Test-match days were limited to five and a half hours, and the idea of a minimum over-rate was not yet a twinkle in the eyes of the ICC. In the first Test I covered overseas, the overall scoring-rate was 31 runs per hour. Pakistan's priority under a military government was saving face, England were content with a draw. The result of a cricket series is often the result which both sides consider their second-best option.

Britain's prime minister Jim Callaghan met General Zia ul-Haq during the one-day international at the Gaddafi Stadium in Lahore. These ODIs were interspersed between Tests, not designed for separate squads. Supporters of Benazir Bhutto, whose father had been deposed as president by a military coup, had packed the stadium for the earlier Test match. They were labelled 'volatile', as if by nature, when they were seizing a rare opportunity to demonstrate to foreign media their distaste for unelected dictators.

Days at the cricket crawled. Pakistan's opening batsman Mudassar Nazar set the tone in Lahore by reaching his hundred in 557 minutes, to this day the slowest in any Test. He scored 114 in almost 10 hours, whereupon Geoffrey Boycott ran down the pitch to the first ball of England's reply and smashed it over the bowler's head for six. No. He could have, but he didn't. Boycott's 63 consumed 267 balls and almost six hours. The only drama was political demonstration. That Britain had left India so precipitously in 1947, making unhappy consequences inevitable, had no part in the conversation.

We were sitting beside the runway at Hyderabad airport, or landing strip, after the second Test. A hut sat beside the tarmac, along with a few benches for passengers awaiting a plane. England had been skittled in their first innings by the most passionate bowler I have seen when his dander was up: Abdul Qadir (Dale

Steyn kept calm by comparison). But Boycott and Brearley, vice-captain and captain, had kept Qadir at bay on the final day until shortly before the close when Brearley had got out for 74. All the batsmen I had bowled into form in the nets were unrequired.

'I got obsessed with the concept of the purity of the not out,' Brearley philosophised. Boycott had got obsessed with scoring a Test century, unbeaten. This was his favourite milieu: the scope to bat all day, without any need to take any risk (the target set by Pakistan's declaration was 344, unimaginable then, even though the 80-odd overs consisted of eight balls). Boycott paced himself perfectly, not to knock off the target but to reach his century by the close. As the game drifted to a draw (14 out of 15 Tests in succession between England and Pakistan were draws), while everybody else was shutting down, Boycott was on fire. In the first three innings of Tests, he averaged less than 48; in the fourth innings he averaged 58. He was England's all-time master at batting out for a draw.

The single reason why England asked for the extra half hour at the end of the second Test was not because a result was in prospect, but so that Boycott could reach three figures (another rule which the ICC was forced to alter, so there had to be the prospect of a result in order to claim extra time). By the end of the third Test, everyone was so stultified by the series it was called off with an hour to go. Explaining to Ginger why a cricket match could end in a draw after five whole days was almost as challenging as watching one.

England's captain by then was Boycott. The only time I saw him give his wicket away was in the practice game before the Karachi Test. Brearley's arm had been broken by a ball that kicked from the Karachi Gymkhana turf earlier in the game. Boycott's response straight afterwards, when he saw a left-arm spinner, was to run past the ball far enough to make sure he could not get back to his crease before being stumped. England lost narrowly to a Sind XI.

Boycott was *the* England cricketer of the 1970s, even when he spent three years refusing to represent his country (Achilles was not going to play under a captain he did not respect). I have to declare an interest: I saw his maiden first-class hundred, in the Roses Match of 1963 at Bramall Lane, featuring cover-drives and back-foot forces of orthodox beauty. Bryan Stott, a left-hander at number four, and Boycott at five had rescued Yorkshire from a bad start: by the time I had scurried down to Bramall Lane with my mum after school, both batsmen had reached their 80s (I can picture the scoreboard on the Grinders Stand as if it were yesterday). Stott reached 143, Boycott 145. Brian Close followed, stumped for nought, and I like to think that Fred Trueman's 18 not out before the declaration consisted of three sixes. It was like going to the theatre for the first time in an audience of 10,000, seeing Olivier, Gielgud, Sher and McKellen starring together; I was hooked. Years later I heard that when Boycott returned to Yorkshire's dressing-room, and saw his senior partner in their match-winning stand of 249, he said words to Stott to the effect: 'I scored more than you.'

When Boycott was England's captain on their tour of New Zealand which followed Pakistan, he was run out by Ian Botham because England needed quick runs for a declaration. Boycott, after his two-hour 26, sat in the dressing-room stewing with a towel over his head. Naturally enough, being on his Test debut, Clive Radley approached his captain to ask how he was to bat in this situation when he went in. 'I couldn't give a fxxxing stuff.'

Circumstances had fashioned Boycott into what he was. He had not been selected by a grammar school after his eleven-plus, until a teacher at the last moment squeezed him into Hemsworth Grammar. His father had died, broken by coal-mining; his mother (the mum who could have middled many a ball that England batsmen missed when he was subsequently commentating) had to look after the family. When I saw Boycott bat for England, he burned. Was it resentment against the world that was trying to get him out? No wonder his nickname was Fiery. No wonder he kept the ball on the ground. No wonder he never got himself out except for that one occasion in Karachi, in a one-day game when his first-class average was not at stake.

I should have known better by the time we played in a media match in Jamaica on England's 1985–86 tour of the West Indies, when Boycott was forging a career as a radio commentator while still playing for Yorkshire. My bowling was never more effective, or never closer to effective, as it was in the West Indies because local batsmen – in this case a combined media team were playing a Red Stripe Brewery XI in Spanish Town – charged so fast they had no chance of getting back if they missed a leg-break. Boycott, at extra cover, fielded a ball off my bowling on the half-volley; he only had to dive to catch it. But he had not brought his batting gloves and bat out from England to field, he wanted to keep his eye in. 'Go on, stick him at number three,' I suggested to our captain, Tony Becca of *The Gleaner*, when he asked my advice about our batting order. 'He likes number three.' OK, it was petty, but we would have had no chance of knocking off our target if Boycott had opened. He scored a sedate, match-losing 30-odd. And afterwards, when he had lost his gloves, I did help search for them. He was as upset as a parent who had mislaid a child.

From the perspective of the same dressing-room, or on the same field, a cricketer is very different from when seen from the press box. I had seen Boycott before in all his glory, after knocking on the door of his hotel room, but in that dressing-room in Jamaica I saw how powerful his chest and shoulders were: he could have hit many a six had he tried to, but going aerial involved risk. In his 36-match ODI career he never hit a six, yet he could still score 105 off 124 balls in Sydney against Dennis Lillee and Jeff Thomson when his place was being questioned.

On the evening after he had scored his 100th first-class century, for England at Headingley in 1977, I saw him at the team hotel bar, which was not a place he often frequented, and some admiring supporters were present. But I saw not a single teammate sharing his elation (and only about half the players had gone on to the dressing-room balcony to applaud). This being England, an inevitable factor was class.

From my reading of Yorkshire cricketers through the ages, most have been lower–middle class or, increasingly, middle class, and a sizeable number freemasons, pillars of society (self-appointed). Boycott and Trueman were odd men out as the sons of miners.

On England's 1986–87 tour of Australia, we were stuck in Perth for a while before Christmas, because a triangular ODI tournament had been dreamed up to celebrate Australia's winning of the Admiral's Cup for yachting. (Few tour photographs could be funnier than the sight of spreadeagled journalists clinging to the cabin roof of yachts, like stranded octopi, on the Swan River, while the Aussie crew stood and held nothing except their tinnies.) One evening those journalists who were unattached, on both sides, congregated in a hotel room and it was decided we should all take a turn at singing a song or reciting a poem. Bobby Simpson, Australia's nearest counterpart to Boycott as an opener who never gave it away, refused to participate. I was next, and can't sing (I was forbidden to sing at school), so I summoned up a couple of verses about the Jolly Miller who once lived on the River Dee. He worked all night from morn to night, and he was always to be heard singing:

> I care for nobody, no, not I
> Because nobody cares for me.

And I was rather thinking about Boycott.

Test No. 9

Karachi, January 1978

A press conference was held shortly before the third Test because England's tour management – the manager and sole coach Kenny Barrington, and captain Mike Brearley, his arm in a sling — wanted to issue a statement. Pakistan's board had invited three of Kerry Packer's World Series players — Imran Khan, Mushtaq Mohammad and Zaheer Abbas — to play in the third Test: the players were at a loose end in Australia at the time. England were not at all keen on a sudden shift in the balance of power: Pakistan would have become favourites to win the third Test. England, however, objected on ideological grounds: they believed official cricket had to hold the line and not re-admit WSC players whenever they were free. This statement, read out by Barrington, declared that England would not play the third Test if Pakistan selected their Packer cricketers. 'No Packerstanis' was the headline.

I am set against press conferences except of this kind, when a new policy or an important development has to be announced, like Jonathan Trott flying home after, or even during, the Brisbane Test of 2013–14. The press conference has since become the staple diet of cricket journalism. Officialdom thus controls the narrative: an opening batsman has made a king pair in the previous Test, so his partner is put up for an interview. Anodyne noises will be emitted: this partner says he is not worried about Blank, he is just going through a bad patch, ideally he will come good, etc etc. The newspaper headlines will therefore be on these lines: 'England unfazed by Blank's nightmare run.' Done and dusted is the journalist after sharing in the transcription of these quotes, writing a few paragraphs of introduction, padding the rest of his piece with these quotes, and filing.

If I were buying a newspaper to read its cricket coverage, I would expect the correspondent to do more to earn his or her corn: to examine Blank's king pair in the previous Test in some detail, to see any pattern of dismissals emerging, to watch him in the nets, to talk about him with other England players and coaches, to attend the press conference and listen, yes, but merely to bear it in mind as the propaganda that it is. I would want the correspondent's considered view on whether Blank should be dropped or not, and where his longer-term future might lie, not a load of orchestrated propaganda. When Blank retires from Test cricket at the end of this series, the reader will then be less surprised.

England's tour party in 1977–78, in addition to 16 players, consisted of Barrington, a physio, and a scorer who was an accountant by profession and had to double as baggage manager. The physio was a source of humour, though he undoubtedly did not view himself that way. If a cricketer was injured anywhere below the waistline, his likely diagnosis was 'tight hamstrings'. For any professional shortcomings, he sought to make it up to the players by being their fount of local knowledge: in Pakistan he knew where the very best deals for carpets were to be had, after requisitioning the team bus to go to the bazaar first. He would sit at the front, the lone passenger, with the driver to one side, beneath him. After more gullible England players had splashed out, they would discover that his 'discounts' and 'special deals' amounted to a higher price than normal.

It is fair to say that egotism has been a feature of some England physios: the chance not only to be seen with the players, but to tell them what to do, can prove irresistible. A zenith, of sorts, was reached on the opening day of the Adelaide Test in 1994–95: the physio was keen to put the players through their paces in front of the gathering crowd of England supporters. It was one of those days of the Adelaide summer when the wind arises in the Simpson Desert and blows across the Oval, drying it out. At 40°C, this is another world from England where we think of wind as cooling. Shuttle runs, sprints, press-ups, the lot – the England players were driven towards dehydration and exhaustion – whereupon they lost the toss and fielded all day after an early, straightforward catch went down. Darren Gough alone seemed impervious to the heat and was still running by the end of day one. Limitless were the long-term benefits of this training session, no doubt; more immediately England lost.

Most respected of England's physios? Craig de Weymarn would be my guess, especially after he had been injured in the course of duty yet returned to the fray. The injury was nearly as bad as a gunshot when he was doing throw-downs in the nets and Ben Stokes hit the ball straight back at his unprotected face (masks or helmets have since been worn for this task). Most loved? Probably Laurie Brown. He had been a trainer for Manchester United so he was accustomed to dealing with stars, and he had been through troubles of his own so he did not get overexcited in his position.

The number of non-playing members of an England party escalated after the 1990s. The less competent the head coach, as a rule of thumb, the more backroom staff he wanted so as not to expose himself. Had the Professor Parkinson who worked out the law about the right number of people to compose a committee – usually between seven and 10 – applied himself to the correct ratio of players to non-playing members of an England touring party, it might have been three to one or thereabouts. It is a bad sign when they are almost equal in number. It is healthiest when players have to think for themselves first, and only call on support when they need it.

Test No. 10

Edgbaston, June 1978

Pink with pleasure, an England batsman on his Test debut had swivelled and pulled his first ball for four. He wore no helmet, so he could be seen shyly smiling. Most initiation ceremonies involve pain or humiliation; this was a help-yourself long hop from a Pakistan bowler who would never have been playing if the tourists had picked their Packerstanis. Liaqat Ali's only selling point was that he was bowling left-arm.

Nevertheless, an outstanding talent had announced himself. Graham Gooch, three years earlier, had begun his Test career with a pair, Ian Botham's first impact was as a bowler, but here was David Gower scoring instantly. Edgbaston's crowd – and

I was right in it, rather than the press box, meeting a friend – was euphoric. Throwing a youngster in at the deep end was to become a theme of the Ben Stokes-Brendon McCullum era, but it was a post-war rarity. Len Hutton and Denis Compton had swum before the Second World War, but Brian Close had sunk in his first Test aged 18 and on his first tour at 19. There was no pathway into the England team except the County Championship, until schoolboy or Under-19 tours prompted by the start of jet travel. Gower had scored one Championship century in 1976 and another in 1977, yet his first-class average was stuck in the lower half of the 20s. He could not build an innings, could not resist the temptation of seeing if he could score off every ball. Limited-overs cricket was more his cup of impatient tea.

Cricket journalists used to profile a player from the time he made his first appearances for his county, and the scores he made. Social or formative background counted for nothing. I have always been interested in these influences. They make each player unique: whether his parents had a garden without a front fence so the boy was forced to hit the ball square of the wicket, for example. When Gower represented England, I interviewed not only him but his housemaster at school and it was obvious that here was a bird of more colourful plumage than his contemporaries. At Grace Road he was surrounded by old sweats like Ray Illingworth and Jack Birkenshaw, the Kens Higgs and Shuttleworth. Why was he playing for Leicestershire, not Kent where he had been schooled, and where he would have been hailed in the Band of Brothers and I Zingari tents as a second Cowdrey? When Illingworth had instructed him not to dress so scruffily, he had access to a dinner jacket in which to turn up for breakfast next morning.

Relaxed, 'laid-back': Gower was to strike me as anything but. If he had been born with a silver spoon in his mouth – and his family motto was in Latin – he had no wish to be Burlington Bertie, and he clipped his vowels accordingly.

His father, I learned from David's housemaster at King's Canterbury, had been the highest of achievers. Richard Gower had been the school captain; he had been in the first XI for cricket and hockey for four years, and for three in the first XV, before winning a scholarship to Cambridge. He had written two books on East African languages after becoming a district officer in Tanganyika in 1942. Upon independence there, he returned to England to become the registrar at Loughborough University, before his sudden death when David was seven.

When the son was 15 he was called to his housemaster's study and asked what he was going to be in ten years' time: 'the captain of England,' said David, and he was to be only one year out. Inner steel, and an ambition to reach the top, lurked beneath diffidence; it was in the genes. His was a family of naval officers and consuls. Admiral Sir Erasmus Gower was governor and commander-in-chief of Newfoundland on his death in 1814. But Gower, as he publicly admitted in later life, is naturally shy. He grew up in Dar-es-Salaam, in a house on stilts as he remembered, with servants rather than friends of his own age to play with. When thunder struck, his father dying, he was packed off to boarding school.

Richard Gower was such a paragon of academic and sporting virtue that the son chose not to compete, directly. Any risk of his obtaining a scholarship to Oxbridge was obviated when he was doing the history paper in the Oxford entry exam and chose to answer a question outside his syllabus: 'about King Arthur or King Alfred, I can't remember which' he told me disarmingly. Instead, at University College, London, he dabbled in law for a year, or rather in hockey, before giving up. He was not a complete rebel though, not a waster, and was playing club cricket for Loughborough Town when spotted by Leicestershire. The image of dilettante was only ever a mask; he has always cared deeply about cricket, having picked up a bat in the garden as a boy and played left-handed, whereas his father had batted right-handed. He was always going to be slightly different. It is significant perhaps that he said he did not recall the anecdote about telling his housemaster his major ambition when he was 15; overtly he did not care to be such a high achiever as his father, and hid behind the unpretentious vowels of middle England. Internally, my guess is that he yearned to be worthy of him.

When Gower captained England for the first time, in Pakistan in 1983–84 after Bob Willis had kept on running to the end of his tether, it was to the manner born. He was the new district officer doing his best for the people under his jurisdiction. England had gone 1–0 down on a turning pitch in the opening Test in Karachi. Pakistan were content for the last two matches at Faisalabad and Lahore to peter out, yet runs still had to be scored and honourable draws achieved. Gower responded to this call of duty with seven-hour centuries, 152 and 173*, in each Test. He played Abdul Qadir's wrist-spin with apparent nonchalance and scored the most runs by any batsman in a three-Test series in Pakistan until Harry Brook in 2022–23. Gower's family motto is 'frangas non flectes': you can break but not bend us.

We assume that an England tour of Australia is – or used to be, before it resembled a business trip – one long lark in the dorm. Yes, it was, until the losing begins in earnest and you take it to heart. You can keep spirits up in the two traditional ways of cricketers on tour; but in this instance we were on the train across the Nullarbor from Adelaide to Kalgoorlie in 1986–87, so only the alcohol, not the philandering, was available. The majority of players and press preferred to fly to Kalgoorlie via Perth, but a few preferred an overnight compartment on the train and, as mine was next to David Gower's, I eventually knocked, and found him in the depths. During the summer he had been rudely sacked mid-series as England's captain. The first half of his reign had been a triumph, apart from the 5–0 whitewash by West Indies in 1984: England had won a Test series in India, and had trounced Australia 3–1 in 1985, when Gower had scored more runs – to this date – of any England batsman in a home

Ashes, 732 at 81. The following winter, had England's touring party been selected by a panel of Alexander the Great, Hannibal and Napoleon, and captained by any one of them, England would still have lost 5–0 in the West Indies, as at home in 1984. West Indies had tanks, England pop-guns. So Gower was fired, essentially for losing the first two Tests of the 1986 season against an Indian side captained by Kapil Dev and filled with medium-pacers who could nibble it around. By this tour of Australia he was also breaking up with a long-term girlfriend and drinking too much. Captain at 26, yes, only a year behind schedule. Fired before 30, not what his father would have wished.

Kevin Pietersen, in 2012, was the only other England player I have found in this similar state of thinking that everything is stacked against him, and of feeling pulled in all directions as only the famous can be. Both Gower and Pietersen were always on the road, badly in need of a break, only nobody in authority was listening. They had to keep playing or retire, there was no alternative then. For more than 20 years Mark Saxby has been responsible for ensuring that England players do not succumb to depression. He began as team physio, and when a cricketer is on the table, unwinding, this is often the time he is going to reveal inner thoughts. Saxby evolved into becoming the players' psychotherapist, so understated, yet so valuable, that Michael Vaughan declared after winning the 2005 Ashes that Mark was England's 12th man.

This 1986–87 tour was the one when Martin Johnson of *The Independent* wrote, after a poor warm-up in Perth, that England 'can't bat, can't bowl, can't field.' Yet in Brisbane, on the eve of battle, they galvanised. I heard that on the morning of the first Test at the Gabba, nerves kicking in, the dressing-room toilets were naturally occupied. The following conversation was heard over the walls and doors to this effect:

> Mike Gatting, England's new captain: 'What number do you want to bat, Lubo?'
> Lubo (Gower's nickname): 'Don't mind.'

Gatting: 'I'll go three then.'

Gower: 'OK.'

Gatting, aware that Allan Lamb insisted on batting at number four and nowhere else: 'You all right at five?'

Thus was a vital re-jigging of England's batting order agreed. And why not do it spontaneously? There's something to be said for coming to this decision the night before, in the team-room, lengthily and collectively; and something to be said for making it in the quiet before the storm. Gatting scored 61 at number three, and Gower 51 at five, a platform for Ian Botham's hundred at number six. Gatting and Gower scored either side of 400 runs in this series, and England won 2–1.

For the 1989 Ashes in England, Gower was captain again, and it was a horrible reversal of the 1985 series: England lost 4–0 instead of winning 3–1. He was somewhat let down by selectors who chose 29 players for the six-Test series, and by players who signed for the second rebel tour of South Africa in the course of it. Terry Alderman became the only bowler to take 40 wickets in a Test series twice. Graham Gooch was still being pinned half-forward; 19 of Alderman's 41 wickets were lbw.

After this series, Gower went back to Leicestershire where he was still captain. In those days it was what it said on the tin: D.I. Gower (Leicestershire and England). Not England and Leicestershire. It was the county that paid your salary, England topped it up.

In the sixth Test at the Oval, Gower had batted sublimely, for a couple of hours, until he got out for 79: OK but not great, considering he had only one century in the six Tests. Back at Grace Road, against Essex, who were becoming the power in the land (five championships from 1983 to 1992), and who were captained by Gooch (Essex and England), Gower wanted a hundred, to reassure and reassert himself. In the first innings, he was lbw Pringle for 0. Second time he opened, which was rare. Enough of this nonsense. He played shots — shots, not strokes, his usual fare, because so much animus went into them. He was hitting the ball with something akin to ferocity, with whiplash wrists, none of that caressing stuff. He made his hundred all right, 109, though Leicestershire still lost by 10 wickets. And that was it for Gower at Grace Road: it was his last Championship game at the ground he had graced. At season's end he went to Hampshire. The move did not really regenerate his England career. He played 11 more Tests, but at the age of only 35 he was gone, his face not fitting into the more disciplined, or less individualistic, tracksuited regime of Micky Stewart and Gooch.

It was only long after Gower had been dumped by Sky as a commentator, when we were doing a Q&A session in Cape Town, that Gower recounted the journey he had made in a car with his parents from Tanzania, as it was to become, to South Africa, camping as they went. He made it sound like a segment of ideal childhood. I had always thought him, beneath the surface, closer on the scale to highly strung than laid-back; and it was when speaking passionately about wildlife in Africa that the fire within most visibly burned.

Test No. 10 (still)
Edgbaston, June 1978

In response to Kerry Packer's World Series paying large salaries, the Test and County Cricket Board found sponsorship for England players for the first time, so they could be paid something like what they were worth: hitherto they depended on the benefit awarded at the discretion of their county if they were not to retire impecunious. Cornhill Insurance put in £1m spread over five years. For their tour of India in 1976–77 England players had received £3000, for their tour of Pakistan and New Zealand the following winter they had been paid £5000, and now their fee for a home Test was going up from a few hundred pounds to £1000 per match.

The media were buttered up to use Cornhill in headlines and match reports. Sponsorship in English cricket had consisted of PR girls dressed in golden attire handing out packets of free cigarettes during the Benson and Hedges Cup, launched in 1972. Cornhill supplied a hot lunch and all the wine you could drink. Starting with the morning session at Edgbaston in 1978 you would be offered wine – a refreshing *rosé*? – by Crawford White, who had lately retired as the cricket correspondent of the *Daily Express*. 'Chalky' knew his cricket, having bowled to high amateur standard, while his journalism was remembered for his intro after Tony Greig had scored a hundred in a Calcutta Test: 'It was a case of ton-up Tony here today.' Convivial, no longer austere, was the inner sanctum. Gower was not alone in being pink with pleasure.

Kingston upon Thames, on several occasions

'I didn't, I didn't want, I didn't want – to make a smell.'

This is the saying I most associate with Sir Leonard Hutton, the phrase I heard him say most often. If it sounds strange, or laughable, or barely comprehensible, a paraphrase would be: 'I didn't want to rock the boat' – as much for the sake of professional cricketers as for his own career.

Hutton had been placed in a unique position when appointed England's first professional captain of the 20th century (professionals who had toured Australia in the 19th had appointed one of their kind). He had to walk on ice at its thinnest: the Establishment was waiting for him to fail. Come the 1953 Ashes, when England had not beaten Australia in a Test series since Bodyline in 1932–33, Hutton was handed a team that included his own chairman of selectors, Freddie Brown, an amateur of course, to monitor the dressing-room. Imagine that: no safe place for Hutton to speak. When England toured the West Indies in 1953–54, so I heard after both parties concerned had died, E.W. Swanton invited Hutton to dinner at his house in Barbados and told him that if he stepped down, to allow an amateur to captain England in Australia in 1954–55, he would personally ensure that Hutton received a knighthood in four years. (The end-of-tour reports by the England captain spelled out ever more clearly during the 1950s how prone E.W.S. was to interfere.)

Ghostwriting on behalf of England captains has been a privilege of my job: Sir Leonard himself, Mike Atherton, Nasser Hussain, Michael Vaughan, Andrew Strauss, later to be knighted too. It might sound an unethical practice, as it can indeed be, but not in my experience. The England captain, especially if he is playing a game, does not have the time to sit down at a desk and write down his thoughts and somehow dispatch them. He needs a secretary (or even amanuensis) to record these thoughts for him, and file them on time. What is unethical is when a cricketer, who may have a substantial contract with a newspaper, tells the journalist to write what he – the journalist – likes, and not to bother him. There have been players who have not read, let alone written, books and articles bearing their name. But the England captains I have ghosted have dictated their copy and insisted on reading and vetting the final version.

In an ordinary press conference, as in a lecture, you are restricted to asking questions which are topical. While ghosting, on the other hand, you can slip in – 'off the record' – questions you always wanted to ask. 'Len, what was Gubby Allen really like?' Allen was the *eminence grise* of post-war English cricket: it was symbolic that he lived in a house behind the pavilion at Lord's and had his own back-gate key to the ground. Weighing up every word – truthful in obedience to his Moravian upbringing, diplomatic as he was compelled by circumstances to be – Hutton replied: 'I didn't, I didn't go to Lord's – to see him.' The master of understatement would follow up by looking at you with piercing blue eyes, and nod, to make sure you fully understood.

So there I was, aged 23, walking to Sir Leonard's house in an expensive cul de sac in Kingston upon Thames in Surrey.

Soon after retirement he had emigrated from Yorkshire: he did not want to be pestered for autographs, and memories of his 364 in the Oval Test of 1938, every single day. At least I was well-prepped in addition to overawed. At school I had given the impression of being a very diligent pupil. Whenever a teacher or prefect walked round the library, I was immersed in a large tome such as *The Atlas of Medieval Europe*. One of the several books by Len Hutton to be found on the shelves – *Cricket Is My Life* or *Just My Story* – was tucked inside.

He might take me to his golf club, where he was treated with due reverence. But he was probably treated with reverence from the moment he first played a cover-drive – so late, right under his eyes – in the Yorkshire nets, whereupon Herbert Sutcliffe took him under his wing. Or else he would talk at home in his armchair over a coffee brought by Dorothy, Lady Hutton. He had a boxer's nose, and, when he was in civvies, you did not immediately notice that his left arm was three inches shorter than his right, following the war-time accident and three operations (until the Second World War he was averaging 67 in Tests). He would wear a suit, an expensive grey suit with a few beige colours designed to blend in, not stand out. And often that phrase: 'I didn't want to make a smell.' He weighed every word. He had to: one word out of place and the process of a professional cricketer becoming the England captain would have been set back another decade.

(The following paragraph is in parentheses, dear reader, because I cannot double-check it. Len, so reserved by force of circumstance, did not communicate easily with his children, like many a father in Britain. One son, Richard, became a fine all-rounder at Repton, Cambridge and Yorkshire: he played five Tests and would have played more if Tony Greig had not emigrated from South Africa. Richard grew up, so I heard, believing that his father did not rate him and did not even bother to watch him play. Len, meanwhile, was so nervously keen for his son to succeed that he would hide behind a hedge to watch, so Richard would not see him and be distracted.)

Len became an England selector in the 1960s but he was not especially keen on watching: he had been there, done that, having played three Test series against Don Bradman's Australia and having won Ashes series at home and away, the first England captain to do so, amateur or professional (Percy Chapman had been appointed for the last Test of 1926, then won again in 1928–29). He was more relaxed, if never voluble, as an *Observer* columnist. He could be found in the press-box bar at Lord's at the back of the Warner Stand, having a quiet one with the jovial barman Pete (I hope Pete put Len's whisky down on the house). Denis Compton was cricket correspondent of the *Sunday Express* – in that he dictated some thoughts to his ghost after a few stiffeners, often on the subject of how unfavourably Ian Botham compared to the all-rounders of his day – and to the end these two gallants of post-war English cricket did not warm to each other. An England supporter might have thought Hutton and Compton had so much in common, fighting off Ray Lindwall and Keith Miller, but they were rivals rather than friends, rivals for the nation's affection, no less. As England's opening batsman, and a second new ball could be taken after only 55 overs, Len was compelled to be a Roundhead; Compo was free to act the Cavalier down the order. It is often thus. Mike Atherton and Alec Stewart played a hundred Tests together, and many times opened the batting together, yet they never went out to dinner together, except on official functions, according to the former. We must not romanticise the tough old business of Test cricket and playing in a team; especially in the eras before central contracts, it was every man for himself.

After a couple of whiskies, on top of the Cornhill lunch, Hutton would remain taciturn. Compton got louder. 'Denis and Bill,' Sir Len said one afternoon in the Lord's press bar, referring to Bill Edrich, Compo's boon companion for Middlesex and England. 'On that '46–7 tour [when England's players celebrated in Australia their release from rationing], they should've been sent home.' Once he trusted me, the most confidential thing

Len said was: 'Don. He should have been done for insider trading.' His dealings with the Adelaide stock exchange were still rankling, decades later. Hutton had bettered Bradman's 334 as the highest Ashes innings, but Bradman had won two and drawn one of the three series in which they had been in opposition. When *The Observer* sent Hutton to Australia for one last tour, in 1982–83, they obviously wanted us to visit Bradman in Adelaide, for what would have been an epic reminiscence. Len rolled back the years. He reverted to his most watertight forward defensive stroke, and said no.

Test No. 23
Lord's, August 1979

If you play or watch cricket, you can learn something every day. If you write about it and watch, rather than merely look, you can learn something about cricket and, often, about writing too. Exhibit A is the fourth day of England's second Test against India in 1979.

Ian Botham's impact on English cricket, indeed on national life, was greater than anyone's since W.G. Grace. Taking into account his actions off the field, especially his charity walks, he was Ben Stokes to the power of two, or three lions in one. It is not hyperbole to say he was almost a young King Henry VIII: he made people believe a golden age was at hand. He seemed capable of anything. He walked from John o'Groats to Land's End to raise money for leukemia research when it was an unfashionable children's charity, and the mortality rate plummeted. Botham did not compose *Greensleeves*, but Henry probably did not either.

Going into the second Test of this series against India, Botham had 94 Test wickets: six more in this match and he would become the fastest to reach 100 in terms of matches. It was little more than two years since he had jogged up at Trent Bridge in the

Ashes Test of 1977 and delivered a long hop which Australia's captain Greg Chappell carved into his stumps. The debutant celebrated with such panache that he made it look as if he had bowled the ball he had intended.

On day one at Lord's, Botham took five wickets in India's first innings as they were skittled for 96. England took a massive lead then, after the rest day of the Sabbath, send India back in again on Monday morning. Mike Brearley gave Botham the first over from the Nursery End. Botham's wife, Kathy, is nursing their baby Sarah in Q Stand (no women allowed in the MCC pavilion), while other members of his family are at the ground to see him take the wicket that will beat the record held by the Antiguan Andy Roberts.

Taking guard – leg-stump – to receive Botham's first ball of India's second innings was Sunil Gavaskar. 'Oh God, not Ian,' Gavaskar said to himself. 'Not the first over, not the first ball. He is going to get me out. I am going to be his 100th Test victim.'

We know this, and a whole lot more besides, because a journalist who was outstanding at research was at work that day. Dudley Doust was a sports writer for *The Sunday Times*. As he was an American, who started on the *Kansas City Star* and had read Tom Wolfe on writing techniques, he came to cricket from a completely different angle – and bringing with him the priceless commodity of goodwill. He resembled an academic, lecturing perhaps about Wolfe, wearing a jacket and glasses tied behind his neck otherwise he would have been forever losing them. He had hit it off with Brearley and written one book for, and another with, him. As he was blessed with the England captain's imprimatur, Botham had agreed to Dudley writing an authorised biography (*Ian Botham, The Great All Rounder*, 1981) with all the access that entailed. Dudley was an indefatigable researcher, a bloodhound for telling details. Thus, on the first morning of this Lord's Test, he arrived outside Botham's hotel room with the porter who was bringing his morning tea and newspapers. Dudley observes Botham shovelling sugar into his tea, and getting out of bed – the tree-trunk thighs make him look 'more like a rugby prop forward than cricket's first modern superstar' – and combing his 'sandy blond hair long and curly at the neck and thick in the moustache; this style, while currently fashionable, gave him the stern look of a Victorian gambler or, sterner still, the menacing aspect of a Mississippi riverboat gambler.' Yes, the hint of menace. Botham was impeccably behaved when I hired a canal boat during the Bath festival for a trip up the Avon after close of play, but a Somerset player was bound to be thrown into the river, like Nigel Popplewell.

Botham had wanted his 100th wicket during India's first innings. Having taken 99, he signalled from second slip to John Lever to bowl wide at India's tailenders; but this was no Gymkhana game, Lever shook his head, and bowled one tailender, while David Gower ran out the other with one stump to aim at. Hereabouts England had, I would say, their finest fielding side before the 21st century: twinkle-toed Gower on one side of the wicket, lulling the batsman as if he were a leopard slumbering in afternoon heat, Derek Randall, all limbs and animation, on the other side, Alan Knott or Bob Taylor behind the wicket, Botham or Tony Greig at second slip with Brearley safe in between.

Botham did not take a wicket in his opening spell of India's second innings before lunch; Gavaskar's premonition was not immediately fulfilled. It was the convention in Test cricket then *not* to warm up before an innings: no throwing a medicine ball on the ground or bowling on the outfield into a coach's mitt. John Snow, who won the Ashes for England in 1970–71, told me that for his first ball of a spell his loosener was 'controlled width', because the batsman who threw his bat at a wide ball, certainly at the start of a spell, would never hear an end to the castigation. Botham spoke to Doust about his looseners: 'They used to be awful – usually a half-volley or a long hop delivered at half-pace – and worth four runs, but now I've got the speed up to about three-quarter pace.' The Test bowler today bowls the same pace spell in, spell out, day in, day out. Before speed guns, analysts and coaches, a pace bowler's range of speed was far wider: Colin Croft of West Indies could veer from 70 mph, when ambling in on a cold morning in Manchester, to 90-plus with steam up.

For two further overs before lunch, Botham switched to the Pavilion End and bowled all 12 balls at Gavaskar, but on a sunny day and with a docile pitch the ball was doing nothing. Here the essence of Botham began to kick in: like Dennis Lillee or Imran Khan, he was a hunter by nature. On the Lord's groundstaff and in the Somerset nets, supervised by Tom Cartwright, he had accuracy and conventional swing drilled into him; the conventional epithet for Botham originally was 'the Somerset medium-pacer.' But he wanted a wicket by any means and his sheer willpower can bowl people over. He tried bouncers but also innovated by using the width of the crease. 'I can't think of a bowler in the world who uses the crease as much as Ian does,' Gavaskar tells Doust (who has previously flown to Bombay to do a feature on Gavaskar for *The Sunday Times* magazine). 'When he runs in at you, you have no indication which way he will swerve. When a seam bowler goes wide of the crease, you can normally expect an inswinger, but from out there Ian is just as likely to bowl an outswinger.'

At the lunch interval Botham pulled off his boots and sweaty shirt, drank a glass of orange juice, smoked a cigarette (permitted in the dressing-room then), ate three slices of beef and some ice cream, washed down with several cups of tea heaped with sugar. At 3.20 p.m., with India batting nicely for a draw, Botham came back for his 11th over. He had been wound up by Bob Taylor: 'For Heaven's sake, you Gorilla, let's see some aggression this time.' Brearley: 'Come on, Guy, where is all this fire we hear about?' Bob Willis, injured for this match, explained later to Doust: 'To get that little extra out of Guy, you've got to insult him.' In Q Stand Kathy Botham, having run out of baby food, has gone to shop outside the ground.

Botham began his 12th over at 3.27 p.m. Gavaskar was batting fluently, too fluently for his own liking, to the point where Botham can hear the batsman telling himself: 'Concentrate, concentrate.' So India's opening batsman let the first ball of this new over pass. And perhaps most strangely of all, as we approach the climax to this story, Doust is standing in the press-box bar at the back of the Warner Stand, where there is no view of the ground, just of the garden behind. I nip out to tell him when Botham starts this new spell. 'I don't want to watch,' Dudley said. He wanted to reconstruct the historic moment from scratch, from minus square one so to speak, without any images or impressions in his mind, by talking to all the protagonists involved, from the Lord's groundsman to the umpires, and to Botham's family as well as the players.

Botham, sensing Gavaskar's euphoria, fancied his chances. He experimented by almost halting in his run-up before delivering a slower ball. 'Here comes a crap ball,' thought Mike Hendrick, filling in at second slip. Gavaskar seized too eagerly on this long hop. He middled it but it flew in the air to the left of Randall, who leaped to his left, but he was wearing a helmet, as he was fielding close for Phil Edmonds bowling at the other end, and umpires had begun to refuse to carry helmets. Randall reckoned he would have caught it if unimpeded.

'Bad luck,' says Edmonds at mid-on, before tossing the ball back to Botham. 'You wouldn't want to get your 100th wicket with a strangle.' Botham was annoyed, not so much because of the dropped catch but because Edmonds, as a spinner, did not look after the ball's shiny side: he did not smooth away blemishes. After rubbing the Dukes ball on his right thigh, Botham decided on a bouncer for the third ball of the over. The infamous Lord's ridge, on a length for a bowler from the Pavilion End, remained an issue, if only in batsmen's minds. Botham aimed for it to get unpredictable bounce, and the ball duly leaped at Gavaskar. He, being the Little Master, relaxed not only his bottom hand on the bat but both hands. The difference just prevented the ball, having been gloved, from reaching Brearley at first slip on the full. 'He has the skill, patience and stamina to become the greatest record-breaking batsman of all time,' Sir Leonard dictates to me during this series; and Gavaskar eventually knocked Geoffrey Boycott off his pedestal of 8114 Test runs.

Following Gavaskar's close call, Randall recalled the fourth ball to Doust. 'Ian was so worked up you could see the foam coming out of his ears. He started his run-up with two long, walking strides, then he bounced three or four strides. When he does that, his blood is up.' This fourth ball lifted and beat Gavaskar outside off stump. The 100th wicket remained elusive.

For his fifth ball, Botham swerved wide in the crease. Not knowing which way Botham was going to swing it, Gavaskar gave himself an extra milli-second by moving back then, still euphoric, aimed an expansive cover-drive. This time the ball stayed low, flicked the outside edge, and just carried to Brearley's left hand as he fell backwards. I can see it as if it were yesterday. It was as if Brearley was keeping wicket back in his student years at Fenner's, and a batsman had finely leg-glanced, so that he had to throw himself to his left to catch the ball in one hand.

Gavaskar – this was another age – offered his right hand in congratulation to Botham who steamed towards Gavaskar and, unwittingly, past him. In Q Stand Botham's mother thumps the collarbone of the woman beside her and shouts: 'He's done it! He's done it!' before noticing she is a policewoman. Kathy, at the Grace Gates on returning from the shop, hears the roar and is told by the gateman: 'Your husband's done it!' More surprisingly, perhaps, she is allowed back into Lord's.

If I have quoted excessively from the late Dudley's work, I hope he – as a mentor – and his publishers will forgive my admiration for his eye for detail. I did help him, by supplying Sir Leonard's phone number. He had been watching on television at home in Kingston, and he compared Botham to

Keith Miller, saying that Botham at 23 was as good a batsman but not quite the bowler. Why? Because Miller was more sideways on when he delivered. Botham opened up his left side a touch too soon, so the ball swung away from the right-hander a moment earlier.

It was an incisive point, to be remembered after April 1980. That month, in the absence of England central contracts, found Botham playing for Somerset against Oxford University in the Parks. It was cold; Botham, while bowling at students who were never going to make cricket their profession, injured his back. In the rest of Botham's career, his outswinger resurfaced rarely and seldom for long. Before April 1980 he took 139 Test wickets at only 18 runs each; afterwards it was 244 wickets at 34.

It was on the two consecutive England tours of Australia, in 1978–79 and 1979–80, that I learned about technique. In England, cricketers and journalists tend to prioritise temperament. In Australia they prioritise technique (every player has talent, otherwise he would not be out there in the first place).

My tutor was a coach from Queensland named Toot Byron, who had played grade cricket in Sydney. 'Look how far his hands are away from his body,' he would say as an England batsman wafted outside off stump and edged to slip. In England, at almost every level, we have an infuriating tendency to say 'bad luck' when a fielder drops a catch. It is not bad luck: there is a cause behind his dropping it. 'He did not get his hands up to the level of his eyes,' Toot would point out when a fielder missed a skyer.

Batsmen in England can all too often get away with a fallible technique by scoring plenty of runs on slow pitches, where their front-foot technique is limited to a half-forward push, never a full stride when one is necessary. Balance is deemed to be sufficient. But it isn't sufficient, not in Australia, and not for England's batsmen when it matters most, in the Ashes. My two favourite right-handed exponents technically? Martin Crowe and Jacques Kallis. Their front toe would point to mid-on when they played an on-drive.

I learned more about another technique when on the same flights as the England cricketers. This generation had some gifted players, world-class performers, ahead of the Australians in this respect. On international flights I would normally have a seat such as 47D, towards the back, but on domestic flights in Australia we were all mixed together in economy and I could watch some experts at work. The chemistry was extraordinary in this age before AIDS. Air hostesses buzzed at being chatted up by these international sportsmen, of whom Australia still saw few. The object of the exercise was for the hostess to call in sick as soon as the plane had landed, so she would not have to take the next flight back to her port of origin but could stay the night. All about technique.

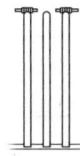

Do not be fooled into thinking he was one of the Flower Pot Men. Mike Brearley, with his speed of thought, was in charge alright. He leads England out for the first Test in 1978 at Edgbaston. David Gower, making his debut, naturally trails behind. See the mental strain involved in fast bowling for Bob Willis. Chris Old and Bob Taylor follow.

The rumour was that Ian Botham could get away with any practical jokes in the England dressing-room until the 1980–81 tour of the West Indies, when he found out that Peter Willey had stronger forearms. David Gower and the late David Bairstow make up this quartet at the Oval Test of 1979 against India.

How not to chase a target. Australia, set 151, are bowled out off the last ball of the 67th over for 121 at Edgbaston in 1981. Ian Botham, who had taken five wickets for one run, and Bob Taylor are especially jubilant.

1980s

Test No. 30

Trent Bridge, June 1980

If a football team is losing 17–0, both sides might call the game off. England in the 1980s lost 17 Tests against West Indies, and won none, but there was no escape. England had to plough on, into the 1990s, against the world Test champions.

Little did we realise that the gap between the two sides would yawn into a canyon after England lost the opening Test of the 1980 series between them by only two wickets. Bob Willis was just as effective as the West Indies fast bowlers, taking nine wickets in his flat-out efforts to help his captain and friend Botham, but at the climax of the run-chase (209 the target) Andy Roberts clubbed England's medium-pacers to get over the line.

All the West Indies players, except for Faoud Bacchus of Guyana, had or would soon play county cricket. So whether West Indies were playing England at home or away, they had the knowledge of local conditions. From losing 1–0 in that rain-affected series in 1980, to losing 2–0 that winter, to losing 5–0 in 1984 and 1985–86, and back to 4–0 in 1988 with one draw, England were a welterweight boxer pinned against the ropes by a heavyweight, round after round: specifically, perhaps, Joe Frazier because he was the boxer whom Viv Richards most admired. England lost five of those 17 Tests by an innings, three by ten wickets, two each by nine wickets and by eight wickets. My composite image is that England would be dismissed around teatime on day one (often after they had naively picked two spinners and chosen to bat first); Desmond Haynes and Gordon Greenidge would reel off derisive boundaries – not so much 'in reply' as a contemptuous laugh – by the close of the first day, and when one of them was dismissed on the second morning, Viv Richards would stroll forth, fix the bowler in the eye – not that the bowler would dare look – and whip his first ball through midwicket for four. Game over.

Test No. 35
Lord's, August 1980

The Centenary Test set off on the wrong foot, and there it stayed. The inaugural Test in England in 1880 was staged at the Oval, with consequences which can be said to have been long-lasting, but the enterprising Surrey secretary Charles Alcock was no longer in charge a hundred years later and the Oval was falling apart. Staging it at Lord's was historically inappropriate – yet far more lucrative. So while the Centenary Test at Melbourne in 1976–77 ticked every box (except for a decent fee for Australia's players), everything went wrong during the one in England. It was no celebration of cricket. Rain washed out 10 hours, or rather a combination of rain and the finickiness of umpires Dickie Bird and David Constant did, and a couple of used pitches on the square should have been better covered.

The umpires did not sense this was an occasion unlike a normal Test. Cricket, for the sake of the sport's popularity, had to put on a show rather more interesting than the umpires walking out to make futile inspections, while MCC members felt ever more irate and ever more entitled to vent their ire. Australia's captain Greg Chappell tried to make a game of it by setting England a target of 370 in six hours; he only had two pace bowlers so there would have been a lot of spin. But his counterpart Ian Botham was hurting: having damaged his back in the spring, he had averaged 18 against West Indies during the summer and, having made nought in his first innings against Australia, did not want to play ball. While captain, my impression was that Botham had too much on his mind to build an innings.

This Centenary Test, however, suited one player down to the ground. The scene was set for him to bat all day. His captain put no pressure on him to go for the target. The crowd was happy enough until they realised that England were not even thinking of going for the runs.

As the match was petering out on the final afternoon, I returned to my hotel near Lord's with an Australian girlfriend. Sir Neville Cardus himself had declared that a man who goes to a cricket match solely for cricket is like a man who goes to a pub solely for drink. When we returned, blithely, Boycott had advanced his score from 63 not out to 79 not out.

I would not want to leave the reader with the impression that Boycott always batted defensively. He was brought up in the three-day Championship. Messrs Close, Illingworth and Trueman demanded wins for Yorkshire, not draws. On 5 June 1971 I bunked off school to hitch a lift and catch a train to Leeds to see the first day of Yorkshire v Nottinghamshire. Boycott led from the front like the Yorkshire captain he now was. He scored 11 centuries in his 24 Championship innings that season at an average of 109. Admittedly, Yorkshire finished 13th out of 17, and only three counties registered fewer batting points, but on this occasion at Headingley they were all over Notts and won by an innings. I remember Barry Stead, left-arm pace, running in, over the wicket, and Boycott just opening the face of his bat to off-glance four: he would never have risked nicking off in a Test. He was dismissed for 169 before I scuttled back to Leeds station. He also made 169 in the Roses match that season. In later years I told him that in 1971 he was always getting out for 169: he liked that one. Walking back to boarding school that long summer's evening I was revitalised, nothing less. I might not have been depressed, but I was very subdued for the four years after my mother died, and talked little to anyone. At last I was seeing what the outside world had to offer. At last I was now getting the chance to play cricket, after raising a side myself to play against Yorkshire village teams. At last I was living again.

Trinidad, January 1981

Before your feet touch the ground, at the bottom of the aircraft steps, you know you are somewhere different in the cricket-playing world. It can only be the West Indies, or conceivably Sri Lanka. The plane's air-conditioning has already disappeared into the mists of time; a film of sweat has covered your skin, a warm and agreeable sweat which feels as though it is oiling your bones.

If it is night-time and you have arrived on an island-hopper, and the pilot has stilled his engine, it can only be a West Indian island. Dominica, for one, has an airport called Canefield. In the surrounding vegetation, cicadas sound like an old waterwheel rhythmically turning.

My first West Indian destination was Trinidad, and I arrived, as we all do, under the influence of Christopher Columbus. To obtain funding for a second venture he had to write up the commercial possibilities of his first discovery (not that he reached the mainland of America). Luxuriance, nature at its most bountiful, the vast potential of a new and paradisiacal world: this was his sales pitch on returning to Europe, and he somehow fixed these images inside our wishful imaginations. We envisualise the West Indies as fertile and soft when the reality is often hard and barren, especially after original rainforest had been burned down for sugar plantations and soil eroded by wind.

Trinidad has some strips of sand, but the main beaches are in Tobago. England played their opening match – a four-day first-class game against the President's XI, or effectively West Indies A – on Trinidad's west coast at Pointe-à-Pierre in the centre of the oilfields. We breathed petrol fumes for four days. Oil production had started in the 1930s, and as in every oil-producing country the vast majority of people had derived little or no benefit. Some revenue had gone into roads (after the train system had been scrapped), and a television station. One tangible benefit for all to see, and hear, was the oil drum: sawn in two, it became the staple of steel bands. In 1981 the streets of Port-of-Spain were safe enough to walk round in the evening to see the pan-yards as everyone prepared for Carnival.

Something always fertile in the West Indies has been the encyclopaedia of forenames from which parents have chosen. Everton Mattis, Timur Mohamed and Thelston Payne were in the President's XI, besides Jeffrey Dujon and a couple of useful bowlers called Roger Harper and Malcolm Marshall. I wanted to see them; but no, on the first morning the PR manager of the oil company wanted to show off the refineries of Pointe-à-Pierre. As I was still the most junior journalist, and working for a Sunday paper, I was delegated. This PR officer was Indian, like half the population of Trinidad and Guyana: mostly lower castes, and therefore darker, transported by the British from Uttar Pradesh to work plantations. Let us call him Vijay. We climbed into his expensive new car and he drove around the refinery on a smooth road (Tar Lake was close by), before inviting me to his house for a drink. Geoffrey Boycott was warming up in the game – he had stroked his first boundary after 80 minutes' batting – but refusal would have been rude.

Having parked outside his spacious bungalow we went inside: finely furnished it was too. While I sat on a sofa, trying to ignore the fumes, Vijay disappeared, maybe to order tea or coffee from a servant. When he came back, a few yards behind him trailed his wife in a dressing gown. Vijay introduced her as ill; she said hello, and mustered a smile weak and wan. She gave me the impression she was often ill, before returning to her bedroom. Vijay, however, was delighted. I had seen her. And he had demonstrated, proved, that his wife was white.

I had of course read *Beyond the Boundary* by C.L.R. James: a set text ahead of any tour of the West Indies. I was not convinced about his portrayal of W.G. Grace as the soundest English oak with a heart of gold (in his native Downend I questioned a couple of ancients whose fathers had known the Grace family, and both simultaneously said they were all 'pigs'). But James's description of notable cricketers in Trinidad, like Learie Constantine and Wilton St Hill, are unsurpassed. So too of the nuances in local society, based on colour and class. After Vijay had shown me his trophy, immediately James's statement came to mind: the most obvious evidence that a man has arrived in West Indian society is that he has married someone lighter than himself.

After the warm-up in the oilfields, which featured a dazzling hundred by Dujon when he frequently struck England's off-spinners over midwicket with what would come to be termed a slog-sweep, we flew to St Vincent, then returned to play Trinidad in another four-day game, before the first Test in Port-of-Spain. England lost it by an innings. The second Test was cancelled: Guyana's president Forbes Burnham thought he would gain more kudos from his electorate by invoking the Gleneagles Agreement and banning Robin Jackman, who had flown from South Africa to replace the injured Bob Willis. These were desperate days in a dank team hotel, below sea level, waiting for tropical downpours to cease and politicians to decide. Guyana had already been bled so dry by Burnham (Swiss bank accounts according to rumour) that imports were unaffordable. An Indian family staffing the hotel shop had little more than local biscuits and curled, dusty postcards for sale. I was so bored I went to the local golf course, where three or four old clubs and balls remained for hire unrotted.

So far the West Indies was not conforming to the CGIs – the Columbus-generated images. The third Test was staged in Barbados. Much more like it – so long as you weren't batting. The Barbados attack in England's first-class game against the island featured Sylvester Clarke, Marshall, and Wayne Daniel. None could squeeze into the West Indies team. In the first innings of the third Test, England were blown away for 122 by Andy Roberts, Michael Holding, Colin Croft and Joel Garner.

'I think you've lost him,' the female receptionist said around midnight at the hotel which England had always used in Barbados. It stands on a beautiful beach and has a wooden pier leading into the Caribbean: after they had won the 1934–35 Test in Bridgetown, the closest of games on a wet pitch when the highest total was 102, England's cricketers had leapt from this pier into the sea before catching their ship. She and I watched as a stretcher was carried past reception into the waiting ambulance, a sheet pulled over the face. Ken Barrington was dead, aged 50.

It took something for a former player to earn the complete respect of Ian Botham, but England's captain felt it for his coach. Barrington, physically, more than a decade after his retirement, was as strong as any of the players, or stronger, as Brendon McCullum would later be. I had bowled a few balls in the nets at Sydney when Barrington, having not played for an age, miscued the first couple before launching what was then a pull-drive, now a slog-sweep, which might still be travelling through space had there not been a net. Yet he was the first England cricketer who had mental health issues in the public eye. He cared and worried so much. He almost never played his natural attacking game because he had been dropped after one Test – after one innings of five balls – for the next four years. Chest pains and anxieties forced his retirement aged 38, but they never went away. The day before he died he was beating himself up for hurting Graham Gooch's hand in fielding practice, before living through every ball of England's collapse.

Not until the fourth Test did this tour of the West Indies fulfil Columbus's billing. England had just won a game against the Leeward Islands in green Montserrat (this was before a volcano inundated two-thirds of the island in lava), so the tourists were in good humour, as was the whole of Antigua. Two events had blended into one carnival: Antigua's independence from Britain and Viv Richards's wedding, although you could not tell which was primary. Somerset supporters were numbered in their hundreds. The Recreation Ground in the centre of St John's overflowed as if flash-flooded. A day was lost to rain but nothing, naturally, could stop Richards marking the twin occasions with a century.

Decolonisation made life harder for England's cricketers. The best cricketers from all round the world used to be attracted to county cricket because no other competitions existed during the English summer, and therefore no other way to earn a living by playing cricket. Between England players and their Test opponents was no great animus, other than when un-neutral umpiring raised temperatures. But people in some countries where England were touring perceived the players as representatives of the British Empire, as if they were wearing pith helmets. In 1983–84 Pakistan and New Zealand gleefully defeated England for the first time; in 1984 England endured at the hands of the West Indies their first 5–0 defeat since 1921. Antigua was one of the last Caribbean islands to gain independence, and I could see what it meant during Antigua's inaugural Test in 1981. One of the local photographers was a Barbadian of middle age. Throughout the 1980s, whenever West Indies beat England, he was more than triumphant, he gloated; he felt the significance and symbolism so deeply – imperial Britain humiliated – that I tried to see it as nothing personal. I have wondered if, circumstances reversed, I would have reacted the same as he did. Slavery had gone from the West Indies, but racial and colour consciousness were alive and kicking, as Vijay had shown. From Antigua slavery had gone only within the last generation: a worker on a sugar plantation could not transfer to another one without the permission of his master, right into the 1950s. There being no escape from your plantation and no other jobs, this was still slavery in all but name. Even in 1981 the most important fact in Antigua was conspicuous by its absence: not one single, hated, cane was any longer grown.

In Jamaica, for the fifth Test, I first saw what had been a traditional phenomenon: the pitch so polished you could see your reflection. Not the actual features of your face reflected by the Sabina Park pitch, but the outline of your head and body, as if in a distant mirror. The groundsman twisted and turned his roller as he walked down the pitch to remove blades of grass above the surface, leaving a sheen off which the ball bounced and sped. The key to this technique was that grass roots remained below the surface. On most West Indian grounds nowadays no grass is apparent, only baked mud, which favours nobody except the flat finger-spinner.

In Jamaica I also met Allan Rae, opening batsman on the West Indians' Ramadhin and Valentine tour of England in 1950. He was a lawyer and leading administrator: attributes that go with opening the batting? In Trinidad I had met another of West

Indies' former opening batsmen: Clifford Roach had scored the first 50 for West Indies in Test cricket, in 1928, and their first double-century, in 1929–30, yet he was given little more than a line in Michael Manley's history of West Indian cricket. Roach sat in a wheelchair while he talked: he had lost both legs to diabetes, in addition to suffering a lack of recognition for his pioneering batting.

Rae told me that after Everton Weekes had made 129 in the Trent Bridge Test of 1950 a short, dapper, well-dressed gentleman knocked at the door of the visitors' dressing-room and said: 'Is Mr Weekes here?' On hearing the affirmative, he said: 'May I speak to him?' On meeting Weekes, the little old gent said: 'Well, I've seen the greats from Victor Trumper onwards and I think that was the greatest innings I've seen. Good day to you.' And, according to Rae, it was George Gunn.

A century on, we can see how far ahead of his time Gunn himself was. As an opening batsman, he was renowned for walking down the pitch against pace bowlers to throw them off their length. I have not heard of any other opener who did that before the arrival of white-ball cricket.

Test No. 42
Headingley, July 1981

It was comfort-eating. England were on the verge of going 2–0 down with three Tests left, and virtually no chance of winning the Ashes. Australia had reached 50 for one, strolling to their target of 130. Cornhill Insurance served lunch in the press box only on the first three days of a Test; it was awkward to cater for the last two when the match might be over. All the Sunday newspaper journalists (and other freeloaders) had gone, leaving the hardcore of about a dozen dailies. Four or five of us decided to nip out to Brett's, the well-known fish-and-chip shop round the corner from Headingley, and beat the crowd by leaving the ground shortly before the lunch interval. It was going to be a long journey home after another defeat. Graham Gooch was going to drive me to Bristol, where he was playing for Essex next day, and he currently could not buy a run against Terry Alderman and expected the selectors' axe. That would be one long haul.

We heard a roar as we walked up St Michael's Lane. We heard another roar as we walked up Kirkstall Lane. So what? What's a couple of wickets compared to haddock and chips cooked in beef dripping, doused in salt and vinegar? We scented lunch, not victory.

We were back in time for the resumption all right. Bob Willis was simulating a runaway steam engine, now Mike Brearley had given him the Kirkstall Lane End at last, right arm pumping like a piston, Afro hairstyle for a funnel, eyes bulging. Still, how could Australia, having totalled 401 for nine declared in their first innings, fail to knock off 130? On the previous evening, when Henry Blofeld had kindly given me a lift to our Ilkley hotel, I had mentioned the possibility of a draw if it rained on the last day. England were only 124 ahead with one wicket left, but if Ian Botham could add a few more to his overnight 145, and if Bob Willis could hang around, and with 10 minutes between innings, and if Australia scored at only 2.58 per over as they had in their first innings, and if there was a bit of bad light like that which had stopped play around teatime on day four, and if it rained...? No, this was getting stupid. In the back seat I ceased my straw-clutching. Blowers said there was no chance of escape.

Shortly after lunch on day five I was pacing up and down at the back of the press box like a pre-natal rehearsal for when my children were due. England had started catching flies, after dropping clangers first time round. Trevor Chappell was Australia's number three, not Ian or Greg, and he was much more limited. (St Peter's College played against other boys when Trevor attended, whereas they had played in the Adelaide adult grade competition when the older two brothers were there.) In his first innings of 27, spanning more than two hours, this Chappell had been dropped by Gower at third slip off Botham and by Botham at second slip off Willis. John Dyson had been dropped by Botham in the gully off Graham Dilley when 57, according to my notes, while blocking and edging to 102. And Australia's captain Kim Hughes had been dropped by Gooch at first slip off Botham and went on to 89. At least Botham's bowling had been generating chances again. After his liberation from captaincy, he had responded to the reinstated Brearley's jibe about having become a 'side-step Queen', and was hitting the pitch harder, even if the outswing was reduced to little more than 'shape'.

England had followed on after they had been dismissed for only 174. Batting had been fiendishly difficult against Alderman, who had Gooch lbw for two, Dennis Lillee and Geoff Lawson. Boycott had batted 89 minutes for 12 – his eye well in – when Lawson pitched just outside off and hit his leg-stump. When England batted again, the second clutchable straw was that Botham's batting had reactivated. His first-innings 50 had been his first half-century since his first Test as captain. In his 12-Test reign, albeit against the toughest opposition in West Indies and Australia when his back-foot defence was challenged, he had averaged no more than 13.

Botham's second innings of 149* in the follow-on was riotous, when he threw his bat as if in a benefit match. (In those days, if a player ever had a Sunday off, he would play in a teammate's benefit game: my club, Hinton Charterhouse, had staged a couple for Somerset players, putting a thousand pounds into the kitty each time, and the second was one of the rare occasions when Botham kept wicket.) Graham Dilley and Chris Old had thrown their bats too, and Hughes 'took pace off' only briefly, even though Ray Bright had bowled Botham for nought in the previous Test at Lord's. Botham then had been bowled behind his legs first ball, sweeping like Peter May at Old Trafford in 1961, not getting his bat down horizontal and low. Botham never stooped to conquer.

The pace quickened and drama intensified. Nobody at Headingley knew what the outcome would be. Dyson was caught hooking Willis down the leg side by Bob Taylor. Rod Marsh hooked, too, and I had to rush down the steps in the press box to see Dilley, almost underneath the stand, hold the catch at fine-leg. Even at 75 for eight Australia were not beaten. Bright and Lillee added 35 in four counter-attacking overs and made me feel sick (it couldn't have been the dripping?). Lillee cut Willis twice for four. In the same over Willis pitched up and a diving Mike Gatting caught the chip to mid-on (we were in no position to jest that Gatting was always ready to dive for a chip). Soon it was over, the second occasion in more than a hundred years that a team had won a Test after following on. England had won by 18 runs to level the series, Willis eight for 43.

Gooch was driving south. He might have been the sole person interested in English cricket who was not ecstatic. He mentioned that Marsh and Lillee had both placed a bet on Australia winning when the odds were 500–1 against, but they had not been hiding anything, it was just what Aussies did. Gooch dropped me off in Bristol that evening, then scored 35 next day against Gloucestershire in a NatWest Bank Trophy match of 60 overs a side which Essex won. He was to be dropped during this series, but not yet, not while the iron was still red-hot.

Test No. 43

Edgbaston, July–August 1981

We convened outside the press box on the last afternoon. It was a Sunday – not any Sunday but the second Sunday of Test cricket in England – so again only the hardcore of us daily journalists remained (I was covering for *The Observer* and for a Scottish newspaper the rest of the week). As Australia ground very slowly towards their target of 150 – they reached 87 in the 50th over with only three wickets down – and a 2–1 lead, we discussed what the story, the angle, was going to be.

'Has to be Brears dropping Border when he was only eight.' A ball from Bob Willis had kicked and carried to first slip.

'Who was that England captain who said to one of his fielders "you've just dropped the Ashes?"'

'I think it was Gubby Allen. England had gone 2–0 up in '36–7 then somebody must have dropped Bradman and England went on to lose 3–2.'

After this preliminary discussion we returned to the press box in the Bob Wyatt Stand, which had a grand view of the game, positioned at the City End just above ground-floor level, therefore not too high. Through opened windows you could almost touch the spectators' resignation. Australia's grind continued. Targets before the 21st century were not 'chased', they were gradually 'pursued'. This was a Sunday-afternoon walk, at the most, as Brearley forced them to sweat for every single.

A breakthrough was made when John Emburey dismissed Graham Yallop for 30, but that still left obduracy incarnate at the other end: Allan Border. With four wickets down, Australia passed 100, only 51 more to win. Batting was difficult because the pitch was dry, the odd ball bouncing unevenly. Brearley's 48 was still the highest innings of the match. England had posted only 189 and 219. Brearley had let Gooch drop down the order to number four, where he escaped being lbw half-forward to Alderman and contributed a pair of 21s before being dismissed twice by Ray Bright. Australia had scored 258; Kim Hughes said afterwards they should have made 300, and they might have done but for a couple of run-outs from mid-on and mid-off. Bob Willis had rekindled his Headingley fire, but he was burning out during this fourth innings. Australia's batsmen appeared to have nothing to fear, except fear itself.

Because this fourth day was a Sunday, as a concession to churchgoers, play did not start till noon. (Bob Taylor and Mike Hendrick were the only churchgoers I knew to attend of the England team in this era.) Edgbaston's crowd – in deference to the Lord's Day, or because Australia were heading for 2–1 up

– was quiet, sedate, restrained, even in the Hollies Stand. Well into the afternoon, Australia were 105 for four, needing only 46 to win. Brearley was conjuring up a final throw of his dice: John Emburey, still clamping the batsmen down to less than two runs an over, to be partnered by Peter Willey's part-time off-spin. Emburey at last made one of his off-breaks pop at Border: five wickets down, and both ends now open like pubs on a Sunday. Brearley said afterwards that Emburey got Border and Yallop in the nick of time.

Already Botham had bowled in Australia's second innings, but little more than tidily: eight overs for nine runs and no wickets. Brearley, holding back Willey, poked the bear for his final throw (his only other bowlers, Willis and Chris Old, were almost spent). Botham was brought on at the Press Box End – and I would swear that simultaneously, around the country, at least a dozen other bowlers were bowling much like him. A run-up that was far from flat-out, a rotation of the right arm, medium-pace, accurate as medium-pace should be, but nothing more than that – except for two extra ingredients.

One ingredient was Botham's willpower: once roused, nothing was going to stand in its way. Second added ingredient: Edgbaston's crowd, especially in the Hollies Stand, once Rod Marsh had been yorked middle stump and Botham, having conceded a single, embarked on a burst of five wickets for one more run.

Botham would drink alcohol prodigiously for months on end, then abstain for months on end, such was his willpower. Here it was like he had acquired the taste for wicket-taking again, after abstaining during his captaincy. Having yorked Marsh, he had Bright leg-before next ball. Lillee waved at, and just missed, the hat-trick ball. Soon he edged Botham for real and Taylor dropped it then, tumbling, caught the rebound. Edgbaston was transformed into euphoric-cum-ballistic. Botham bowled Australia's last specialist batsman Martin Kent then their last man Terry Alderman. Botham had huffed and he had puffed and he had blown the oldest enemy's house down.

England, having been at the wrong end of the game until its last half hour, had gone 2–1 up. Brearley told Edgbaston afterwards that he had 'never known a crowd like that in a Test in England'. As for Prometheus Unbound, Brearley said Botham now ran in 'in an uncomplicated way – if he does anything, he does it quicker now.' Note the proviso 'if'. There was nothing inherent in his bowling – not its speed, not its trajectory, not its lateral movement – that had spreadeagled Australia. It had been Botham's choreography and force of character which had overwhelmed them.

The dropped catch? What dropped catch? The one that Brearley missed off Border. Oh, that one. Never mind. Good old hindsight. That was worth a passing reference, at most.

Test No. 44
Old Trafford, August 1981

On the Saturday of the fifth Test, the Ashes were back in the balance. England were 2–1 up (one to play) but, after taking a first innings lead of 101, their batting had frozen second time round, in the face of Dennis Lillee and Terry Alderman. Alderman, before his shoulder injury, sailed to the crease like a yacht being blown by a strident wind up the Swan River in his native Perth, before whipping over his arm at fast-medium. England had only one left-hander, David Gower, to counteract his outswingers.

Lillee, to this stage in cricket history, had earned as much as anyone the title of the world's finest-ever fast bowler. I had watched him in the nets that morning, Old Trafford offering as close a vantage-point as any Test ground in England. Lillee had the idiosyncratic gesture of reaching up with his right forefinger to flick the sweat off his brow while stalking back to his mark. On this third morning he 'warmed up' for the best part of an hour before the start, steaming in full pelt at Graham Yallop (Yallop had been appointed the Australian board's official captain during World Series Cricket so there was little love lost). Lillee stormed back to his mark after each (supposedly practice) delivery in the nets, flicking sweat away. It made you realise the impact Fred Spofforth had on England in 1878 when bowling his fastest. Black-haired and scowling, as portrayed in *Punch*, Spofforth was the original Demon, Lillee his reincarnation.

Flogging himself before the start, or resumption, could only have occurred in the amateur, or pre-scientific, era: Australia's bowling coach, had there been one, would have been insisting that Lillee had to stop bowling, that he was in the red zone already. Lillee had bowled 24.1 overs (four for 55) in England's first innings, Alderman 29 overs. They did not get much rest. Australia were dismissed in 30.2 overs for 130. I have seldom listened to radio or television commentary during a game: I prefer to concentrate on what lies in front. But after Australia had collapsed I tuned in to *Test Match Special* and listened to Alan McGilvray, the visiting guest commentator. He was dyed in the wool, having played 20 first-class matches for New South Wales. The last time Australia had been dismissed in fewer overs had been on a wet pitch at Edgbaston in 1902, but he made only the briefest reference to Australia's collapse. No, what mattered was that Kent had scored a maiden Test fifty. Never mind those batsmen who had failed, and why, and effectively losing the Ashes. It was all about the promise of Kent, who played three Tests. Patriotism accentuated the positives long before coaches did.

Second time round, Lillee and Alderman were doing all the bowling again. Rodney Hogg and Geoff Lawson were unfit, so Australia had called up a whipper-snapper who had been playing for Gloucestershire, Mike Whitney, fast-medium left-arm, but Lillee and Alderman were not going to let him bowl with the Ashes on the line, or Ray Bright, a flat left-armer who had taken some wickets at Edgbaston in the previous Test but only because the pitch was turning.

England had closed the second day at 70 for one, a lead of 171, in sight of safety and the urn, so we had assumed. Whereupon Lillee and Alderman swept aside England's top order like Lillee flicking a bead from his forehead. With England stalled on 104 for five, Australia were back in it. England were effectively 205 for five, the pitch drying and flattening out, and they had come to a standstill: in the morning session of 28 overs they had scored 29 runs for the loss of three wickets. Graham Gooch had been Alderman-ed again on the second evening; Geoffrey Boycott had barely added to his overnight score; Gower, Brearley and Mike Gatting had all fallen to Australia's counter-thrust either side of lunch. England had taken all of 69 overs to post their 104 for five. Alderman had bowled right through this third morning from the Warwick Road End, while Lillee permitted Kim Hughes to give Whitney a couple of overs before lunch.

It was making quite a story, England's seizing up in sight of the Ashes, for *The Observer*'s first edition. I had to dictate my own copy so I was simply writing on a notepad, no need for a typewriter. The drawback at Old Trafford was that the phone I was hiring was in a booth at the back of the press box, where no more than a glimpse of a few white figures was to be had. Even Botham was relatively becalmed — taking more than an hour to reach 28, while Chris Tavaré continued to block for dear life — by Lillee and Alderman, who refused to say die.

Lillee and Alderman took the second new ball. All hell let loose. Lillee, like the *City of Truro* breaking the 100 mph barrier, steamed in anew from the Press Box End — I could see that much from the booth while dictating — and Botham kept hooking him into the Warwick Road Stand. The first eight overs of the new ball yielded 66 runs, and it was not Chris Tavaré who was unleashing, he was still hair-shirting. Normally Botham's sixes did not travel great distances: he hit sixes frequently (in the first-class season of 1985 he was to hit a record 80), but not far. He was too classical a batsman for that, having been brought up at Lord's to keep his left elbow up. The index finger and thumb of his right hand touched the bat handle, they did not clench it as T20 power-hitters do. This ball was new, however, this pitch had dried out as pacy, Lillee was giving all he had in his last-ditch attempt to win the Ashes, and some of Botham's hooks at his bouncers were flying deep into the Warwick Road Stand, almost on to the railway line. Lillee was to bowl 46 overs in this innings, and 70.1 in the match, Alderman 81. Inconceivable, or never permitted, now.

While Botham ripped into Australia, I ripped up my match report. I told the copytaker I would ring back shortly with a new version and returned to watch Botham. After taking 53 balls to reach 28, he needed only 33 more to surge to his century. His six sixes were then an Ashes record. Old Trafford imitated Edgbaston: it was a primeval roar when Australians dropped two half-chances. I had to ad-lib, which I normally hate doing, to get the job done.

On the Monday, after the rest day, John Woodcock told *Times* readers that Botham's was the greatest innings 'of its kind' that had ever been played for England. In the middle of the wood at the time, I had not stood back to see the tree itself, but I deferred absolutely to his judgment: he had been covering Test cricket since 1950. All I would add is that subsequently Graham Gooch, in his unbeaten 154 against West Indies at Headingley in 1991, and Ben Stokes in his unbeaten 135 against Australia, also at Headingley in 2019, equalled Botham's 118 at any rate – or, I would say, surpassed it, if only because Gooch and Stokes had more Test-standard bowlers to face than the two that Botham had.

After one sweet dream we do not expect another to follow. Yet in the summer of 1981 we had three sweet dreams in a row – albeit some nightmarish moments in between. Australia were winning the Headingley and Edgbaston Tests, on top throughout, until the lion roared and the kangaroos fled. England nearly let Old Trafford slip.

Between Botham's Headingley and Old Trafford hundreds it was easy to draw a distinction in retrospect. England went on to win 3–1, just hanging on for a draw at the Oval thanks to Alan

Knott's batting and Botham's bowling. 'Beefy' was too drained to batter the Australians again, but he still bowled more overs than anyone else in the match, 89. It was another heroic effort: had England won the series only 3–2, it would have looked less impressive to posterity. Botham took 10 wickets then went to bed and slept, so I was told by the late Peter Roebuck (he and Botham were then friends), for 24 hours.

Botham also enabled England to draw that sixth Test – they clung on with seven wickets down – with some psychology of which Brearley would have been proud. Australia had a debutant called Dirk Wellham. He reached the nervous nineties as the end of the fourth day approached. Botham kept on urging him 'Don't give it away.' Wellham eventually scraped enough singles to reach his hundred, but by then it was too late for Kim Hughes to declare. He waited until the fifth morning. Thus England had to face the second new ball for only a handful of overs, because then it was available after 85.

After the series *The Observer*'s chief sports writer Hugh McIlvanney wanted to interview the year's hero. McIlvanney seldom ventured into cricket, but he had recently come as close as anyone to capturing the charisma of Viv Richards. An interview with Botham was arranged for the hotel outside Lord's: I was to be present to introduce and facilitate. The interview turned to the centuries at Headingley and Old Trafford – and Botham almost dried up. He was not trying to be awkward (it has been known), he was simply at a loss to explain. He saw the ball and hit the ball, fearlessly, as Bazballers at their best were to do. I suggested that Headingley was hitting whereas Old Trafford was batting; and, after a pause, he agreed. Beyond that? Dudley Doust would have spoken to other England players, and some Australians, but what else could have been wrung from Botham himself? We will have to wait until an encephalogram, placed inside a helmet, can monitor the brain activity of a batsman in the course of a great innings. Botham had been inspired and, after some conscious thought while building his innings, he had ascended into a realm which mortals do not know.

Mumbai, or Bombay as it was then, November–December 1981

I went to India a few days in advance of England's 1981–82 tour. Firstly, India's prime minister Indira Gandhi was thinking of invoking the Gleneagles Agreement because Geoffrey Boycott had represented Northern Transvaal and the reserve opening batsman, Geoff Cook, had also played in apartheid South Africa. Second, I had never visited India before, having missed the Golden Jubilee Test in Mumbai in February 1980 when Ian Botham had beaten India almost single-handedly; instead I had gone from Australia, where England had been powerless to avoid a 3–0 defeat, to Fiji, which had some ingredients of a serious cricket-playing country (like a tribal chief who had played first-class cricket in New Zealand). Third, I was going to write a tour book about this England tour of India; to do that properly one has to research more widely and dig deeper than a journalist normally would.

Fourth, I was 27. Time to begin to think about marrying and settling down? I knew she was the one the moment I saw her, skipping down the steps of a hotel in Poona, oblivious to a new wide-eyed admirer. Apologies for having told the story before but I would like to stress here that it happened exactly thus, word for word.

She said she was half-Bengali, half-Pathan. I said: 'Some of my favourite drinks are cocktails.' She promptly replied: 'Cocktails can give you a hangover.' Decades on, my head has not cleared.

The first Test, at the Wankhede Stadium, degenerated into disputes about umpiring that are mercifully never seen in this era of neutral umpires. Sport is intended to be fun and to bring people together: this first Test was full of hatred, racist abuse, accusations of cheating by both sides. I am in no position to judge. What I can say is that nobody then was in a perfect position to judge. Indian television was in its infancy and could not offer replays, slow motion or otherwise. The players of both countries interpreted events subjectively and, therefore, very differently.

All I could do on the rest day of the first Test in 1981–82, when England's captain Keith Fletcher was seething in the team hotel (no official press conference), was to visit one of the umpires, Swaroop Kishen. During England's first-innings collapse Swaroop had awarded a very close run-out decision to India; he had no part in the proceedings when England's middle order faced the left-arm spin of Dilip Doshi and started sweeping, and mis-sweeping, and missing, and lost four wickets in five overs to Doshi. It should be noted that Doshi was bowling from close to the stumps, almost wicket to wicket. Swaroop's ample physique was such that Doshi could not have got in close at his end. England hereabouts were trying to accelerate after Boycott and Chris Tavaré had combined in one of their lengthier partnerships, when the scoreboard stood almost as still as time itself: they added 92 runs off 59 overs.

After the International Cricket Council took umpires under their wing during the 1990s, and introduced match referees, then TV umpires (who can be more influential than men in the middle) and fourth umpires (fixers to help the on-field umpires with local knowledge), a team of Test Match Officials would be accommodated in – if not the same hotel – then the same standard of hotel as the players. On this occasion, while players and media enjoyed one of the great hotels of the world in the Taj Mahal (old wing, for preference, please), Swaroop was billeted in the clubhouse alongside the Wankhede Stadium: a sign of the lower status accorded to umpires by the Indian board. I found him in a frayed vest and cool, loose trousers. He sat sideways on the edge of his bed, and it was soon manifest that, whether or not his colleague Ramaswamy had something up his sleeve, Swaroop had nothing to hide.

'We have all practical facility here [meaning the clubhouse]. We have tea and breakfast in the morning,' Swaroop said, before mopping his brow (no air-conditioning in his room). 'Where I come from it is snowing now. I come from Kashmir originally, Srinagar is my native place but I have subsequently moved to

Delhi. It is very hot now in Bombay, so I came here to acclimatise two days before the Test match.'

Swaroop offered me betel nut from an old tobacco tin: a mild narcotic that has long eased life in the East. His mouth was currently stained dark red; so are the lower reaches of many a wall in India. Between chews he talked me through the particular challenges of umpiring a Test match in India, of which he had stood in seven previously.

'In Bombay, when England batting, there are 40 to 50 thousand people shouting every time ball hitting the pad, and in Calcutta, my God, there are 90 thousand people all shouting! But you must concentrate. It is a selfish thing but you must concentrate, to save your skin and give umpiring in your country a good name.'

Swaroop paused to mop. 'Never has the Indian board given me instructions about what to do on the field, never, never. You must always give the right decision, and God alone is your judge.' He also referred to 'the sanctity of the game'.

For standing five days in the sun, Swaroop and his colleague were not being paid anything like what the cricketers received. 'Before several years,' Swaroop said, 'Test umpires were receiving 250 rupees (equivalent to £15 in 1981-82) and travelling by train, but now we fly by air and receive 2,500 rupees.'

The point here is that Swaroop, and most Indian umpires at first-class level in his time, were basically amateurs. They held jobs in government departments, which were generous in granting unpaid leave – for purposes like umpiring – but not so far as their salaries were concerned.

How much had he played? Of all the umpires who had officiated in Tests in India after their inaugural home series in 1933–34 against England, not one to that point had played first-class cricket. They were masters of hypothetical and abstruse regulations, for example, was the batsman out if the ball had split in two after being hit and a) the cork or b) the leather had been caught? Most English umpires have always been gamekeepers, who know all the poacher's tricks, and never mind the theoretical:

having retired from playing one season, they umpired first-class games the next.

Swaroop said he had been 'a one-down batsman' in club cricket. I liked that description of a number three. I would like to be referred to as a 'nine-down batsman' when stuck at number 11. He had umpired his first league game at 18 and 'after 30 years I had my first Test match in 1978. After 30 years,' he repeated with justifiable pride. There must have been hundreds or thousands of other contenders.

Other Indian umpires whom I watched, before the ICC introduced neutrals, did not always seem to be motivated by the same high principles as Swaroop. One or two seemed intent on being the star of the show, signalling a six histrionically even before the ball had landed inside the boundary. Looking back, they were trapped in time. After World Series Cricket had been wound up in 1979, all the existing Test countries professionalised their players, sooner not later. Test umpires in the 1980s were meanwhile left to their own unresourced devices: no sight or hearing tests, no information on how umpires in other countries were operating or reacting to new developments, no official guidance on how to interpret Laws. They were trapped, plumb in front, between rocks and hard places.

At the end of this tour, when finishing off my book *Cricket Wallah*, I predicted: 'Not many years hence, although the game grew up thousands of miles away, India is destined to become the capital of cricket.' I did not have the gumption to realise how television would govern Indian cricket once the government had lifted the lid of Pandora's box, allowing neo-liberalism, or neo-conservatism, to take over the economy, but I did add up two and two and two. Having the biggest cricket equipment-making industry was one factor behind its inevitable growth in India, enabling the expanding middle class to afford bats and balls. So too the decline of hockey, once the switch to artificial surfaces was made and India were no longer regular Olympic gold medallists. So too the wealth of writing about cricket in newspapers, magazines and books, in several more languages than English. The traditions of Indian batsmanship, the intricacies of their spin bowling, the enormity of their stadia, the insatiable enthusiasm for this non-contact sport which did not prioritise huge physiques, the popular desire to semi-deify star cricketers, they all added up. And within 30 years the eight captains of the franchise teams in the inaugural Indian Premier League – all-time greats like Sachin Tendulkar, Rahul Dravid and Shane Warne – were ascending the podium in Bangalore for the opening ceremony, as fireworks illuminated the night sky and cricket's future.

Test No. 49
Calcutta, January 1982

'Do you want to come to an orphanage?' Mike Brearley asked.

He had retired from playing, and now had a newspaper contract that funded his visit to India for England's tour. Head gamekeepers in cricket morph speedily into poachers: England captains have scarcely put down a ball before they pick up a mike. Len Hutton entered the press box shortly after his retirement as England's captain in 1955: never, ever, confrontational, always roundabout if not positively circuitous in his approach, he looked at Michael Davie, who was covering cricket for *The Observer*, and nodded at the typewriter: 'Is it – is it useful?' This was his way of proposing that he should become the paper's columnist.

In India, Brearley had met Mana, whose people in Ahmedabad had been supporters of Mahatma Gandhi during the Salt Marches and independence movement. Mana had contacts in Calcutta (now Kolkata) who had been instrumental in setting up the SOS Children's Village in the city, in order to accommodate the many orphans in Bengal, many, though not all, the result of famine.

'Isn't it a sad place?' I replied. At school, when we had hosted an annual visit by disabled children, I did not volunteer, I scarpered.

'No, it's quite the opposite,' Brearley said, using 'quite' in its absolute not partitive sense. 'It's a happy place.'

When we went to this SOS Children's Village in the reclaimed area of Calcutta known as Salt Lake City, it was not a happy place: it was filled with joy. The kids, of both genders, were the complete opposite of spoilt brats; any simple thing like a biscuit or pencil was a treat to be savoured. They lived in bungalows of 10 to 12 children, supervised by a mother who herself had been turfed on to the streets (Siamese twins, for example, were discarded because they were considered unlucky). Older girls would help look after younger children. Everybody kept an eye on everyone else. All were orphans who had thus acquired not only brothers and sisters but a mother too. It was such materially simple joy. Of my preconceptions and stuffed-up English reserve, I've never felt so ashamed.

All altruism can be seen, *au fond*, as being rooted in selfishness. Whatever that truth, I started sponsoring a girl there: like many of them she had been so malnourished in infancy that she would never grow to full height. On England's next tour in 1984–85, I persuaded a couple of the players not involved in the Test to play a game at the Village on the rest day. The boys went up to the age of about 14 and two teams were assembled. I had brought a bat and tennis balls, and the playground normally used for football and netball was requisitioned. This was Bengal: football has usually been the main sport, ahead of cricket, before the IPL at any rate. I compare Bengal to Italy: the temperament, love of food, the literary culture, where Tagore has similar stature to Dante but is rather more recent. Nobody else's verse has formed the lyrics of two national anthems.

We played a game of 20 overs per side. Neil Foster was in competitive mood with ball then bat. Batting first, Vic Marks's team (including me) made a decent total before Fossie enjoyed one big over (tennis ball sailing over bungalows) off Victor's bowling. At the end of this over a boy, aged perhaps 12 or 13, studiously walked up to Victor, took the ball from him and marked out his pace bowling run-up, as if to say 'no more of this rolled English off-spin!' The lad restored order and we narrowly won. It was an afternoon which could hardly have been happier for all involved; older girls watching with a baby on their hip were wide-eyed with excitement too. Fossie, back in the England team, took 11 wickets to win the next Test.

In the era when England tours were tours not business trips, a PR day would often be factored into the schedule. Typical was a visit, on England's first tour of South Africa after readmission, to a township club in Kimberley by the name of Yorkshire. David Bairstow, Jonny's father, had either coached or played there so a link existed. England players got off the bus, milled around, saw how rough and shabby the field and pavilion were: no sprinkled lawn like white club grounds. Hands were shaken, smiles, protestations of friendship, a shirt or tracksuit presented, group photographs in front of the sign saying Yorkshire for the newspapers at home; then everyone back on the bus, return to the hotel, move on. I do not know if there was any follow-up, whether England or Yorkshire CCC kept in touch with Yorkshire CC.

The ECB's corporate affairs advice was that the England cricket team should not be associated with one particular charity: it was to be an afternoon here on this tour, an afternoon there on the next. I would have liked to see all the eggs in one basket for, say, five years, then the outcome reviewed: long-term involvement with the England cricket team would surely have raised the profile, funds and sponsorships of a particular charity that worked in Commonwealth countries. (A charity, that is, which did not spend too much of its income on generous salaries and benefits for its white middle-class, mainly male, administrators.)

Brearley's recommendation should have been more than adequate to start: SOS Children's Villages was established in Europe after the Second World War to look after orphans of all persuasion. I told Nasser Hussain when he was England's captain about the one in Calcutta, and about Brearley's endorsement and the subsequent pick-up game. Nasser immediately said 'let's do it' – and his team did, during a visit to Calcutta during a one-day series. I was not present but it was reportedly an occasion of wild enthusiasm if not bedlam, as ordinary fans tried to enter the Village to watch England's cricketers. It must have raised, apart from money, the status of the orphanage in the eyes of Calcutta.

Test No. 51
Kanpur, February 1982

It was hard to smell a rat in the centre of India's tanning industry. Muslims did the work of turning cow hides into leather garments and shoes, and the obnoxious smell permeated Kanpur. The Hotel Meghdoot was nothing to telex home about either, a concrete pile for teams and media. At the reception desk on the ground floor, a Bakelite phone protruded from black wires, and occasionally the outside world intruded, as now.

'Phone call for Mr Graham!' shouted the receptionist in the bare and basic lobby, in order to be heard above the players returning from the ground. This was called Green Park, as the only thing in Kanpur's city centre that was not the colour of dust.

'Zap, it's for you,' people said helpfully.

Graham Gooch pushed his way through to the desk. It was a long-distance phone call. He bent over the desk to hear better. But then he would have had to bend over the desk to hear if the caller had been in a room on the second floor, so we were none too suspicious.

Several minutes this call lasted, and now we know what it was about. Dr Ali Bacher was calling from South Africa to find out if the deal was sealed: whether Gooch had gathered a team of England players who were sufficiently disaffected to set off to South Africa almost as soon as they had returned from India. A lot of them were feeling disaffected: they had been traipsing around India for two months since the opening Test in Bombay, and the score was still 1–0 to India. None of the five subsequent, mind-numbing, draws ever suggested a definite outcome. To give a flavour of the competitiveness, all 11 England players bowled in the fifth Test in Madras.

I did not criticise the England rebels of 1981–82 half so much as those of 1989–90. Gooch's players did not know the lie of the land when they went on this unofficial tour – beyond the large payday. The later rebels, recruited by Mike Gatting and David Graveney, knew what they were doing: that they were bolstering South Africa's government at a critical moment when it was struggling to preserve apartheid.

The immediate consequence of Gooch, Geoffrey Boycott, John Emburey, Derek Underwood and John Lever from this touring party, along with seven other players in England, heading off to South Africa was a three-year ban. (The cricket correspondent of the *Evening Standard*, John Thicknesse, was inconsolable: when Underwood had made his Test debut, Thicknesse had placed a bet that he would take 300 Test wickets, and now he was stuck for eternity on 297.) Politics and ethics aside, the most serious loss to English cricket was Gooch, who, unlike most of the others, was still in his prime. Seldom has any opening partnership papered over so many underlying cracks as Gooch and Boycott had done in the 1980 and 1980–81 series against West Indies. Boycott, aged 40, was seen to his finest advantage as his defence soaked up the new-ball thrusts while Gooch took the attack to the West Indian fast bowlers like nobody else in the world could. Instead of losing 1–0 and 2–0, England without this pair lost their next two series 5–0.

England's remaining players, who had not succumbed to the lure of krugerands, became a tight-knit unit to prevent any further defections. It was an understandable and healthy reaction up to a point. My observation is that most Test countries at most periods have, at best, only 10 or 12 cricketers of Test class (Australia were a major exception in the McGrath-Warne era when they had a superfluity of batsmen). But this unprecedented player-power evolved into something a little too strong. England under Bob Willis did well to lose the 1982–83 Ashes by a margin of only 2–1, but the series loss in New Zealand in 1983–84 was England's first there, and they even lost a one-day game in Fiji en route, befuddled by a mystery-spinner far ahead of his time called Jock McGoon. From New Zealand, England went to Pakistan and chose not to play a single warm-up game on pitches a world away from the ones they had been playing on. It was a foretaste of the future when tours consisted of nothing bar Tests, but there was not even a camp of a few days in the UAE by way of preparation. When David Gower took over the England captaincy during that tour of Pakistan, administrators at Lord's ensured that he was on a tighter leash.

Test No. 58

Faisalabad, September–October 1982

One of my very few regrets is never to have seen Imran Khan play a Test against England in Pakistan. By the 1983–84 series he was injured, after playing for New South Wales. After the 1987 World Cup had ended in a semi-final defeat for Pakistan, he did not want any part in the Test series that followed (it was poor timing, England having just played five Tests against Pakistan that summer at home). But I did enjoy the sight of Imran bowling in a Test in Pakistan in 1982–83, when the tiger was still in his prime: it was one of five Tests I have attended, out of 500, which did not involve England. I flew to Faisalabad, where Australia were playing the second Test in a three-match series, to see how they were shaping up for the next Ashes and to interview Imran for his profile as one of *Wisden*'s Five Cricketers of the Year.

'To tell you very frankly, I should have been selected last year.' This was what Imran announced at the start of our interview in Pakistan's dressing-room at close of play. Imperious or, merely, lordly? He had indeed played brilliantly for Sussex in 1981, but the five cricketers were selected by the *Wisden* editor alone and unaided. This time he had been selected for leading Pakistan to their first Test victory at Lord's. It could, and probably would, have been their first Test series win in England had neutral umpires been standing: Imran was marshalling Pakistan's tail at Headingley when a patently wrong bat-pad decision was given in England's favour.

Imran, however, did not complain about the umpiring, not now. We talked instead about the Lord's Test: he, as captain, had set what was thought to be a record for any Test in England by not taking the second new ball until the 117th over of England's second innings. Why not? 'Taking the new ball is such a cliché,' Imran replied. Mudassar Nazar, his medium-pacer, had taken six wickets for 32, by far his best Test haul, with a ragged old ball. I could not put two and two together, then. In my defence the term 'reverse-swing' did not exist; but if I had plugged away, as the best bowlers do, Imran might possibly have revealed to me what he had learned about it from his compatriot Sarfraz Nawaz.

Next day I watched it in action again – I watched reverse-swing but still did not know what I was seeing. Imran rounded up Australia's lower order by setting the ball in motion with his arm lowered to the line of off stump, and by directing it initially away from their right-handed batsmen – at close on 90 mph – then making the ball change direction, swerving it in at least a couple of feet, to crash into the batsman's stumps or toes. It was some fusion of magic, physics and pyrotechnics. One of the great beauties of cricket, curvaceous and lethal, is the parabola described by the prodigiously reverse-swung ball. I am so glad to have seen it live in its natural habitat, before neutral umpires were introduced and instructed to check the ball's condition. Wasim Akram and Waqar Younis did not play a Test either against England in Pakistan when they were at peak pace, or Mohammad Zahid, rumoured to be their rival. Thirteen years were to elapse from the confrontation between Mike Gatting and Shakoor Rana in 1987–88, when both men thought they were in the right, until England's next Test tour.

Test No. 62

Melbourne, December 1982

'Bor-der! Boor-der! Booor-der!'

The crowd at the MCG had suddenly swollen to about 10,000 on the fifth morning of the fourth Test, but nobody was counting. Gates had been opened for free. Australia overnight had only one remaining wicket and they still needed 37 runs to win.

An English cynic would say so many people turned up – and they might have watched a single ball – because Melbourne does not offer much else in the Christmas holidays. Not quite fair. Some decent beaches are on offer at St Kilda, even if everything else is closed, apart from the MCG.

Nobody had been chanting Allan Border's name when he came in to bat on the fourth afternoon. It was on the Australian selectors' lips though: he was expected, and expecting, to be dropped for the fifth Test after a lean series. It was the closest he ever came to be dropped during his 153 Tests in succession, a world-record sequence until bettered by Sir Alastair Cook.

This was a unique Test in several ways. For the first time in a completed match all four totals fell within a span of 10 runs: England 284 and 294, Australia 287 and 288. The result equalled the smallest margin of victory recorded to that point in terms of runs: three. The MCG became the first ground to stage 75 Tests – yet the problem of its square had still not been sorted. Australian Rules churned up the pitches all winter. A shocker of uneven bounce had been served up for a recent Test against India, and the Melbourne Cricket Club wanted matches to last more than two or three days, given crowds in their tens of thousands. This time the square was relaid; then it became the first ground in official Tests (experiments had been made during World Series Cricket) to yield to drop-in pitches, with the tiresome uniformity that entailed.

'Border! Boor-der! Booor-der!' they kept chanting as Australia's last pair of Border and Jeff Thomson edged closer to regaining the Ashes by taking a 3-0 lead.

Of the 74 runs which Australia's last pair had wanted, they had scored exactly half by the fourth evening. Before then, however, an incident happened which dates this game, or rather a non-incident. Norman Cowans was bowling from the Pavilion End, over the wicket as normal, at the left-handed Rod Marsh – and a ball pitching around or just outside his off stump, on a fullish length, shot along the ground. Being angled across the batsman, the grubber went through to Bob Taylor without disturbing Marsh's pads or stumps.

And that was it. England were desperate for wickets – Australia were five down – to claw the series back to 2–1, yet there was no follow-up. The point is that right-arm pace bowlers of this era seldom bowled round the wicket, some of them never. Had Cowans, or Willis, or Ian Botham, or even Derek Pringle at lesser pace, bowled round the wicket, there was a spot to be hit – and even if the ball did not hit that spot, that grubber would have kept preying on Marsh's mind.

We know that 'back in the day' right-arm pace bowlers had side-on actions and, therefore, when bowling over the wicket, they could get closer to the stumps than bowlers of today, who have chest-on or 'split actions' designed to keep the spine straight during delivery. But it is still strange that right-arm pace bowlers did not explore more often the possibilities of round the wicket. Sitting behind the arm in one of the MCG's huge stands (the press box has a restricted view), I was looking around for a concrete pillar against which to bang my head as the overs passed and Australia's middle order of left-handers – Border, Marsh and David Hookes – carried on batting, without England aiming for the Achilles heel.

When Australia's last pair came together, I was less annoyed when England pushed the field back to allow Border to take singles. This was a tactic in its infancy, but at least it had a fundamental logic. The more balls you bowled to the tailender, the more likely you were to take a wicket; and meantime the specialist batsman could hardly hit fours because the field was so widely spread. The trouble in this instance was that Border, having entered the fray like a man whose head was on the block, visibly regained his confidence the longer he stayed in – and he would be strutting for the next ten years. Spreading the field for Border was tantamount to laying down a red carpet for lord and master.

The climax became ever more excruciating. Willis had not trusted his tidy off-spinner Geoff Miller during the partnership on the fourth evening: was it worth a go now, perhaps when Thomson was on strike for the start of an over, in the hope of a wild swing if the ball was tossed above his eyeline? Too late, it appeared. England, in this crisis, went into autopilot and kept doing what they were doing in the desperate hope a break would come their way. Botham bowled again because the other two pace bowlers, Willis himself and Cowans, were exhausted. If anyone was master of this situation it was Border on 62; Thomson, who had restrained himself, was 21.

More than 40 years later, when Border was commentating on a rebound catch in a Test at Perth – Nathan McSweeney at gully pushed the ball towards Marnus Labuschagne in the slips – he was instantly reminded by his co-commentators of the rebound 40-odd years before. Four runs to win. Thomson in two minds – go for the winning hit or tap a single to let Border take strike? – dabbed at a widish ball from Botham that was completely innocuous except as bait. The edge flew high to Chris Tavaré at second slip, one of the best fielders in that position, only these were the days before the gym and core strengthening. The ball flew up from Tavaré's palms as he bent back, the ball going 'over the bar', until Miller swooped from first slip to catch the rebound behind Tavaré. The England players ran madly in all directions in their relief.

Looking back, my guess is that more runs have been conceded by spreading the field than would have been scored if the field had been kept up for both batsmen, although it is only a hunch.

Test No. 76

Edgbaston 1984, and *passim* 1984–'88

Andy Lloyd, as a Warwickshire player, had offered his advice that England should bowl first at Edgbaston in the opening Test of the 1984 series against West Indies, but he was making his Test debut so nobody was fully listening. And not for long was he making his debut: after half an hour, of England batting first, he was hit on the head by Malcolm Marshall and carted away from the front line, not seeing straight or playing again that season, and never representing England again. No such thing as concussion substitutes.

Thus did England set off on the wrong foot against West Indies, and there they stayed for more than four years. England had endured horror streaks before. In their first three series after the First World War, they had lost 12–1 against Australia; in their first three series against Australia after the Second World War, they had lost 11–1. In their three series against West Indies from 1984 to 1988 they lost 14–0. They drew the other game, at Trent Bridge in 1988, thanks to Graham Gooch scoring 73 and 146, and rain.

Such was the disparity between the two sides that sometimes West Indies would have won if they had had one innings and England three. Often it was men against boys. Two England batsmen were very seriously injured by the fast bowling: in addition to Lloyd, Paul Terry never played for England again after his left elbow was fractured. In hindsight it is remarkable that so many escaped unscathed: England, facing an attack of four fast bowlers, quaintly persisted in picking a 'balanced side' with two spinners, which required them to bat first in the vague hope that come the fourth innings they would catch West Indies on a wearing pitch. Except, often, there was no fourth innings. That spinners of advancing years like Pat Pocock and John Childs did escape injury was thanks to the West Indians pitching the ball up – Pocock recorded a pair in two consecutive Tests, but at least lived to tell the tale.

In one of those 15 Tests, the second of the 1984 series, England were in a position to declare – except that they were in no such position. It was just that the chairman of selectors, Peter May, thought they should declare to make a game of it, and told the captain so. This made for an exceptional case of falling between stools. England had either to declare at the start of day five and get West Indies in when the Lord's pitch was doing a little: their target would then have been 329 on the whole of the last day. Or else England had to continue batting on the fifth morning until they were bowled out, whereupon West Indies would have had to score at more than four an over, an almost unprecedented achievement in a run-chase to that point (except at Headingley in 1948 when Don Bradman's men knocked off 404). Gower, bowing to the chairman, batted on until the ball stopped moving around, then declared with nine wickets down. In glorious sunshine on a true pitch West Indies derisively knocked off 344 in 66.1 overs, for the loss of one wicket.

During the Edgbaston Test that was the first in this living nightmare of a sequence, I sat for a while in the crowd. England supporters had the better of West Indian supporters in numbers, but not in volume, given the aid of conch-shells and steel drums. I have never experienced such an excited level of audience participation – such passion – in a theatre or elsewhere, as England were routed for 191 and West Indies replied with 606. In England's second attempt, when Derek Randall came out at number three, a West Indian supporter yelled: 'You're sacrificing him! You're sacrificing him!' – and he was right. Randall had all the strokes of a middle-order batsman; he did not have the defence to be a 'one-down' in England. The supporter was not blindly supporting his team, although West Indies winning in England probably made life easier for him, with a little more respect on the streets. He was passionately involved in the whole drama. So was I. It contained the essential element of spontaneity: West Indian supporters turned up when top-class cricket was to be seen, queued to buy tickets with cash, and participated. By the 1990s they were being phased out by English authorities: tickets went first to those on mailing lists who bought with credit cards.

What made these Tests of the mid-1980s so spectacular was the sight of England players reacting to fast bowling of a speed they had never seen before. In little more than a garage in Bristol, a start-up project called Bola was beginning to make bowling machines, to compete with baseball pitching machines imported from the US, of which English cricket had no more than a handful. When Bob Willis became assistant manager on England's tour of the West Indies in 1985–86, he took a bowling machine to replicate his opponents' speed. But brains, synapses and reactions have to be programmed from an early age, preferably the cradle. In those days Test cricket was said to be 'a step up' because the bowling was faster than anything a county player had seen before. On his Test debut in 1977, even Ian Botham was well behind the pace when he came to bat against Jeff Thomson and Lenny Pascoe, although he had already taken wickets. It was the way it was. Batting in a Test for the first time was like a motorist driving on to a motorway for the first time: everything happened bewilderingly quicker.

In this context it was not shameful if players were afraid. In the Antigua Test of 1981, when Colin Croft was the most threatening of the West Indian fast bowlers, I saw two England lower-order batsmen backing away, not to upper-cut but in self-defence, for self-preservation. The sightscreen was too low at Croft's end when he leaped wide in the crease and angled the ball in at the ribs of hapless right-handers, so sighting the ball was more difficult; but, above all, this was uncharted territory. Here were players who had never been able to condition their reflexes to this sort of speed.

As Tests in the West Indies went untelevised, except in Trinidad, we will never know how fast they bowled. What I would say is that their speeds would vary far more than they do now. A bowler might work up his pace gradually: Michael Holding's over to Geoffrey Boycott in the Barbados Test of 1980–81 became famous for coming at the other extreme of the Richter scale. Croft himself might amble in for Lancashire on a cold day, and steam in on a hot one in the Caribbean, a difference of 20 mph. On the truly frightening day in Kingston in 1985–86, when Malcolm Marshall saw a rival emerging in Patrick Patterson, the pair made Holding and Joel Garner resemble medium-pacers. I think there might be only one objective measurement: when Patterson was tearing in from the George Headley Stand End, when not only the pitch was cracking up but England's batting too, one of his deliveries soared over the heads of the batsman and wicketkeeper and bounced only once before crossing the boundary rope and hitting the sightscreen with the thud of an executioner's axe on the block.

How fast? Too fast.

West Indies occasionally picked the fast-medium all-rounder Eldine Baptiste: not that he was much of a weak link because he set a world record by winning every one of his 10 Tests. This enabled them to play Roger Harper too, and three quicks. Normally, however, it was four out of Malcolm Marshall, Joel Garner, Michael Holding, Wayne Daniel, Sylvester Clarke, Patrick Patterson, Courtney Walsh, Winston Benjamin, Curtly Ambrose and Kenny Benjamin, all of them having Andy Roberts to call on for counsel. He was to West Indian cricket what John Snow was to England's and Dennis Lillee to Australia's: the man who worked out modern fast bowling techniques and how to train for the job. Roberts did not need a high-performance centre: he took trainees to the beach and had them running on sand, then in the sea, and deeper and deeper until their legs were muscled. Roberts showed them how to bowl bouncers cross-seam so they lifted to unpredictable heights, and the most difficult delivery of all: the thumb flipping the ball around in the delivery stride, so fooling the batsman who thinks he has identified the shiny side. (Ghosting a few Roberts columns for *The Sunday Telegraph* was priceless tuition.)

Some critics objected to the West Indian strategy, which had been born out of the failure of their three specialist spinners in Trinidad in 1976: India, set 403, knocked them off for the loss of four wickets and two were run-outs. I do not think anybody has the right to tell cricketers how to play. They are given the Laws, the conditions, the equipment, and it is for them to get on with winning the game as they think best. The Law on intimidation was in place in the 1980s and perhaps should have been invoked more often. A few wanted to view these England v West Indies contests as a race war. All I would say is that the most concentrated and vicious assault I have seen live by one fast bowler against a particular batsman (I did not see Brian Close fending off Holding at Old Trafford in 1976 as I was playing that day) was when Courtney Walsh pounded the daylights out of Devon Malcolm in 1989–90. Not only was the Test staged in Jamaica, both players were Jamaican by birth.

West Indies bowled their overs slowly, down to 12 an hour, so that each of their four bowlers had six overs per session. But the international regulations allowed them to do so – Len Hutton had been the captain to drag it down to 15 per hour – and, furthermore, very few of their Tests ended in draws. I never heard any England player complain about West Indian fast bowling or their over-rate – not even one afternoon on a beach in Antigua, after a couple of us journalists had started throwing a tennis ball at each other from short range at the point where the waves lapped the beach and, like *Bolero*, England players kept joining in. They threw as hard as they could at one journalist who had been writing that they should play forwards more – this against steepling bounce on pitches no longer as well-rolled, even and shiny as they used to be – but they did not criticise West Indies for their methods. England, through the 1980s, just wanted to be able to bowl like West Indies did.

And never a word of sledging. When West Indies were world champions they were silent on the field. Plenty of them had been brought up by their grandmothers, who God-fearingly read the Bible and who would have walloped infants if they had sworn.

Rarely, for an hour or so, or almost a session, a pair of England batsmen could take them on. These counterattacks were fast and furious because West Indies kept their fielders in until a dismissal, never did they admit failure by spreading the field. It might be Graham Gooch, though he was still serving a ban during the 1984 series, or, in Trinidad once, when David Gower and Allan Lamb took the bowling apart, briefly. Both reached 60, nobody else double figures. I do not know whether the phrase 'a ball with your name in it' was used in English cricket after the two World Wars, when the reference would have been too real, but it was current in Test series in the 1980s, when the analogy to bullets was not too tasteless. Most of the time England's batsmen were expecting one.

Bestriding these contests was the king and colossus, Viv Richards: he who strutted/strolled out to bat, chewing his gum, and whipped his first ball through midwicket as if the bowler were a fly. It has emerged that the main motivation of the West Indian fast bowlers when beating England was pragmatic: knock them over as quickly as possible so we can put our feet up, before going back to the summer's grind of county cricket. Richards was cut from another cloth, made for a higher mission. Learie Constantine's mantra, when playing against England in the 1930s, was 'They are no better than we.' First Frank Worrell, quietly, then Richards, proudly, upped it to: 'We are better than they.' By 1988 he had scored more Test centuries in England than any other tourist except Don Bradman; in Tests in England he averaged 64. Richards put into action the words of his contemporary Bob Marley, that we should free ourselves of negative thoughts and liberate our minds. Because he had this mission statement to promote his people, and the power to carry it out, Richards was the most charismatic cricketer I have seen, followed by Imran Khan, then Ian Botham.

Most batsmen after scoring a hundred walk back to the pavilion. In the Antigua Test of 1985–86 Richards pummelled England for 110* off 58 balls, having reached his hundred in the then record time of 56 balls. It was necessary, not gratuitous, pummelling: England had batted out the last day of the Antigua Test in 1980–81 and Richards did not want the same to happen again, not on his turf, so he hit out then got England two wickets down by the end of day four. When two-thirds of the way back to the pavilion, after declaring, Richards, like a great actor, paused – it might have only lasted a second – to acknowledge the applause. I guessed he was taking a moment to drink in all he had done. Richards had brought Antigua to the world's attention. He had made an island of 80,000 people a destination for cricket supporters and tourists in general. He had put Antigua on the map. And, far beyond the Caribbean, it was acknowledged that Black people could perform every bit as skilfully, and in the world of cricket even better.

Test No. 77

Lord's, August 1984

Memories try to be selective. Forgive me, therefore, if I do not raise the will to look back at Sri Lanka's civil war, to which the cricket world was alerted when Tamil demonstrators rushed on to the Lord's outfield on the first day of Sri Lanka's inaugural Test in England. Velupillai Prabhakaran, leader of the Tamil Tigers, was one of the all-time monsters. I have read fairly widely about the civil war while on tours of Sri Lanka, and tried to write about it in *Beyond The Boundaries*. This is as far as I want to go now. Suffice, perhaps, to say that for many a complicated reason, Tamils are not represented in the Sri Lankan cricket team any more extensively than they used to be.

The orthodox batting of Sidath Wettimuny and the jovial hitting of Duleep Mendis were, however, a joy to savour.

Test No. 103
The Oval, August 1986

Ian Botham's first Test since being banned after admitting the use of recreational drugs. Rusty? He took a New Zealand wicket with his first ball, and with his 12th, passing Dennis Lillee's world record of 355 Test wickets. Cautious when playing himself in? He hit 24 off one over to equal the existing Test record, and reached 59 off 36 balls by the time rain intervened: he had another 35 balls to beat Gilbert Jessop's record of the fastest hundred for England, little more than a run a ball.

Australia, 1986–87
So seldom have England won an Ashes series in Australia since the Second World War that a decent sample size hardly exists. Yet, if a trend is perceptible, it is that England have won the preceding Ashes series in England. Such an advantage – which England took to Australia in 1954–55, and 1978–79, and 1986–87, and 2010–11 – forces the hosts to win one more game than England if they are to regain the urn.

England's success in 1985 had been based on Ian Botham, again. Runs flowed all the way down England's order because Australia had so few bowlers of note (several, like Terry Alderman, had been banned for touring apartheid South Africa). What England needed was a fast bowler: they had swing but not pace. So Botham did the job himself. He rolled back the years, extended his run-up, bowled flat-out, and as in 1981 he huffed and puffed Australia's house down.

Some clever psychology too, from what I heard. On the England tour of the West Indies in 1980–81 Botham, then captain, had socialised more and more with the winners, including his Somerset teammates Viv Richards and Joel Garner. He thereby became more detached from his own team, who were losing. In 1985 England identified Allan Border, Australia's captain, as their main adversary and set about detaching him. How about going to Ascot? Do come along with us, AB. It was very matey stuff, in the finest Australian tradition, except Border was not being matey with his Australian players but the Poms. Lesson thoroughly digested, Border went all gruff on returning for the Ashes tour of 1989.

By the autumn of 1986, however, England were in a right mess: reportedly, by their warm-up in Perth, they couldn't bat, bowl or field. But having switched their batting order around for the Brisbane opener, they had Botham to build on their sound start – and he struck what turned out to be his last Test hundred, aged 30. He would have hit many more if he had led an athlete's lifestyle and worked on his fitness. But had he worked at his fitness and kept out of the public gaze – for he was by then as famous as any footballer – and focused more on his own performance, he might never have had those spontaneous surges of inspiration, most typified by Headingley and Old Trafford in 1981.

After taking a 1–0 lead at the Gabba in 1986–7 (to this day the last time they won an opening Test in Brisbane), England competently warded off an increasingly desperate Australia. Come the fourth Test at the MCG, Australia had to win the last two matches, and called in a psychologist to pump them up. They duly came out bristling to play shots, and offered nine catches behind the wicket. Botham had only to jog in and turn his arm over – a pulled rib-muscle had forced him to miss the third Test – to take a five-for for the 27th and final time.

'He bats like Stan McCabe,' Bill O'Reilly had announced to anyone who would listen. For the second Test in Perth, Australia had shunted up to number three a young batting all-rounder. This was Steve Waugh in his first incarnation – a dashing strokeplayer driving on the up through the covers, an adventurous Waugh, not an accumulator at number six – and Tiger, sitting behind the arm in the press box at the WACA, was transported back 50 years to McCabe's similar style.

O'Reilly was the most eminent former cricketer with whom I shared a press box: Sir Leonard Hutton kept too low a profile to appear in a press box and be pestered, and Sir Everton Weekes sat in the radio commentary box, while the modern star-turned-media man confines himself to green rooms and television studios. Tiger would be driven by his daughter to the Sydney Cricket Ground, where he worked as a columnist for the *Sydney Morning Herald*, and collected in the evening. When he flew to another state for a Test he was more available to talk about players past and present, not himself.

On my first tour of Australia, I had seen Tiger chatting with Clarrie Grimmett in the stand in front of the press box at the Adelaide Oval, and would have paid big bucks to overhear, but I did not dare approach. By the 1986–87 tour we were sufficiently familiar for Tiger to tell me how he had started. The epicentre of Australian cricket used to be the nets behind the main pavilion at the SCG; sooner rather than later every player was there assessed. O'Reilly, like his contemporary Don Bradman, was summoned from rural New South Wales. After bowling his own brand of brisk leg-spin off a longish run-up, when everyone was leaving, he met an old man with white hair who asked him how the net-session went. Tiger was discouraged, saying he was not prepared to make the adjustments to his grip which the coaches wanted him to make. 'Good on yer, I was exactly the same,' said the old man. 'I didn't listen to them either – and you won't make it if you do listen to them.' The veteran was Charlie Turner (17 Tests, all against England, 101 wickets at 16.53), who bowled such rapid off-breaks on uncovered pitches in the 1880s and '90s that he earned the sobriquet 'The Terror'. In his 19 Tests against England, in a far higher-scoring era than Turner's, O'Reilly took 102 wickets – more than five per game – at 25 each. Such was his perseverance, his tigerishness, that when Hutton scored his 364 and England posted 900, O'Reilly yielded 2.09 runs per over while bowling 85 overs and taking three for 178.

O'Reilly's message as a journalist was that Australia, to be their strongest, had to revive wrist-spin. Fast bowlers like Dennis Lillee, Jeff Thomson, Rodney Hogg, Geoff Lawson and Carl

Rackemann had enjoyed a golden era until the early 1980s but were petering out. Australia could no longer afford a modest finger-spinner, or a leg-spinner who rolled it rather than ripped it. Australia needed a real wrist-spinner, as a successor to Richie Benaud and Grimmett (and himself).

'Would you take Ray Bright on the next tour of England?' I asked him.

'I wouldn't take Ray Bright on a trip to Manly!' Tiger exploded.

It worked out all right in the end. In the same year that Tiger died, 1992, a young wrist-spinner called Shane Keith Warne made his Test debut. But even now Tiger's message should live on. England established Bazball's reputation by chasing down enormous fourth-innings targets on bland fourth- or fifth-day pitches, without turning a hair and without their opponents turning a ball. Wrist-spin is the hardest craft to acquire, and the most valuable, because it can succeed where no other type of bowling can.

Lord's, August 1987

When was a five-day cricket match not a Test? When it was the MCC's Bicentenary Match. It was a game, not a contest, *Wisden* rightly summarised. I am glad the vogue of the 1980s, for celebrating centenaries and bicentenaries, is passing.

The most memorable moment occurred when Graham Gooch, on 117, advanced down the pitch at the off-spinner Roger Harper. 'When an old cricketer leaves the crease,' the wonderfully evocative song by Roy Harper goes, 'you never know whether he's gone.' Gooch, on leaving the crease, did not know much for a split second either. But once Harper had picked up and thrown down the batsman's stumps, Gooch knew he had gone all right, perhaps the fastest run-out since MCC had been founded in 1787.

Was this run-out an omen? Gooch was representing MCC against the Rest of the World. In hindsight Harper's run-out could be seen as symbolic: his fast flat throw was a warning shot across MCC's bows. The time was coming for their power to diminish.

So long as the governing body of cricket in England and Wales has its headquarters at Lord's, their relationship with MCC will be cosy. Leading men in one organisation cross over to the other; and, even if they don't, the network is in place, so long as one party (MCC) plays host to the other (ECB). Two Tests per year to be staged at Lord's, old boy? Not a word need be said.

My verdict is that MCC preached to the converted only until 1987 at least. They played out-matches against public schools, not getting their hands dirty in inner cities. When they sent tours abroad, for their members to enjoy winter sunshine, they played against local Anglophile elites, not in townships. It was for their members to choose what to do, and they did, but we cannot rewrite history to say that MCC did much to spread the sport around the world. They would often taken an umpire with them on tour to raise the standards of local officials, but that's not game-changing. Not until the power of veto of England and Australia was removed from the constitution of the International Cricket Council in 1993 did cricket grow. We might not care for some of the values of the new rulers, Indian businessmen, but expand it they did.

Tom Brown's Schooldays tells us what MCC was traditionally like. MCC's secretary, during their game at Rugby School, suggests to Tom that he would be welcome as a new member when he comes to town. Self-perpetuation was the main objective, like the monarchy. MCC, now and then, has administered the Laws wisely, for which much credit, but this has not involved great physical effort. *The MCC Coaching Book*, in the debit column, did untold damage by making English batting stupefyingly dull in the 1950s: see ball, block ball.

MCC's first step towards preaching to the unconverted came when their secretary Roger Knight started hubs that spread around the country, inviting state schools – shorn of their playing fields by Margaret Thatcher – to join in training camps at private school grounds, especially in the summer holidays.

This work was expanded when the MCC Foundation was launched as a charity and Sarah Fane (OBE for her medical work in Afghanistan) was appointed chair. The foundation has done truly admirable work since, home and abroad, converting the unconverted to cricket and often some education thrown in. MCC remains important, mainly because of the several million pounds per year that they give to their charitable arm. Owning a Hundred franchise? Won't be a free lunch.

Sour grapes? No, not actually. Soon after I joined *The Observer*, a couple of sponsors filled out a MCC membership form for me to post but, after hesitating, I decided no. A journalist has to be independent, without vested interests, and free to criticise. Sometimes I think my only qualifications to be a cricket correspondent are that I do not have vested interests and that I once worked for E.W. Swanton. Or that I resigned from his employ. Oh, and a bit of experience.

Test No. 115

Faisalabad, December 1987

We know now that the command was issued by the highest level of Pakistan's military government: Pakistan MUST win the three-Test series against England. Pakistan had just lost a World Cup semi-final against Australia at Lahore, and their one-day series against England which followed. The losing had to stop, to save national face and the government's prestige. This task, even more than to Pakistan's players, was up to the umpires.

The cause of the war between the England captain Mike Gatting and the Pakistan umpire Shakoor Rana, the *casus belli*, was their different interpretations of a convention, as I understood it: whether a captain was allowed to move a fielder behind the batsman's back without telling the batsman. The behaviour of Gatting and Shakoor would have been reprehensible in all normal circumstances, but in this highly inflammable context – of active government interference – here was a clash waiting to happen. A clash which overflowed on to British streets and added to racial tension.

We have to go back to the first Test in Lahore. The whole country of Pakistan was flat after losing that World Cup semi-final; so was India, after losing theirs to England. Home advantage was to have been decisive in both semis, but the younger, hungrier and more athletic semi-finalists won through to the Calcutta final. England lost that final – they were always behind the clock in their run-chase, long before Gatting reverse-swept – but they had won the one-day international series against Pakistan 3-0. More loss of face. President Zia ul-Haq cannot have been amused.

Pakistan won the first Test on the back of the best wrist-spin bowling in a single match that I have seen. I see why Graham Gooch rated Abdul Qadir, at his best, as possibly harder to play than Shane Warne. Warne turned most of his deliveries one way, backed by the showmanship of a great magician creating an aura of invincibility. Qadir could turn a ball at any angle in an arc of 40 to 50 degrees, from a big leg-break to a huge googly – and so quick was his arm that, sitting in the press box and watching through binoculars, I had not the slightest clue. It was one whirl of passion when he was in the mood, often culminating in the most vehement appeal. Qadir had the temperament of a Trueman, Lillee, Imran or Steyn, caged in a spin-bowler's body.

Qadir took nine for 56 in the first innings of this first Test, the best figures registered against England: to be exact, 37–13–56–9. England had one left-handed batsman in Chris Broad (David Gower, like Ian Botham, gave the World Cup and this whole tour a miss). Broad lasted more than three hours for his 41 but essentially no England player could hit the ball off the square. In the second innings Qadir added 36–14–45–4.

England made two complaints after the game. One was that the pitch had been prepared – or underprepared – for Pakistan's spinners. I dismissed this complaint. Had it been a minefield, as England argued, their spinners, John Emburey and Nick Cook, would have taken more than six wickets in their 79 combined overs in Pakistan's reply. For the very little this is worth, when we played a media game on the same Test pitch a couple of days later, as an attempt to maintain a few cordial relationships, the ball was turning a bit but never excessively or unevenly. I never saw a Pakistan pitch turn excessively from the last day of the Karachi Test in 1984 until the last two Tests of 2024–25, when electric fans had dried out the Multan and Rawalpindi pitches for several days beforehand.

England's second complaint was justifiable. The umpiring was, in their terminology, 'blatant': in other words, cheating. I did not know at this stage about the higher – or rather highest – authority that had intervened, but Shakeel Khan raised his finger with suspicious frequency. Seven of Qadir's 13 wickets were given lbw. It was so unnecessary: Qadir's wickets would have come anyway, no need to expedite the process. The only question about the result was always going to be the margin of Pakistan's victory: an innings and 87 runs in the event. 'It gives me delectable joy to congratulate you and your team,' President Zia ul-Haq drooled in a telegram to Pakistan's captain Javed Miandad. 'The paces set by your team must now be maintained.' NB MUST.

After the game I interviewed Qadir at his home in a well-off rather than wealthy part of Lahore. Dharampura had been a Hindu quarter before Partition. Qadir's father had come to Lahore from a village near Peshawar – he was of Pathan or Pashtun ancestry – and became the imam of Dharampura's mosque. This was like being granted access to the dressing-room of an Italian tenor the day after he had enthralled Rome or Milan. Qadir had touched the heights in his latest performance: not simply an artist, he was a virtuoso who had done what nobody else in the world could do (nobody between Richie Benaud and Shane Warne).

Qadir emerged from his afternoon siesta in *salwar kameez* and gestured to the sofa. Like Pavarotti, he had his own pastry chef – it could have been his wife, but no females appeared – who sent in samosas. Having eaten two or three, he lay beside an electric fire while an elderly one-eyed physio kneaded his back; after this series Qadir was found to have kidney-stones. By then he had taken 30 wickets, thrice as many as the next bowler in this three-Test series. His closest to an English counterpart, John Emburey, said Qadir was the finest spinner he had seen.

'I am a mood bowler,' Qadir kept saying in very passable English. 'It's all up to the mood.' He had been a fast bowler when young; he revered Imran Khan and once, when presented with a car by Zia ul-Haq, he surprised his captain by presenting the keys to him. When he had made his Test debut, against England in 1977–78, Qadir would leap into the crease in a surging wave of enthusiasm, but he said he had since reduced the leap so his delivery stride – and consequently his length – was steadier.

For the second Test in Faisalabad, Qadir was not so much in the mood, his right side perhaps still hurting. Broad scored an exceptional hundred in which he took the attack to Pakistan's three spinners, while Gatting, full of righteous indignation after Lahore, played arguably his finest innings of 79 off 81 balls. Towards the end of the second day Pakistan's first innings suddenly disintegrated and they were in danger of losing on a turning pitch. The general's words must have sprung to mind about how the paces 'must now be maintained.'

In English cricket, in a leisurely age, it had been the custom for the captain to inform the striker if he was moving a fielder behind the batsman's back. This habit was fading as county cricketers played so many games, including three limited-overs competitions which allowed ever less time for the captain to exclaim: 'I say, Claude, do you mind if I pop square leg back a few paces?' This responsibility to warn the batsman had devolved upon the non-striker, who might simply point with his bat. It had become a grey area, and Laws are tightened up after one is highlighted. In this case, eventually, fielders were forbidden by

Law 28 to move substantially their position after the bowler had started his run-up.

My understanding at the time was that Gatting, fielding close to the wicket as Pakistan were slumping to 77 for five, warned the batsman Salim Malik that he was going to move David Capel behind Malik's back; and that Shakoor Rana, standing at square leg, did not hear Gatting say so. Both men thought they were in the right. Shakoor walked in, waving his arms: 'You are making unfair play.' This is what Shakoor later stated that he had said, but he might possibly have used the word 'cheating' which, if so, would have had a highly inflammable effect on Gatting after what had happened in Lahore. It quickly degenerated into a shouting match. Gatting pointed his right index finger at the umpire; they were in each other's faces, no peacemakers were on hand. But that seemed to be it, the latest chapter in an acrimonious series owing to the absence of neutral umpires. Shouting match over, the protagonists returned to their places, play was resumed, and at the end of the over 'time' was duly called to terminate day two.

The players and most media personnel were staying at the Serena, a new hotel chain, of international standard, owned by the Aga Khan. The umpires Shakoor Rana and Khizer Hayat were staying at dear old Ray's. The England players returned to the stadium next morning all ready to resume on day three. But neither was the pitch rolled nor the stumps inserted. The previous evening several journalists had gone to interview Shakoor: he told them that the England captain had sworn at him (it later emerged that Shakoor had sworn first), and he demanded an apology from Gatting, otherwise he would not continue to umpire.

To abbreviate toings and froings: England went out to field at the appointed time on the third morning, to be told by the groundstaff not to touch the unpitched stumps. The diplomatic row escalated to ever high levels. The Test and County Cricket Board instructed that the tour had to go on, and forced Gatting to write a letter of apology: I APOLOGISE FOR THE BAD LANGUAGE USED DURING THE SECOND DAY OF THE TEST MATCH. SIGNED MIKE GATTING. (NB no mention of who had used the bad language.)

So this third day was aborted in favour of diplomatic manoeuvrings. It was followed by a rest day, distinctly unrestful. We hung round the Serena; pollution from the cotton factories deterred one from going outside much. I started preparing a 'write-through'. I was covering this tour for *The Observer* only and one of the functions of a Sunday newspaper, at least in the good old days, was to provide an overview of a significant week's events: and these in Faisalabad were not precedented.

Match days on a cricket tour are long for players, umpires, media and security personnel but, above all, photographers. I do not know how they develop the stamina to 'set up' their cameras a couple of hours before play, sit in the sun all day without missing a ball, then start processing all the photos and labelling the ones they file to newspapers. On my first tour of Pakistan in 1977–78, the only photographer, Adrian Murrell, had to go to the main post office in each city to file photographs, but as Hyderabad did not have one, he had to take the train to Karachi after a day's play, then return the next morning: unearthly hours. Patrick Eagar would have to persuade a passenger to take a few rolls of film on the flight back to London.

A decade later the one photographer on this tour was Graham Morris. No shortcuts: come the last over of the second day he had to be alert as for the first over, and he suddenly found himself in sole possession of world-exclusive photographs of England's cricket captain shouting at a Pakistani umpire. And the world was interested: American newspapers wanted Graham's finger-wagging photo. There was no rest day in his room at the Serena. Cases of equipment and all kinds of cameras lay strewn around the odd room-service tray, and the phone by his bed was constantly ringing. Some of the main UK newspapers had commissioned him for the tour – hence *The Times* and *Telegraph* might use the same photo on their front page – but not all of them. So his position was: sign up for the whole tour package or no deal, how ever often they kept ringing back to plead for a couple of one-off photos.

Cricket photographers and writers can be easily distinguished in an airport crowd: photographers have shoulders much broader for having carried so many kilos of cameras.

Writers, you might think, have a readier line in wit than photographers. Not so in my experience. Yes, we can manage a merry quip or laboured pun in the press box, but more often it is the cricket photographer who has the gift of the gab and can unleash a stream of funnies. He – although there was a fine female photographer on some England tours, Rebecca Naden – would banter by saying: 'One of my photographs is worth a thousand of your words.' And, well, it was not worthwhile retorting: 'Actually, one of my words is worth a thousand photos.'

I put this gift of the gab down to their needing to persuade a) the grumpy person at the check-in desk to let his excess baggage through for free, otherwise the cost will burn a hole in his freelancer's pocket (if he does not have an agency's credit card) and b) famous people to hold a pose or do something ridiculous. The snapper (the journalist's pejorative term) has to get the triumphant England captain to place a replica of the urn on his head and keep it there until the spray of champagne clears sufficiently for the photographer to take a picture that is usable. This goodwill has to be built up over preceding tours, a relationship developed from the time the youngster is first selected for England, with the photographer sending the player or his parents some snaps for free. It is a trusting relationship, just like writers had with players when I was a lad. In the case of photographers, there are no printed words to which the player can ever take exception.

Not until shortly before the resumption on day four did Shakoor have his pound of flesh in the form of Gatting's written apology. After play had resumed for 12 minutes, the umpires called off play for bad light with an almost discernible smirk, and after an interruption lasting three and a half hours, Pakistan were guaranteed a draw by the end of day five.

'Job done!'

'Job done, what?'

'Job done, General, sir!'

And so toxic was the bad blood that England did not tour Pakistan again for 13 years.

Test No. 117

Sydney, January 1988

It was some hangover, even by Australian standards, by the time Mike Gatting's England party reached Sydney to celebrate the founding of the first Australian colony 200 years before. The country had partied out at New Year. Somewhere in this enormous land – if not Perth nor the Northern Territory, if not in the Kimberleys nor the Dandenongs – a half-consumed can of lager might have been left undrunk on a cold BBQ or a kitchen counter, but nothing more than that. Thousands had bought tickets for the Bicentennial Test and never turned up.

Little did I realise at the time, but it was during this game that the baton began to pass from England to Australia. England continued their high scoring in their one and only innings of 425. Australia, 214 all out, followed on and the worm hereabouts turned. No more soft Australian underbelly, which had been a feature of their last three Test tours of England, starting in 1977. Australia, under Bobby Simpson and a tougher Allan Border, could be beaten in future, perhaps, but there was to be no surrendering ever again. England slowly took their foot off the Aussie throat. David Boon scored 184* in 135 overs as Australia ended on 328 for two. The dullest of Tests moved more slowly than the cavalcade of Legends, each sitting in a vintage car trundling round the outfield, and it had the dullest of endings. It was relieved only by the presentation of a book we had all signed to Bill O'Reilly, on retiring as a journalist aged 82. I'm not sure I read his final column but it might just have been on the subject of England picking two off-spinners, who bowled 90 overs and took one wicket for 205 between them as Australia batted out.

One reason the wheel turned was that Chris Broad played only two more Tests against Australia. Tall, high wrists, abrasive, tucking the ball forever off his hip, he scored 139 in the Bicentenary game, his fourth century in six Tests in Australia. No England batsman has a Test average in Australia like Broad's 78, although Alastair Cook batted like him in 2010–11. That Broad was dropped forever after averaging 39 in 25 Tests might have owed something to his reactions to getting out: in Pakistan he had simply refused to leave the crease, in Sydney he perfectly middled a shot, except that it was his leg-stump that he middled after being bowled. 'Wholehearted' could never be attributed to his fielding, but it could to his batting. A poacher perfectly suited to become England's best match referee.

Tests No. 119 & 120

Auckland and Wellington, February–March 1988

Only once in half a century, on England's interminable tour of 1987–88, spanning India and Pakistan for the World Cup, then New Zealand and Australia, and back to New Zealand, have I got fed up with this job.

The background was England shooting themselves in the foot in the opening game of the three-Test series in Christchurch, on the old rugby ground at Lancaster Park. It was a shocker of a pitch, designed for the native son Richard

Hadlee to break the world record for the most Test wickets: he began the game level with Ian Botham on 373. As he proved dozens and dozens of times at Trent Bridge, Hadlee on a responsive pitch was the most effective fast-medium bowler, arguably, ever.

After Hadlee pulled up with a calf injury in his 18th over, still wicketless because he was trying so hard, England were in with a great shout, even though Ian Botham, David Gower and Graham Gooch had turned down their invitations to tour New Zealand (Botham went instead to play for Queensland). They had only to maintain a crisp tempo after the Nottinghamshire pair of Chris Broad and Tim Robinson had pushed England up to 175 for one in their first innings and fruit would fall into their lap. England needed a victory, too, not having won since the Melbourne Test more than a year before.

This period, however, still pre-dated central contracts. It was every England player for himself. New Zealand in the field, moreover, were expert at lifting the ball's seam: as one of their remaining seamers walked slowly (after Hadlee's injury) back to his mark, the fingernail of his index finger made the stitching prouder to promote seam movement. Monitoring the condition of the ball has become one of the umpires' constant duties, at the fall of every wicket and after every six-hit at least. But this umpiring was home umpiring, very home umpiring. Understandably, and justifiably, given their history of being poor relations, New Zealand's players were very proud of not having lost a home Test series during the 1980s; so were some of their umpires.

England could do nothing about these external factors or 'uncontrollables'. What they could have done was to score slightly more quickly in their second innings. There was rain around – this was South Island approaching the end of the cricket season – and once England had taken a first lead of 151 (a huge lead on a slow seaming pitch), they had to score briskly, get New Zealand in, and give themselves more than a day to dismiss them a second time.

Whereupon England in their second innings batted for 74.1 overs to score 152, a rate of 2.04 runs per over (less than two if you deduct extras). Had Botham been playing, he might have run all his partners out à la Boycott, except perhaps David Capel: he naively tried an attacking shot and was dismissed for nought. Scoring was exceedingly awkward but the urgency was zero – no attempt to come down the pitch or to run quick singles – as England did a convincing impression of continental drift. Among their top six batsmen, the highest strike-rate was 37 per 100 balls. Most of England's players were afraid of getting out because most of the players were afraid of losing their place.

New Zealand had to bat out the last day only and lost no more than four wickets in the process. They faced 77 overs so a second new ball, available after 85 overs, never threatened them.

England had not won a Test during the previous summer of 1987. They did not win one of their seven this prolonged winter. Naturally, they did not win a Test the following summer against West Indies. My head might still have been bruised, from banging it against the crush-barriers on the Lancaster Park terraces, when we reached Eden Park in Auckland.

The last two Tests were the most joyless and negative England played in my time. New Zealand, without Hadlee, did not want to try to win; England, knowing they had blown their chance in Christchurch, could not win because they did not have the firepower on sluggish pitches. Mike Gatting, to give him credit where it is due, when asked how he rated the Eden Park pitch, replied: 'One out of ten.' I guessed the solitary mark was for being 22 yards long. New Zealand blocked, England bowled fast-medium and finger-spin, the ball did not carry to the slips and if it did, there was a chance the umpires might rule that the batsman had not hit it. In the turgid third Test at the Basin Reserve, whose pitch was even more grassless and soulless, eight wickets fell. There was nothing to play for as it was a standard bilateral series, a generation before the World Test Championship made every game worth a few points. There was no chance of a definite result – the conditions, and England's lack of a wrist-spinner, made sure of that – and the crowds were minimal. These last two Tests were pointless in every sense. Never again, please.

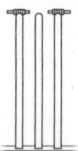

Viv Richards at the end of the Oval Test in 1984. Guess the result of this England v West Indies series? One clue: it consisted of five Tests.

Geoffrey Boycott at his best, or when most valuable to England, fending off Michael Holding and others during the Old Trafford Test of 1980.

When England tours were leisurely paced, often over four months, the many spare moments were often filled by card games, both among players and between players and journalists. Bob Willis (bottom left), Peter Willey (top left), Mike Gatting (top right) and John Emburey (partially obscured) are playing here on the England tour of the West Indies in 1980–81. The manager Kenny Barrington, looking on, has only a few days to live.

The highest percentage of runs in a Test innings for England by a single batsman is still the 61.1 per cent by Graham Gooch against West Indies at Headingley in 1991. More pertinently, his 154★ was the finest innings for England to that point, I would say, until Ben Stokes's 135★ in 2019 on the same ground.

1990s

Test No. 142
Old Trafford, August 1990

Sachin Tendulkar scored his first Test hundred when 17 years and 112 days old, against England at Old Trafford. The current saying is that if you are good enough, you are old enough, but cricket used to be far more hierarchical. In England, at any rate, ripeness, i.e. experience, was all. The youngster worked his passage until he was rated to be fit to join his seniors.

I saw Tendulkar first in the backwater of Trowbridge, where the touring Indians played a first-class warm-up against Minor Counties, on a belter. He was a prodigy, who had debuted at first-class level for Mumbai aged 15 and in Tests at 16, fending off Waqar Younis. But no security guards were needed in Trowbridge to keep fans away. I looked in his cricket bag, at the batting pads of only two straps apiece, which had been given to him by Sunil Gavaskar. I even got close enough to ask him a question and hear his high-pitched voice, just like W.G. Grace's. He seemed completely self-sufficient, and I did not question his age. I am sceptical, though, that Mushtaq Mohammad was actually 17, and a month younger than Tendulkar, when he made his maiden Test century in 1960–61. My guess is Mushtaq shed a couple of years in the chaos of Partition after leaving the Indian port of Junagadh for Pakistan – with all the advantages for a cricketer at junior or age-group level, advantages which a refugee in such circumstances deserves.

Tendulkar used a heavy bat for one so young. The activity in which he had stood out at school – aside from batting – was arm-wrestling. It was no surprise when his forearms kept cutting boundaries behind point at Old Trafford, smacking the ball into the ground, not steering past the slips. It was the season, 1990, when the Dukes ball had fewer threads in its seam so it seldom deviated. Graham Gooch had gorged to the extent of 333 in the Lord's Test and, as it was an eat-all-you-can buffet, 123 in his second helping.

When Tendulkar made a similar century in the Perth Test on his first tour of Australia, it drove commentators into rhapsody. Unlike most of his contemporaries, he was up with the pace in Australia. He did the same on a quick pitch in South Africa, which made John Woodcock lyrical. The young Tendulkar addressed the match situation – India, in those days, were normally out-gunned – and attacked. No wonder Don Bradman likened Tendulkar to his own early self. Sir Everton Weekes, quietly and modestly, told me something similar: that Jessie, Lady Bradman, had told him that the Don thought he, Weekes, had batted like himself.

In the second half of his career there were times when I could not understand what game Tendulkar was playing. He was always superstitious about numbers – 10 on the back of his shirt, 100 international hundreds, 200 Tests – yet there must have been more to it. As in the World Cup Pool A match of 2003 against Pakistan at Centurion, he could still bat divinely, but then a spanner entered the works. After he had cruised to 70, if not all the world then all of India would have been backing him to convert it into three figures. Yet something would stop him, perhaps cramp and he would go off, or he would get out. For one reason and another he took an age to reach his 100th international hundred, and that was against Bangladesh in a match-losing ODI because he batted too slowly.

In the Bangalore Test of 2000-01 when Ashley Giles bowled over the wicket into the rough well outside a right-hander's legs – umpires would not tolerate it now – Tendulkar was content to kick him away. Stalemate. Another Indian right-hander sailed down the pitch and gave himself room to drive Giles over the off side, making the most complicated synchronisation of so many muscles look simplicity. Thereafter, my favourite Indian batsman was Virender Sehwag.

Test No. 144
Headingley, June 1991

England in the 1980s won only one-quarter of their Tests: a startling figure given that Ian Botham was rolling Australia over regularly in the first half of the decade. England, overall, failed to make the most of their resources, whereas Australia knew by the end of the 1980s what they had to do: a permanent head coach, a stable captain (not four in one series as England tried in 1988), a settled national squad over and above their state system, and a national academy to teach best practice.

As one example of this failure to maximise resources, small in itself yet huge in impact, the England captain was made to toss at the start of a Test with the opposing captain to select which brand of ball would be used. England wanted Dukes for their swing bowlers, touring teams wanted Readers because it would not swing. After-you-Claudism went too far. On their tour of England in 1989 the Australians could barely lay a bat on Phil Newport as he swung a Dukes both ways, and they lost a warm-up against Worcestershire so emphatically that I felt sorry it was going to be a one-sided series. It was a one-sided series: Australia won 4–0, and carried on winning until 2005.

That England started the 1990s on a stronger footing, and went on to win one-third of their Tests in this decade, was largely the work of one man. On tour you would see Graham Gooch pounding the streets on his own, perhaps on a grey morning in Auckland down by the harbour. He had begun training with West Ham United near his home. When England captain he would wake up early and go for a run before any other cricketers stirred. Hotels of this era did not have gyms and health clubs. Gooch used what he could to maximise what he had. He scored more runs at the professional level than any other human being, 67,067 of them, overtaking Sir Jack Hobbs; two-thirds were first-class runs, the other third in limited-overs.

One of the all-time shock results – like Bangladesh winning a Test in New Zealand, or New Zealand clean-sweeping 3-0 in India – was England beating West Indies in the opening Test at Sabina Park in February 1990. Whereby hangs the Journalist's Tale. Jamaica is five hours behind Greenwich Mean Time. England had been thumped by West Indies throughout the 1980s, winning not a single Test, so what was more predictable than West Indies winning again after Desmond Haynes and Gordon Greenidge had embarked on another demoralising partnership? For the first edition back home, copy had to be filed in late morning; even if only an hour or two had been played, the piece had to extend to the same length of 800 or 900 words, as at the close of play. When most of us started to file, West Indies were 50 for no wicket and set for another whitewash over pathetic England, it was men against boys, and the sooner our domestic system was changed and an academy introduced etc etc. By the time the first editions came out, West Indies were 164 all out.

'It will taste good tomorrow when it's wrapped around fish and chips,' my sports editor used to say when an early edition report was overtaken by subsequent events.

Not only were we journalists complacent, West Indies were too. Viv Richards batted at number six. England's seamers were disciplined. Allan Lamb made his most valuable hundred. England won by nine wickets. Above all, England under Graham Gooch were fit and hungry, not physically flabby and mentally scarred. It could not last, not after Gooch had his hand broken by Ezra Moseley in the third Test in Port-of-Spain. Gooch's first innings of 84 had given England the lead, and their target was only 151. Gooch sat in the pavilion all padded up as bad light closed in, to give the impression he was going to come in next, but the fracture was so bad the pavilion cat would have had to bat ahead of him.

The greatest Test innings are tide-turners. Gooch on England's 1989-90 tour had started to stem the West Indian waves. In the opening Test at Headingley in 1991 he succeeded where Canute had failed and turned the tide almost single-handedly. For the rest of the 1990s England and West Indies went toe to toe.

The atmosphere of a Test ground in England a generation ago, especially in the North, was far removed from now. Cricket followers still supported their county first, England second. When Ben Stokes staged his epic 135* in the 2019 Ashes he had the whole of Headingley, if not the entire country, behind him; when Jonny Bairstow hit 99 not out in the 2023 Ashes, he was not a Yorkshireman batting at Old Trafford, he was an England player representing us all. For the opening day of the 1991 series the crowd was 8,000. It was damp but, more important than the weather, no Yorkshireman was in the England side. Little over a dozen years before, in a Test at Headingley, Keith Fletcher of Essex was booed for having usurped the place of their own Phil Sharpe. So Gooch, also from Essex, was not exactly transported on a wave of popular sentiment in the Western Terrace.

England had some top six on paper: Gooch, Mike Atherton, Graeme Hick, Allan Lamb, Mark Ramprakash and Robin Smith. But Lamb was approaching the end of his career and Atherton, though already vice-captain, was starting out; while the Test careers of the two debutants, Hick and Ramprakash, never fulfilled expectations, not least their own. If Patrick Patterson, as a speedster, was not fully suited to the conditions – the pitch was so damp that footholes were quickly apparent – then Curtly Ambrose was, and so too Malcolm Marshall after all his Hampshire seasons. Courtney Walsh had sent many a stump flying for Gloucestershire.

Gooch was batting so fluently he became a bit giddy in his first innings: 13 runs had already flowed off Marshall's first over, and when the last ball of it lifted he was good enough to edge it to Jeffrey Dujon. Hick, waving outside off stump at Patterson, might never have seen such vivid pace before; Ramprakash, as he was to do all series, hung on – on this occasion for 142 minutes – without once passing 27. England were all out on the second morning for 198, but West Indies fared no better and it was a captain's innings of 73 by Viv Richards that got them up to 173, 25 behind.

Here began the finest innings by an England captain, so I believe, and the best by any England player until Stokes on this same ground. Gooch batted for seven and a half hours on a pitch that was responsive to one of the all-time great attacks. His unbeaten 154 out of 252 represented 61.1 per cent of his side's total, the highest percentage ever for England. Only two players had carried their bat against West Indies before, Len Hutton and Glenn Turner.

By lunch on day three Ambrose had swept away Atherton, Hick and Lamb second time round: Hick was yorked, the ball edged into his back pad and the stumps, not the luck he needed for a confident start to Test cricket. Showers kept interrupting Gooch and refreshing the fast bowlers. Ramprakash made another valiant 27, as did Derek Pringle, but nobody else double figures. At the close Gooch had scored 82 of England's 143 for six. Advantage West Indies.

The crowd on day four was down to 7,000. Gooch and rain persisted. When he reached his hundred, which came after previous struggles against Headingley's lateral movement, Gooch joined Ken Barrington, Ian Botham and Geoffrey Boycott in having a Test hundred at each England ground. Cuts and off-drives were his main scoring shots, and workings off his legs. Richards hesitated before taking the second new ball; Gooch capitalised, on-driving and pulling Walsh for consecutive fours in the 87th over, whereupon Richards took it and England's last four wickets were snuffed out. Gooch somehow had survived 331 balls.

Gooch, as captain, was not done. England had a steady seam attack of Phil DeFreitas, Devon Malcolm, Steve Watkin and

Pringle, and Richards was not going to let them dictate. He took on a straight ball from Watkin with a pull shot and the ball soared towards mid-off, Gooch, who held it running back. When Gus Logie tried a loose back-foot drive, Gooch was diving at third slip to catch him left-handed. England's winning margin of 115 runs, against the world Test champions, was relatively enormous; and England's first home victory against West Indies for 22 years was, as near as it could be, the work of one batsman – one very fit and brave batsman.

Test No. 148

The Oval, August 1991

Luck levels itself out. Yes, agreed, I believe that, with one proviso: that it evens itself out over a prolonged period.

For the final Test of the 1991 series against England, and for the final Test of Viv Richards's career and captaincy, West Indies gave a debut to a pugnacious left-handed batsman with a leg-side penchant, Clayton Lambert. He made 39 in his first innings at the Oval, the second-highest score as West Indies collapsed against Phil Tufnell's flight. Second time round, he started brightly again and had reached 14 when Ian Botham came on, Lambert went to pull, and he was given out lbw. The appeal was energetic, yes, and the ball was straight, yes, but it was also destined to go straight over the stumps. I would not say there was any significance in the fact that both the umpire, Mervyn Kitchen, and Botham had represented Somerset, but Kitchen might have been swayed by the vehemence of the appeal. This was the Oval in its heyday of bounce and pace. Lambert was 29 and, after suffering the bad luck of a manifestly wrong decision in a promising debut, dropped for more than six years.

When he was 36, Lambert was given four more Tests, as an opener. He made a century too, against England, before being discarded forever. He was the nearest to an unlucky Test cricketer I have seen, deprived through no fault of his own of a chance in his prime years.

Dubai airport, any time

Autumn is the cruellest season. Warmth remains in the sun, the clocks have not gone back, leaves are not falling in earnest, and even if we delay the start till midday to let the damp grass dry, we could still squeeze in 30 overs a side. But no. Tomorrow I have to go on tour and won't be home till Christmas.

My first child – our daughter – was born in 1991. Saying goodbye to my wife, handing over my keys and catching a train to Heathrow, is to have a layer of epidermis removed. My wife and I go through a ritual of squabbling before I depart and desert her: it is easier to leave somebody you are disliking. Saying goodbye to a child is another layer removed, not surgically.

Have to compartmentalise, have to compartmentalise. Go from being a husband and dad to one of the lads.

A tour of Australia lasted four months when I started, from autumn to spring, wiping out the English winter. A lucky escape, but you can have too much of a good thing, even of Australia on expenses. An initiation ceremony for cricket correspondents – thank goodness the only one, because initiation rites are tribalism – was to be asked by one of our number, mid-tour: what is your car registration number, and what is your home phone number (landlines only). I could remember the second, not the first.

Tours of Australia, and subsequently South Africa, spanned Christmas, and, without kids, it is easy for your partner to fly out for the holiday. Tours of the West Indies start, or started, in the new year. Tours of Asia were usually scheduled to allow England players Christmas at home. A Test in Mohali in the week before Christmas would be followed by a stampede to Mumbai or Dubai to catch the flight home on 23 December, and to nod off at the festive table.

Cricket's globe spins faster and faster as tours grow shorter and shorter. England can set off on tour in September. As the

United Arab Emirates waxed, one of their airlines became one of cricket's larger sponsors, and Dubai became the sport's hub, once the headquarters of the International Cricket Council were transferred from Lord's to a business park in the desert. In the middle of the night one could be staring at a carousel, wondering if one was going anywhere, or just round and round like a suitcase. The cricket tour was designed to be an escape from the English winter: what is the point of one in autumn or spring?

Expenses, when I started, were the game within the game. Bill Bryson lifted the lid when he wrote about working in Fleet Street before Rupert Murdoch, so I feel empowered to reveal a few secrets, without fully opening the box.

At the peak – say on a tour of Australia in the late 1970s – the expenses being claimed bore, shall we say, little resemblance to reality. But, and this is the point, they were not expected to bear any resemblance. It was one long gravy train. Some colleagues, the cricket correspondents of mass-circulation newspapers, would reckon to cream off £100 per DAY while on tour. An ample lunch would be served on match days at an Australian ground (the WACA, when Ruby was catering, would offer a three-course lunch with all the wine you could drink from a vineyard a few miles up the Swan River). So you could make do without eating any breakfast – and charge £10 or £12 for that. You could walk from the hotel to the ground and back – and charge £20 each way for a taxi, having scrounged a few blank receipts from a driver in return for an extra large tip (put that on expenses too). You could charge £30 for dinner, again with a blank receipt that could be forged, and double that if you were 'entertaining'.

I suspect that if HMRC had been diligent, they would have discovered that England's assistant manager had successfully managed the stupendous gastronomic feat of being entertained by five different UK newspapers to five different dinners in one evening. Meantime, you just had a drink at the hotel bar, and charged that to entertainment as well. A correspondent for one of the more munificent papers said he could buy a new car on the expenses – every penny tax-free – generated during a long tour. Another carried with him a John Bull set by which rubber stamps would lend a veneer of authenticity to a forgery. *Fair Dinkum Airport Taxis* could charge as much as £60 for the ride from Melbourne airport to the city centre – even if the taxi was actually shared with three colleagues. And at the end of the tour the exchange rate when converting the Australian dollars into pounds – well, the Australian currency was notoriously strong, wasn't it?

Difficulties arose in Asia. Taxi drivers in general do not carry receipt books; many are not literate, and even if you aid your rickshaw-wallah in Kandy with sign language, you lose this game of charades because he does not know what a receipt is. After I had joined the *Telegraph* in 1993, and when classified advertising and circulations went into decline, accountants became ever stricter and demanded a piece of paper for every expense. I was having one particularly bad tour of the UAE expenses-wise: taxis from Dubai to Sharjah or Abu Dhabi cost a fair amount and I could not get a receipt for love nor bribery. Tests in the UAE were always staged in deserted stadiums, because the Baluchis, who do most of the UAE's hard labour, cannot afford to take a whole day off to watch a Pakistan Test match. I did like the two banks on either side of Dubai Creek, where vestiges of the old way of Gulf life could be found among the dhows, ropes and packaged white goods waiting for shipment to Gujarat or Oman. One evening, growing desperate, I found a shop that sold some stationery. I went inside and asked for a receipt book. The man behind the counter was alarmed. He disappeared through the door at the back of the shop and whispering was audible in Arabic: 'Shurtah, shurtah!' 'Police, police!' The man returned with half a dozen receipt books and pressed them all on me. He refused to take any money and bowed me out of the shop. Only in the taxi on the way back to one of those high-rise hotels in Jumairah did I realise: I had forgotten to ask for a receipt.

Even at home, scope was considerable. Those were the days when most newspapers had a Northern Cricket Correspondent, covering Yorkshire and Lancashire (certain dailies today do not have a cricket correspondent to cover the country). One of them lived up a drive on some moors. He not only claimed his 50p per mile, or whatever, for every visit to Old Trafford and Headingley. He backed his car up his drive, so he claimed for 'reverse mileage' in the course of a cricket season.

Starting at the bottom, I was as open-mouthed as the reader may be. When I had written my first match report for *The Observer* and was told to fill in an expenses form, I charged almost one whole pound for the chicken foo yung and chips I got for lunch from the takeaway near Fenner's. Transport? I walked the half-mile to Fenner's, and back. Transport £0.00. Lunch £0.75. Total: £0.75. The next time I was on the phone to the office, it was spelt out – by the deputy sports editor – that I had to play the game, and it would undermine the system for others if I didn't. But soon it was not Virtue which guided me but self-interest. *The Observer* was teetering on the verge of bankruptcy after the Astor family had bankrolled it, and I thought they were more likely to employ me if I came cheap.

When I joined *The Sunday Telegraph* in 1993, I discovered it was still the golden age. My sports editor, Colin Gibson, set a sterling example – or, if on tour, an example in sterling. He was and I believe still is of a generous disposition, and this extended to hiring current and former cricketers as columnists. As soon as Mike Atherton was appointed Test captain in 1993 – and I was allowed to write that Alec Stewart should have been made captain then, instead of having to wait until Atherton had resigned – he was signed up. So was Nasser Hussain, so was Angus Fraser, all on long-term contracts. To them would be added an eminent former player, or two, from the country which England were touring.

In 1980, when the Centenary Test was staged at Lord's, I had been bidden to assemble a list of questions about the cricket of the day and obtain answers from Sir Leonard Hutton, Jack

Fingleton, who had just switched from *The Sunday Times* to *The Observer*, and Bobby Simpson, who was commentating during a lull between being Australia's captain and first head coach, along with Tony Pawson who was my predecessor, and a dear man. (He was versatile: he not only played for Oxford and Kent, averaging 37 as a first-class batsman, he scored against Spurs on his debut for Charlton Athletic. As cricket and football correspondent for *The Observer*, he once covered a match in both sports on the same Saturday. He was so fit, and self-effacing, he told us how he had reached the press box at Lord's one morning when well into his sixties: the long up-escalator at St John's Wood Tube station was so crowded he raced up the empty down-escalator and nearly reached the top, to mounting applause, before subsiding back to the bottom.) The answers by these experts to each question were printed in vertical columns. Now, given the *Telegraph*'s abundant resources, how about bringing the panellists together, preferably over a convivial lunch, so they would figuratively feed off each other? Thus, as I remember, the round table was born.

I might never have had the temerity to sit there, directing the conversation between eminent cricketers, without that prototype experience. Don't look down, don't get vertigo, don't dive under the table. I was heartened to hear that some players who were panellists felt the same. On an England tour of South Africa, *The Sunday Telegraph* had signed Graeme Pollock and Barry Richards. I had to bring them together with Mike Atherton and Nasser Hussain. Both of them were unusually reticent. I asked why, after the round table, and the two current England players, past and present captains, admitted they were in awe of the two all-time greats.

The chemistry of a round table made for fascinating discussions, almost all printable, especially when Ian Chappell was the elder statesman and standing back and seeing the wider picture of how Test cricket was shaping. Photographs had to be taken, too, so I had to pin down past and present players and a photographer at a scenic location at a precise time when they all had busy schedules. One photograph belies the stress as I sit back nonchalantly in the West Indies while quizzing Michael Holding, Mike Atherton and the late Graham Thorpe. To be fair, not once did anyone say what on earth are you doing here in this company? But one round table was fraught. It was 2001, when Hussain was captain – or rather, he was the official captain, but had broken a finger and had to miss the second and third Tests, passing the captaincy back to Atherton. This round table, held in the ECB offices at Lord's, consisted of these two England captains and Australia's captain, Steve Waugh. The atmosphere could have been cut with a knife. Hussain refused even to look at Waugh. Atherton offered some middle ground. It was the intensity of Hussain's desire to regain the Ashes which made him keep his counterpart at a distance. The Australians then were at the height of their powers, almost superhuman. But Waugh was very human that day: he arrived at Lord's with a migraine. Since his collision with Jason Gillespie in a fielding accident in Sri Lanka he said he had been suffering them frequently.

I think the tables turned. When Atherton and Hussain were fighting off South Africa at Trent Bridge in 1998, especially Allan Donald's ferocious assault from round the wicket and into the ribs, I could imagine Barry Richards turning to Graeme Pollock to say they were fortunate to play when they did, then looking back at their TV screen with awe.

Test No. 155

Old Trafford, July 1992

Waste. I hate waste. And what English cricket did with its resources in the 1990s was waste them.

England had an attacking opening batsman of rare quality. England had always preferred cagey, dogged openers to blunt the new ball, and would spurn aggressors like Charlie Barnett, John

Jameson and Colin Milburn. But the tempo of Test cricket was changing under the influence of limited-overs cricket, specifically 50-over internationals; and England had found a swordsman who could put new-ball bowlers to flight in Alec Stewart.

After a tough novitiate at number three, mainly against West Indies and Australia, Stewart made his first Test century against Sri Lanka at the end of the summer of 1991. He entered a purple patch: two centuries and a 63 in five innings in New Zealand when he was promoted to open; he followed with his highest Test score of 190 against Pakistan at Edgbaston, when he hit 31 fours; then at Lord's, when Waqar Younis and Wasim Akram began reverse-swinging, he not only top-scored in both innings, he carried his bat second time round (74 and 69*). So he could defend, as well as blaze through the covers off either foot, and pull. So what did England's selectors and management do? After an innings of 15 in the third Test against Pakistan, they made Stewart keep wicket.

Stewart was to shed the gloves occasionally and buoyantly resurface at the top of England's order, as when he scored a century in each innings in the Bridgetown Test of 1993–94, ending the West Indian unbeaten run in Barbados which stretched back to 1934–35; or when, captaining in Australia, he passed the gloves to Warren Hegg for the Melbourne Test of 1998–99, scored 107 and 52, and led England to victory by 12 runs. What a waste overall. When Stewart was not keeping wicket, he averaged 46, and when he was opening the innings as well, England had a top-class and complementary opening pair in Mike Atherton and him.

Of Graeme Hick's 136 first-class hundreds, six were in the cause of England. Of Mark Ramprakash's 114 first-class hundreds, two were for England. Hick was not forgiven for disappointing expectations after that toughest of debuts against West Indies at Headingley in 1991: a duck against Curtly Ambrose followed in his only innings of the second Test, and a 43 in the third was insufficient to give him a run in his favourite position to settle down. Thereafter, he was not only in and out but up and down, right down to number eight on a couple of occasions. Hick's conditioning with Worcestershire and abroad had been to stride out at the fall of the first wicket and, without having to think about the game situation, play his strokes. Being more of an off-side player, he was unlikely to have a Test average of 52 to match his first-class average, but had he been given an extended run in his favourite position it would surely have been in the 40s, not 31.

Like Hick, Ramprakash was not only in and out but up and down the order. He had six or more innings in six positions. He was most fluent when called into the England Test side at short notice and expectations, not least his own, were realistic. For the rest, I suspect, they felt too insecure to give of their best to England, a team which did not trust them to do what they did in county cricket – and in the period when county cricket was stuffed with fine overseas pace bowlers.

Atherton, Stewart, Hick, Graham Thorpe, Ramprakash and Robin Smith: England could have won more than one-third of their Tests in the 1990s with that batting line-up, if consistently selected. Jack Russell to keep wicket and bat at seven, followed by Dominic Cork or Craig White, Darren Gough, Andy Caddick and Angus Fraser. Hick could turn his off-breaks hugely and would have sufficed as the only spinner in most English conditions, with Phil Tufnell specialising in Asia. As another example of the waste, Gough scored two fifties in his first 10 Test innings and averaged 34 as a bowling all-rounder; subsequently, his batting was allowed to atrophy at numbers 10 and 11, and in the rest of his England career he averaged 10.01.

Test No. 173

Lord's, July 1994

'It doesn't look good,' said Tony Lewis. England's former captain, and the BBC's presenter of Test cricket, had been a predecessor as *The Sunday Telegraph*'s cricket correspondent, so it was kind of him to pop into the press box to tip me off. The TV cameras had spotted Mike Atherton putting his right hand in his pocket, picking out some dirt he had collected from the ground, and rubbing it surreptitiously over one side of the ball.

These were the days when at least one Test bowler got away with using a bottle-opener to rough up one side of the ball. By comparison with such practices, dirt was subtle. It was not expressly against the Laws either: the ICC and MCC had not got around to limiting legal substances, which could be used on the ball, to sweat and saliva.

It is a shame in a way that the dark arts of fast bowling were brought into the light of day. I never saw an England bowler reverse-swing a ball a greater distance than Darren Gough did in this very match against South Africa, until the alarm was sounded. Craig White was another who could lower the release-point of his right arm, for Yorkshire and England, and describe the same beautiful arcs. It brought the focus back to where cricket began: the bowler no longer forcing the batsman to fend off short balls but trying to knock over his stumps. Amid the uproar – Atherton was fined £2000 – little attention was paid to South Africa winning their first Test against England since readmission by 356 runs. Such was the calibre of the tourists' pace bowling, after a generation out of the international arena, that no England batsman reached 40.

No subtlety was involved in South Africa's readmission. In what I thought was obscene haste, they rushed to the West Indies for a one-off Test. Most Barbadians also considered it to be obscene haste as they boycotted the match (subsequent research by the University of the West Indies proved that the non-selection of the Barbadian Anderson Cummins was a secondary issue). What mattered was that Shell had to rehabilitate their global image after ignoring the boycott of apartheid South Africa.

In South Africa's three-Test series in England in 1994, Gary Kirsten bowled two wicketless overs of rickety off-breaks: the sum total of their reliance on spin. If there was to be subtlety, it was to involve Hansie Cronje's brand of match-fixing. Spin bowling did not play a part until their domestic first-class cricket spread beyond the white community. Meanwhile, the athleticism of their fielding and discipline of their work ethic were wonderful to behold.

Test No. 188

Johannesburg, December 1995

My sports editor had issued the instruction already, even before Mike Atherton had finished his innings. Please could we – that's me – ask Athers to write immediately about his 185★ that had defied South Africa, as if the Wanderers had been Rorke's Drift. He had shaken hands with the opposition, and joined his main partner, Jack Russell, in walking off the field, and there was Muggins talking to him the moment he had crossed the boundary rope. Athers was in a world of his own: he admitted afterwards that he was in that exalted state called the zone. He was calm, even serene, neither tired nor sweaty, not out on his feet. He said he would write the piece, after he had got away from it all and gone fishing with England's assistant manager John Barclay (nicknamed, appositely in this context, 'Trout'), and could look back at leisure.

A couple of days after the Johannesburg Test, at an impossibly gorgeous Cape Dutch winery near Franschhoek, I interviewed South Africa's head coach, Bob Woolmer. He was adept at putting an angle, his angle, across to the media, but I had conversed with him before. He said, for quoting, that he was surprised that England had not gone for their target of 479, but this was propaganda: England were five wickets down before they reached the halfway stage, and it would have been folly to go for their target. I bought Woolmer a case of six bottles of the local wine (on expenses).

A few years later, when both were still columnists for *The Sunday Telegraph,* Atherton and Nasser dined at my house and at a moment when they were the only two sitting at the table, one said to the other: 'You know, we're both going to be remembered for our worst moment.' Atherton was referring to the dirt-in-pocket affair; Nasser to when he raised his right arm and patted his back on reaching a century, his indignant gesture when he had pointed to the number 3 on his shirt, not in a backwater but at packed Lord's during a one-day international. I am genuinely delighted that both have been proved wrong. Atherton, as a player, will always be recalled for his monumental defiance at Johannesburg, and later against Allan Donald at Trent Bridge, Nasser for grabbing the England team in 1999 and dragging it from the depths into mid-table respectability.

South Africa, 1995 to date

On a human level, nothing has pleased me so much as South Africa's growth into the first successful multiracial Test team, winning the World Test Championship final of 2025. (Zimbabwe integrated sooner but have never been successful.) A national sports team that is multiracial could be a template for other sectors of society to follow, or a substitute for integration, a fig leaf. That is another issue.

South Africa was such a beautiful country when I first visited in 1995, but its society remained so ugly: people of different races seldom looked each other in the eye, which is the starting point for human relationships. England, mind you, were having troubles of their own. England's head coach and tour manager, Raymond Illingworth, had come into the job a decade too late by his own admission, too long after his playing days. He came from a generation that had grown up in Yorkshire after the Second World War before any non-white immigration into Britain, and retained those attitudes, pretty unreconstructed. He had been my special hero in the Yorkshire Championship-winning team of the 1960s, but times had moved on, and I don't think Illy had.

Devon Malcolm, in the last Test of the 1994 series, had enjoyed his finest hour when he had blown away South Africa at the Oval. (Ian Chappell said that Malcolm should always be selected for England as one of five bowlers, and simply asked to bowl as fast as he could.) When England played their opening first-class game at Soweto – a contrast to their opening warm-up game at the Oppenheimer's private ground which was not for public consumption – Nelson Mandela had personally congratulated Malcolm on his nine for 57. Illingworth seemed to want to cut him down to size and sent him off for naughty-boy nets with the bowling coach, Illingworth's contemporary, Peter Lever. Malcolm needed TLC all right, but not Technical Lever Changes.

Mandela had been elected president in 1994 yet it was as if bantustans still existed, so rigid was the economic and therefore social stratification (outside the boardroom, where a few non-whites had to be incorporated). If you saw a hundred private cars, every single one of them would have a white driver. If you saw a bus in Cape Town, it was filled with Cape Coloureds; if in Durban, with Indians. If you saw a pick-up truck, every single man packed into the back was Black African, with a white driver sitting in the front and a Black foreman beside him. Mixed marriages had always been banned under apartheid. Nowhere did the races overlap, even or especially on the cricket field.

South Africa did not select a non-white player during their three-Test series in England in 1994 nor for the first three Tests of 1995–96. When an 18-year-old left-arm spinner from the Cape Coloured community was selected, he turned the series South Africa's way, so there could be no accusation of tokenism: off the 107.1 overs by Paul Adams, England scored only 231 runs. Soon Makhaya Ntini bowled his way into South Africa's Test side, gradually followed by other non-white pace bowlers. But at close of play the picture stayed the same: the Black bowler sat on his own at the back of the bus. He batted at number 11 too. Ntini, after his career, said he would often run back to the team hotel to avoid this embarrassment – and however senior he was in the side, the wicketkeeper would call him 'Boy'.

My favourite Test on England's first tour after readmission was in Port Elizabeth, at St George's Park, which had staged England's inaugural Test in South Africa in March 1889. It is a ground on a hill above the port's cranes and rail tracks. The original Elizabeth, after whom the city was named, lived in a large wooden house overlooking the sea, and set out from there to do her good works like founding a hospital. (The 1889 match should not really be counted as a Test – the strongest case is for South Africa's first Test to be dated to their 1907 tour of England – but Mrs Dunell, the home captain's wife, stitched the name of South Africa on to the team's caps, so it was a test of their national strength, while England's side consisted of amateurs game for an interesting winter and a few pros to do the hard work.)

Early 1996 at St George's Park saw a phenomenon like no other in Test cricket, not even in the West Indies at Carnival. Along one side to the left of the pavilion ran an old wooden stand, the sort you might have sat in when, or if, watching Derbyshire at the Racecourse Ground in the 1950s. And from this mundane setting – though not unsightly because the roofs of St George's Park are painted green – emerged a sound that I had never heard before, the sound of joy unconfined, the sound of freedom.

A local church band plays during a Test at St George's Park to this day. Its members, who might be given free tickets by the ground authority, drift in during the first hour of play and quietly tune their instruments. By noon the horns and trumpets and larynxes have warmed up and they sing – 'Shosholoza' is one favourite, 'Stand By Me' another – and even if you are completely tuneless like me, you get carried away, transported. These singers, only two years earlier, were barely people in the eyes of the South African government, and yet here they were, not bearing grudges, not talking about past grievances, but belting out their music with joy unconfined. I would guess, privileged Englishman that I am, there can be no joy in this world like that of new-found freedom. These South Africans – from the vast majority of South Africans – were no longer deprived of their voice, of their vote, and they celebrated accordingly. They dwelt on each song, without rushing, and why would you rush now if you had spent all your life until the last two years as a non-person, as merely a source of manual labour, all your life un-free, until Nelson Mandela was released and elected president?

Over the years, of course, the joy of freedom has been followed by a certain disillusionment. Where are the decent jobs that pay a living wage, where is the wealth from the nation's minerals? Yet in the 1990s there was hope. Around Port Elizabeth, car assembly factories were built by multinationals and a Black workforce hired. In this city, before anywhere else in South Africa that I saw, a Black middleclass began to grow – and some of the church band members may have been in their number. Not only freedom, but bread on the table for the children, and dignity, and the chance of education at last. The cricket seemed irrelevant, which indeed it was by comparison: what mattered was that the people in a public stand at this cricket ground had a future, finally, and were happy – gloriously, intoxicatingly happy – to sing of it.

In the afternoon (I hope they were given some lunch) the band would start up again for another session of half an hour or so. Their music would put a spring in the step of the South African cricketers, and it should have been in the step of all who heard it. The whole ground would rock uninhibitedly, yet calmly, even serenely, without shouting or discord. I would still be humming, if not buzzing, at close of play when I would return to the hotel in Summerstrand in time to change and run down to the beach with a boogie board to splash through the waves. The sea has warmed slightly after heading north from the Antarctic to embrace the Indian Ocean. After a day at the cricket, zing-zing-zing and away we go to the beach! Some of the best things in life are free, like the music at St George's Park and boogie-boarding in the waves at sunset.

One day my wife and I were frolicking with our boogie board as a cluster of African women stood and cautiously splashed in the waves. I was dense: I was wondering why none of them were swimming until the realisation dawned that they were never permitted to go anywhere near this beach, except to clean it. And how or where would they have ever been given swimming lessons? But, oh boy, were they happy to enjoy the sea. They politely refused at first but my wife and I gradually persuaded a couple of them to have a go on the board and naturally their smiles were radiant after the sea had swept one of them up the beach, with all the exhilaration entailed in feeling powered by waves; and we left them to it, with the board, to enjoy at last what their own country offered.

A real change in racial attitudes took a whole generation, and no doubt more in many individual cases, but South African cricket got there in the end. When positive discrimination was tried, white cricketers protested that merit should be the sole criterion for selection and it was no longer a level playing field – but then it never had been. Since the beginning most South African Test cricketers have attended elite schools which have exemplary playing facilities for cricket and rugby. One of these players who scores a Test hundred has come a long way; but a township kid who scores a Test hundred has come vastly further and in this sense has shown more merit, because he had no back garden where his family could bowl at him from infancy and who could drive him to practices and games. The multiracial South African team still consists largely of the products of elite schools, but they had become far more diverse in their selection of pupils.

Harare, December 1996

Sign language does not come more obvious. When you write a piece about a player which he does not like, he blanks you – and might even do so for the rest of his career. If you write a piece he likes, he might offer a smile in appreciation. On a couple of occasions I have had a written response saying thank you. One was a letter from Paul Allott when he was selected for England in the early 1980s (I knew he would go far – as a commentator). The second was an email from Mark Wood – 'appreciate it' – after a piece about the happiness he brought to the field whenever the occupational hazard of injuries allowed. Which two England players would you want beside you in the trenches: I opt for Wood and Liam Plunkett. Platoon sergeant? Paul Collingwood. General? Andrew Strauss.

Once I was Taken to Task. On England's inaugural Test tour of Zimbabwe, I was summoned to the headmaster's study. John Barclay, now the manager, and Mike Atherton, still the captain, were 'disappointed' with my preview in *The Sunday Telegraph*. A preview used to be a staple of Sunday journalism: to look ahead to the Test series that was beginning the following week, give a feel of the host country and its cricket, analyse the state that the England players were in, and predict the result.

I had written that England were not in the right frame of mind to win the opening Test in Bulawayo, even against the lowliest country. The signs were that some players did not want to be in Zimbabwe at all. At a reception at the start of the tour the England players, far from mixing with Zimbabwean people and players, had huddled among themselves. It was unsightly and I wrote as much. (England had yet to resort to a gushing statement that 'we are here to embrace the culture', which means heading to the nearest golf course.) *Wisden*, in its tour summary, was to agree: 'It was hard to think how England could have made a bigger mess of their first senior tour to cricket's ninth and newest Test country ... They had accomplished the rare double of failing to win a single match of significance while adopting an approach widely regarded as unfriendly, aloof and, thanks to one crass comment from coach David Lloyd, downright rude.' His 'we flippin' murdered 'em' came after the first Test had ended in a draw with the scores level.

Here was another example of England failing to make anything, let alone the most, of their resources: this tour on which they drew the two Tests and lost the three one-day internationals, while the Zimbabwe players were sufficiently astute to conduct a charm offensive towards the visiting media. England set off on the wrong foot and there they remained. I am not being wise after this event. When the itinerary was announced, England were busy being feeble in the 1996 World Cup, defeating Holland, as some ignorantly called the Netherlands, and the UAE, while losing to four other countries. Dennis Silk had recently been appointed chairman of the Test and County Cricket Board, and we shared an enthusiasm for Siegfried Sassoon (his was based on personal experience). I tried to advise him the proposed schedule was going to cause trouble. Only the England captain in those days had the undisputed right to take his wife or family on tour, a vestige of the era when he was always an amateur and could do what he liked. Every other England player was frowned upon if he wanted to take a wife or girlfriend on tour, although an exception might be made for a tour of Australia, allowing families out for Christmas provided the individual player paid for them. Otherwise the official attitude, whether of the TCCB or ECB, was that England players were servants, and jolly lucky to be paid at all for representing their country, and should concentrate on doing what they were told.

It was apparent to me that, if there was a will, there was a way to allow the England players to have their families in Zimbabwe for Christmas. On Boxing Day, instead of starting the second Test, play one of the three one-day internationals. No need then to go to bed early on Christmas Day: have a *braai* around a pool at lunchtime. But the itinerary was not rescheduled; and Atherton, whose back was playing up, and Barclay, decreed that no player should be allowed to have any companion on the whole tour of Zimbabwe and New Zealand from late November to early March. I did not bend over to be caned in the headmaster's study; the tour should not have been arranged as it was.

Lord MacLaurin, Silk's successor after his career in business (Silk had been a headmaster), flew out to Harare to see for himself and crack a whip. 'Lord MacLaurin and I were horrified by what we saw in Zimbabwe,' said the ECB chief executive Tim Lamb. 'We were not happy with the way England presented themselves. Their demeanour was fairly negative and not particularly attractive,' according to *Wisden*'s tour review. And why was that? In large part because they were not permitted to see their wives, partners or children over Christmas, or at any other time in the space of four months.

'Atherton, initially handicapped by his chronic back problem, and Graham Thorpe both lost form completely.' The cricket world has since learned why in Thorpe's case: he was going through a domestic crisis. In New Zealand, at Napier, we talked at length. I was in a similar boat with two young kids I wanted to see growing up, but I had flown home between the Zimbabwe and New Zealand legs. Thorpe did most of the talking; shy initially in company, the dam would burst when he unburdened himself of his troubles. Nobody in the England management team made a sounding board. A player was left to sink or swim.

So many England players of that generation, including Thorpe, had marriages which ended in divorce. I would look at them as they came down to breakfast and count how few had lasting relationships. Their job made them almost unattainable. Their employer washed his hands of the wellbeing of his employees. On any cricket tour of four months the temptations will become harder and harder to resist, not least out of loneliness. Only when Duncan Fletcher became head coach in 1999 was there any progress beyond this antediluvian approach – or, let us call it plainly, this inhumanity. Suddenly somebody in authority, Uncle Duncan, was interested in the person as well as the player.

One immediate change that was made by Lord MacLaurin was to allocate single hotel rooms to all players, instead of making most of them share, apart from the captain and perhaps the vice-captain. This alteration was made with the best of intentions, to help them sleep better – in larger beds, not singles – and improve their efficiency. Sharing a room had often worked as a smooth arrangement: Graham Gooch and John Emburey were birds of a feather wanting to shack up together. But it was a fractious relationship if one player wanted to listen to his radio until the early hours, like Phil Edmonds. A few players got on each other's nerves and grew to hate each other.

It is almost 30 years since the new system of allocating every player his own room was introduced – and too soon to say whether it has been an outright success or not. Most of the time, yes, it is right to give every player his own space. Nevertheless, the fact remains that a certain type of personality would prefer not to spend all of his nights and much of his days on his own when far from home. You have to wonder if one or two of the players who have found touring too stressful would have found some comfort in sharing with a teammate: when Marcus Trescothick was struggling in Pakistan towards the end of 2005, when Mike Yardy was struggling on one-day tours, when Jonathan Trott was overwhelmed in Australia in 2013–14 to the extent of flying home during a Test (after he had been dismissed twice). A cricket tour can be the greatest fun. But, because it can last so long and take the player so far from home and family, it can grow into the opposite extreme, of living hell. England's Test cricketers now inhabit a healthier world, with someone who specialises in their mental wellbeing always in attendance or on call. It would just have been nice if there had not been so many nervous breakdowns before getting there.

Test No. 204

Edgbaston, June 1997

This nine-wicket victory was the prototype of England's Ashes triumph in 2005. Ian Chappell, albeit an Australian, would have been pleased. England attacked, for once, and Australia quailed, for once. It was a fine example of bullies – including Shane Warne and Glenn McGrath – not liking to be bullied. This was the only Test between 1987 and 2005 which England won when the Ashes were still alive, and Nasser Hussain's 207, his highest score, made for a happy column.

It helped that Australia's captain Mark Taylor had been very short of runs, so much so that his place was being questioned by the Australian media before the match. It really helps in a five-Test series if the opposing captain is vulnerable or injured: Andrew Strauss's task in 2010–11 was helped by Ricky Ponting's broken finger. But Taylor came good with a century in his second innings here, and Australia rallied to retain the urn and take a 3-1 lead into the final Test.

In this opening match, England were set 118 to win and knocked them off, for the loss of one wicket, in only 21.3 overs. Here was another 'outlier', a foretaste of that future when England would regularly score at five and a half runs per over. In the 20th century Test sides approached a small target as if treading on eggshells and often surrendered the initiative. They tried to absorb the pressure imposed by bowlers, when there was never going to be time to reap the rewards by hitting them when they tired. Australia, though world Test champions in all but title, batted as slowly as everyone else in a run-chase, the classic being the Sydney Test on South Africa's first tour of Australia since readmission: crawling, not chasing, in pursuit of 117, Australia could not achieve two an over before being dismissed for 111 in 56.3 overs. It was not until the 21st century that players realised that Parkinson's Law, of work expanding to fill the time available, should not be applied to run-chases.

Barbados, March 1998
It is not the job of a journalist to be a mover or shaker. There are times, however, when a cricket correspondent has to express an opinion, and at certain moments that opinion can exert some influence on a public debate: notably when no succession-planning has taken place and various candidates offer themselves as the next England captain.

Before the England and Wales Cricket Board had heard of succession-planning, the scene could resemble a medieval court. 'The King is dead! Long live the King!' Yes, but who should the next king be? we whisper among ourselves behind the arras. Who's in, who's out, as King Lear said? X is the most successful county captain, Y is England's one-day captain, and Z, while young, captained England Under-19s, and England A, and is a leader in the making. These are the nights of intrigue, if not long knives.

Complicating the issue is whether the candidate in question is a columnist for your newspaper or a rival. The protocol is – old-fashioned courtesy dictates – that one does not say anything disparaging in print about someone who is, if only temporarily, a colleague. Tricky. Thus it was in 1993 when Graham Gooch was coming to the end of his reign and even those yeoman shoulders could no longer support the weight. The ailing king knows his time has come; he looks around the dressing-room to identify his successor. It is all very medieval. Will the ailing king do the gallant thing and fall upon his sword, or will he have to be pushed?

In the summer of 1993, while the 40-year-old Gooch's England were being steamrollered by Australia, the realistic choice lay between Alec Stewart and Mike Atherton. Stewart had already led England in two Tests abroad, losing both, but scoring a fifty in each, and there was a good chance that he would give up wicketkeeping if he were captain and be a swashbuckling opener. However, swashbuckling batsmen have always tended to rein themselves on being appointed captain, to demonstrate more responsibility.

Atherton was only 25. My reservation was that he had been drawn by circumstances, if not nature, into a defensive mindset: he told the story of how he had been set upon by thugs, who had spotted his uniform, on his way home from Manchester Grammar, and had curled himself into a ball until they stopped kicking him. In his three seasons playing for Cambridge University, his back had always been against the wall, and the objective a face-saving draw. He had seen winning cricket for Lancashire, but this was usually one-day cricket. I thought it was right to wait, and to appoint Stewart, only Atherton had just been signed as a *Sunday Telegraph* columnist.

I expressed my view in print, in favour of Stewart, then ducked out. The vote went in favour of Atherton. His England sides resembled, initially at least, his Cambridge team, doggedly hanging on for a draw, rather than attacking and aiming to win. To put it another way, the style was not Bazball.

Do captaincies always have to end in tears in mid-series or straight afterwards? They seemed to do so before succession-planning. Atherton felt he should resign after the 1997 Ashes had resulted in a 3-2 defeat, a commendable scoreline for England in the context of recent Ashes series. He was persuaded to carry on for a tour of the West Indies by Lord MacLaurin, the ECB chairman, and rightly so, I thought. Having passed over Stewart in 1993, there was no urgency to go back to him now. But the luck of the toss kept going against Atherton: he was losing the Test series against West Indies 1-3 when winning the toss could well have made it 3-1. He spread the word that he was going to fall on his sword at the end of the sixth Test in Antigua. He was stepping down, as well, from captaining the one-day side in the 50-over series which followed in the Caribbean.

No actual throne was involved. In Barbados, however, there was a Mini Moke for the England captain's use. One day it was Atherton's. Next day Adam Hollioake was driving merrily around the island with his Surrey mates. Atherton should have been opening in England's one-day team: slow pitches made 220 off 50 overs a winning total, and Atherton was well-versed in grinding out the ones and twos as a one-day opener, but Hollioake did not want his predecessor in his side. King one day; a foot soldier, unselected, the next.

Outside the hotel shop on the golf resort in Barbados where we were staying, Nasser Hussain would mooch and stare in the window, without going inside to buy anything. As we talked, he said he should be the next Test captain. I had to disagree, on the basis of timing. It would be a festering sore in the Test side if Stewart were never given the chance: he would have legitimate cause for complaint if he had never led England after those two Tests as Gooch's deputy. But I gave Nasser my word that he would be my candidate after Stewart.

In the summer of 1998, South Africa, blessed with all-rounders and fast bowlers, went 1-0 up against Stewart's England. Who should stem the onrushing tide but Stewart himself, in a match-saving seven-hour 164 at Old Trafford, then Atherton and Nasser, fending off Allan Donald and Shaun Pollock to level the series at Trent Bridge. England have not been the best at every facet of Test cricket in my time, but they have been in this regard: former captains, who have gone back into the ranks after resigning the captaincy, have not rocked the boat and have fought every mite as hard under their successors.

Test No. 229

The Oval, August 1999

England this summer unveiled the perfect template. For failure. No wonder some of the crowd booed at the end of the fourth and final Test against New Zealand. In the affairs of men (women might be more coherently organised) a time does come for public protest if anything is to improve.

After staging the 1999 World Cup in the first half of this season, England left a legacy all right: one of complete incompetence, a masterclass in how not to stage and participate in a global tournament. The opening ceremony was symbolic when showers over Lord's turned the fireworks into damp squibs. England were not knocked out in the qualifying stage: they knocked themselves out, by blocking in sight of victory against Zimbabwe, scoring their last nine runs in 30 balls (Neil Fairbrother consuming 23 of them to score seven), with Andrew Flintoff 'in the sheds', instead of bolstering their net run-rate. Australia's semi-final against South Africa was as tight as a tie could be, and widely considered the most absorbing limited-overs game to be played to that point, and decided in favour of Australia on net run-rate. Meanwhile, the hosts went out at almost the same time as the tournament's theme song was released.

Almost any team would have struggled to become even more shambolic, but not an England side governed by people who did not prioritise the national team. Feuds between the players and a chap appointed by Lord MacLaurin — Simon Pack, solid background in the Marines you know — kept erupting. Pack had decided that the afternoon before the first Ashes Test in Brisbane in November 1998 was the ideal time (for him, not for the captain Alec Stewart) to discuss World Cup contracts. Unbelievable. Would the England captain then be otherwise engaged? Graham Thorpe boycotted an event when contracts were grudgingly signed. How Not To Pull Together. As for the head coach, David Lloyd or 'Bumble', he was temperamentally too ardent for England to succeed.

England won the opening Test of 1999 against New Zealand emphatically at Edgbaston. It was their nightwatchman Alex Tudor, though, who made the runs: and in yet another case of everyone failing to connect with each other, Thorpe hit the winning runs when Tudor was 99★. Atherton, who opened the batting, said afterwards that England would win this series 4–0. So deep and unending was the downward spiral, however, that New Zealand secured their one and only Test series victory in England, 2–1. Such was the shambles that by the end David Graveney was selecting the team: someone who had never played nor studied Test cricket until, with the rebel tour of South Africa under Mike Gatting forgotten, he was appointed chairman of England's selectors. For the fourth Test at the Oval, the series 1–1, Graveney sacked Mark Butcher, not only as stand-in captain but as opening batsman, brought in the dogged county opener Darren Maddy, and selected the weakest tail that England have ever fielded: Andy Caddick at eight, Alan Mullally at nine, Phil Tufnell at 10, plus Ed Giddins, who contributed 27 runs between them. England were bottom of the world Test rankings, ranked below every country including Zimbabwe.

New Zealand were also adhering to a perfect template. But perfect for success. It is said that radical change is only brought about by a financial or moral crisis, and in New

Zealand's case it had been both. After a tour of South Africa that was disastrous in too many ways to list, the New Zealand government appointed an academic called John Hood to draw up a constitution for all national sporting bodies. Cricket bought in. Their structure had been the same as England's: their executive board consisted of representatives of each major and minor association. In other words, the representative for Lower Whakaratatatui was only interested in the financial and other benefits he could obtain for Lower Whakaratatatui. The national side generated all the money, but the tail – county chairmen in England's case – wagged the dog. So no central contracts in England, no national academy or centre of excellence, as in Australia: just make the players channel most of their energies into their county and hope they might be fit when selected for England.

Reap what you sow, and in the 1980s and 1990s England's board – the Test and County Cricket Board until 1996 when the England and Wales Cricket Board took over – sowed nothing. Ian Botham's brilliance papered over the cracks in the 1980s, but by 1999 they had expanded into fault-lines. To this day the ECB's executive board is not a patch on New Zealand's, which consists of eight great and good persons including at least two who have played Test cricket. Members of the ECB board often appear to be nominated and selected precisely because they do not have any experience of cricket, so they can be steered wherever the executive wants.

Test No. 230

Johannesburg, November 1999

Duncan Fletcher wrinkled his nose when he smiled. Most of the media took against him from the beginning, so he did against them, but I was fortunate to set off on the right foot. When Duncan had coached Glamorgan in 1997, and immediately took them to their third and last Championship title, one of his leading players had been the opening batsman Steve James, and he kindly put in a word for me. Duncan and his wife Marina stopped for a pub lunch on the way from his home in Cardiff to Lord's to discuss his England appointment. As a shy country boy, Duncan was taken aback by large numbers of cameras and people but, one-on-one, he was friendly, amusing, un-egocentric, almost avuncular, and how can you dislike a grown man who wrinkles his nose in a boyish smile? He also saw the game of cricket in a way that was, in my experience, unique.

On England's last tour of Zimbabwe in 2004 he borrowed a car and took me and a photographer, Rebecca Naden, to visit the farm where he had grown up, for a feature. It was about an hour out of Harare, and on the way he told us about his former job in the transport department where his ingenuity was given scope. Duncan came up with a new system of car registration numbers that was so clever I could not understand it when he first explained it – Rebecca could – let alone now. It was based on his insight that, in the event of an accident, the victims made a mental note of the letters of the other car involved first, then the numbers (or it could have been the other way round); and if they could recall the three letters, and the make of car, it would be relatively easy to track down the car itself. No wonder he looked at cricket from an untypical perspective.

When Duncan was growing up, as a boarder in one of Zimbabwe's fine schools (comparable to South Africa's elite schools in their sporting facilities), cricket was a sport of the white community, which decreased from 250,000 before independence in 1980 to 80,000 afterwards. They played it in the capital, and Bulawayo, and at country clubs where children were encouraged to play tennis and rugby and swim – all the sports that make a cricketer into an athletic fielder. The only non-white player of note was a batsman Ali Shah, whom I interviewed. He said that Duncan, as captain, would not back him initially, but once he played a brave innings, it convinced Duncan to support him. Compelled to do national service, Duncan was a captain in the army before the national cricket team. I had to check he had not transferred the same attitudes from war-time to peace-time. As Duncan was the first non-England player to coach England, due diligence was in order.

After we had turned off the main road on to a track, the farmhouse was a couple of minutes further on through the fields. The Fletcher family had sold up long ago and Duncan did not know who the new owners were. We pulled up outside a spacious bungalow – four bedrooms? – but nothing opulent or flash, simply functional. We went to knock on the door. Nothing was locked. Nobody was in.

After walking round the farmhouse, Duncan saw three African labourers at the far side of one of the adjoining fields. He walked over and for a good 20 minutes they all leaned against the wooden fence and talked. When he returned, I asked which language they had used, and he said they had all been speaking Shona. We waited further but the owners did not come home. It must have been a stable society for them to have gone out for hours, to town or into the fields, without locking up.

On returning to the outskirts of Harare, he pointed out the house where he had to court his future wife Marina by climbing over the wall. She was always his first concern, and when he worked to make the ECB more considerate of the welfare and family life of their employees, in other words the England players, I could understand where he was coming from.

Duncan started at the bottom: England were sent in on a damp pitch in Johannesburg and their score was soon two runs for four wickets. He had not been party to the selection of this England squad – he thought it his duty to work out his three-year contract as Glamorgan's coach, without leaving them in mid-season to succeed David Lloyd – but on this tour he could evaluate them. One he rated was an uncapped batsman who looked the part the moment he entered the England dressing-room for the first time: he deported himself as if he belonged, even in the first practice game. This was Michael Vaughan. Exactly the same was to be said a few years later of Andrew Strauss.

In Bloemfontein over dinner one evening at the start of this tour with his captain and senior pro, Nasser Hussain and Mike Atherton, both *Sunday Telegraph* columnists, they seemed to attune quickly to each other's wavelengths. It was not like that when Duncan's appointment had been first announced – and Nasser shouldn't mind if I say so now. He went nearly apoplectic when the new England coach was announced: he knew about Keith Fletcher, of Essex and England, but Duncan who? From where? Zimbabwe!!! This selection was largely the work of Brian Bolus, a former England player renowned for his pad-play and perhaps the most defensive batsman they ever picked (Bolus-ball was the opposite of Bazball), and he made a fool of himself when drunk. Yet he still deserves credit for researching the subject and making the right choice for head coach. Duncan brought stability where there had been chaos. If you have a *Wisden* containing the 1997 Glamorgan averages, you can see the same 11 performed most of the Championship season: for their 17 games, 14 Glamorgan players were selected. For the four Tests against New Zealand in 1999, 18 England players had been selected.

From today's perspective, defeating West Indies is small beer, but at the start of the 2000 season this objective seemed as taxing as regaining the Ashes: not for 31 years, since 1969, had England won a Test series against West Indies at home or away. By then though Duncan had seen enough – and, like the future management team of Brendon McCullum and Ben Stokes, his identification of England players was not based on statistics in county cricket. He knew his own mind and which players should receive one of the new central contracts that Lord MacLaurin had introduced. In addition to Vaughan, Fletcher looked at Marcus Trescothick and his back-foot play when he was languishing in Somerset's middle order, and saw an England opener. Trescothick and Vaughan were to give England first-wicket partnerships that rivalled the scoring-rate of Ben Duckett and Zak Crawley, and exceeded them in substance.

Defeating Pakistan in Pakistan was another objective, as England had not done so since their inaugural tour of 1961–62. Defeating Sri Lanka in a Test series in Sri Lanka, where Muttiah Muralitharan ruled every roost, was another objective if only because England hitherto had played them in one-off Tests. Defeating West Indies away was another (not since 1967–68 had England done that), and defeating South Africa away yet another (not since 1964–65 had England done that). Very top of the wish list was the Ashes, held by Australia since 1989. And Duncan was to supervise all these achievements, firstly with Nasser as captain, then with Vaughan, without ever seeking to take credit for himself.

Duncan called himself a consultant, although his title was head coach and he was the manager of the touring party. In other words, if a crisis occurred on a tour, he would be the one to decide whether it should continue. It has always been the case in my time that the manager has held this power, except once. When England had disintegrated into disarray again, post-Duncan, in a feud between Kevin Pietersen and Peter Moores as captain and coach, Andrew Strauss was given the ultimate say on England's tour of the West Indies in early 2009 when he was the official captain for the first time. It was an extraordinary exception to this rule, and a manifestation of official trust in the new captain from the outset, and it was because Andy Flower was the batting coach, not the head coach that he was soon to become.

Behind his sunglasses, which gave him a far sterner image than the reality, Duncan observed everything on and off the field, but said little, and always in unison with his captain. The four previous England head coaches – Micky Stewart, Keith Fletcher, Ray Illingworth and David Lloyd – had, to greater or lesser extents, been keen to be seen in charge. Duncan saw and did things differently without ever, from what I saw, writing notes down. He transformed England's playing of spin immediately, from inept sweepers into imperious centurions on turners in Asia, notably Trescothick and Graham Thorpe. He noted the angles at which opposing batsmen should be attacked: if there was a single tactic which won the 2005 Ashes, it was Andrew Flintoff going round the wicket to Adam Gilchrist. He saw England slip fielders drop chances offered by right-handed batsmen that went to their left-hand side – and suggested they should place their dominant hand on top when catching to their left, overturning convention. Duncan was not looking for 'one-percenters' as his successor Peter Moores was to do; he was re-assessing all the orthodoxies of English cricket to see if they were still best practice.

On an England tour of South Africa after Duncan had retired, he agreed to meet Nasser for dinner in Cape Town (Duncan was living down the coast in Hermanus). They had not met for years, and neither was the type to have a Christmas card list. It was touching to see them greet each other again: the warmth, respect, affection. Duncan wrinkled his nose, even Nasser smiled. I should have played the newshound and eavesdropped on every word, but they deserved their time together, and I lingered over ordering drinks at the bar, and obtaining the receipt. (I would also have bought Brian Bolus one had he been there.) Duncan never courted the media, as he did not think it was part of his job to say things that would generate headlines. The country boy took a mischievous delight in not giving the media what they sought. He has, in consequence, never been accorded his official due. Vaughan has said he was England's best coach.

The last time I saw Duncan was on my last England tour of South Africa in 2019–20. He was still living in Hermanus, but inhabiting another world, nothing to do with sport. His eagle eye had turned to eagles: birdwatching was his passion. About 900 different types of bird had been identified in southern Africa and he had spotted more than 600 of them. If he heard on a WhatsApp group of a bird he had not seen, he and Marina would drive together, and he would photograph it and she would catalogue it. He had not given up cricket – he asked after 'Sammy

Curran', whom he had first encountered in Northampton at the age of three and already hitting practice balls over his parents' house – he had simply moved to other interests, taking with him that ingenious mind. He made me think of the saying that there are people who do, and people who take the credit for what has been done. He was much happier, too, at the opposite end of a camera.

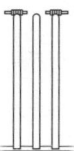

Once upon a time England played first-class matches on tour outside the Tests. Here we go to Jamaica v England in 1990. Had we known that England would win the subsequent Test, their first win against West Indies for 16 years, we would have been merrier.... So playing a red-ball game before the opening Test of a series is not a bad idea.

Against expectations: England captain Andrew Strauss celebrates with Graeme Swann who has just dismissed Australia's Michael Hussey in the Oval Test of 2009 to regain the Ashes 2-1.

2000s

Test No. 234

Centurion, January 2000

Well, well, would you believe, South Africa are making a game of it. Good old Hansie!

Please remember the context before condemning this gullible folly. It had been raining through days two and three and four. The Lake Hotel in Centurion is conveniently close to SuperSport Park, only a few minutes' walk, but the surrounding attractions are limited to a small shopping mall. The players and most journalists therefore prefer to stay in Johannesburg, at Sandton, which has a big shopping mall. After two months away from home, and three days stuck in a hotel, the thought of the flight back straight after the game was one of the few reasons for living – until Cronje's declaration on the last day cheered up hundreds of equally stir-crazy England supporters and set a target of 249 off 76 overs. Yes, of course I should have smelt a rat – it was barely more than three runs an over – but South Africa, 2-0 up, had already won the series so it was a dead-rubber, and England's batsmen had been tied down all series by the relentless quality of South Africa's quicks.

Looking back with the wisdom of hindsight, what was really suspicious was that Cronje never shut up shop when England caught up with the run-rate – when the whole ethos of South African cricket then was making certain you did not lose. He could have brought back his opening bowlers – only 76 overs needed to be bowled, no need for a spinner – after three days of resting. Yet Cronje brought on his part-time left-arm spinner (Paul Adams had broken a finger earlier in the game) and Pieter Strydom, on his debut, proceeded to bowl six maidenless overs for 27 runs. Why was he bowling to a spread-out field that allowed England so many easy singles? Because Cronje wanted

England to stay in touch with the asking-rate and not to shut up shop for a draw. One side or the other had to win, otherwise Cronje would not get his match-fixing fee of 53,000 rand (about £5000) and an infamous leather jacket.

Cronje, whatever else he may have been, was a wheeler-dealer with, as he himself confessed, 'an unfortunate love of money'. It proved a fatal flaw: he had done a contra-deal which allowed him to fly for free on cargo flights from George airport to Johannesburg, including the plane that crashed. When some details of his match-fixing emerged during the inquiry by the King Commission, Cronje could be seen to have siphoned off more than his share of some deals. He abused the power of his captaincy in more ways than one. As with many official enquiries, the scope was limited by the timescale – it examined little more than a year of his career – but what was revealed made it apparent that Cronje liked to pick on non-white players: less established, more vulnerable, easier to bully, easier to filch a higher commission from.

When the transcript of Cronje's phone calls with a match-fixer were revealed by Delhi police, it struck me immediately as genuine. I had the advantage of having interviewed him at Grace Road when he was playing for Leicestershire, and the strangest interview it was. I saw him briefly before the start of play and he said let's meet in the pavilion at lunch (Leicestershire, a major team in those days under the coaching of Jack Birkenshaw, were in the field). The lunch interval passed, and as the players came out again he said we would meet at tea. Which we did, but an interview at a tea interval can be 10 minutes at best. I do not know if he had anything to hide then: I doubt it – this was 1995 – but during the lunch break he might well have been doing some kind of wheeler-dealing. He was definitely not stuffing his face as he was very fit and lean. In any event, I had made some acquaintance with his speech patterns, and the transcript rang true.

On a later tour of South Africa I went, at Judge Edwin King's invitation, to his house in Cape Town. He said, a little too hurriedly, that he had been under no political pressure to close down the inquiry – just when the depth of Cronje's involvement in match-fixing was becoming apparent and liable to damage the reputation of 'the new South Africa'. But King was still annoyed that Cronje had got away with little more than a life ban from cricket, and his reputation was still largely intact within the Afrikaner community. King had announced that Cronje should be granted immunity from prosecution only if he told the whole truth, yet he had been granted immunity after telling part of it. So annoyed was King that he gave me the phone number of the Scorpion who had investigated Cronje (the Scorpions were a unit set up by SA's democratic government to investigate corruption, and were so good at it they were closed down). In a bar in downtown Cape Town, the Scorpion told me that Cronje had held 16 bank accounts, some of them joint, in the Cayman Islands. All were illegal.

It has been the failure to land a single big fish, and to give him an exemplary punishment, that has allowed match- and spot-fixing to grow into what it is today. Only the exposure and punishment of a top international cricketer would have sent a warning to players in every cricket-playing country – a warning not to get involved, ultimately, with one of the world's biggest mafias, perhaps the biggest. It is the duty of the fourth estate to be eternally vigilant, as nobody else seems to be, but the harsh reality is that UK law demands a standard of proof – cheques, bank statements – that is never going to be met in a paperless age. The fundamental trouble is that corruption, whether in the real world or sport, offers something for almost everybody involved: only the truth and the integrity of the activity itself are losers. Every year or two the ICC's Anti-Corruption Unit surfaces triumphantly to say that a marginal Sri Lankan player has been caught and banned, or that a Zimbabwean captain has confessed. Then the waters close over and the sport carries on, along with the game within the game.

Ever more T10 and T20 tournaments spring up around the globe, whose sums never seem to add up: large player fees, expensive hotels and costly flights, yet few spectators and peanuts for a broadcasting deal. Is it being broadcast on television, specifically in South Asia? In that case, in the time-lapse between the ball being bowled and the outcome being seen on a screen, in those 15 seconds all sorts of bets can be placed. World-class, honourable, players can join in the short-form fun and a big payday. All they have to do in return is turn a blind eye: even if they do not score a run, they lend veneers of respectability to the tournament.

It is one more reason to stick to less corruptible red-ball cricket, specifically Tests.

Test No. 238

Lord's, June–July 2000

After Curtly Ambrose had bowled the first ball of the opening Test at Edgbaston, Courtney Walsh had run towards him and celebrated. Premature? Not really. That first ball had soared from a length over the heads of the England batsman and West Indian wicketkeeper, and on TV commentary Richie Benaud said he could not understand the cause of this celebration. He soon found out: no England player passed 34 in either innings as they lost yet again to West Indies, by an innings and in three days. Same old, same old.

Apparently the second Test at Lord's was an exciting match. I know it was a close one: England, worm-turning, won by two wickets after Darren Gough, Andy Caddick and Dominic Cork ran through the West Indian second innings for 54. But exciting? How was any journalist expected to know that?

This was the first Test when the new Lord's media centre was in action. It was called by some 'iconic' but it resembled no icon I had seen. Its shape was pleasing, and formed an agreeable ultra-modern contrast to the late-Victorian pavilion opposite. But if it looked like a spaceship, it was almost as hermetically sealed as a spaceship, save for one window that could be opened in the *Test Match Special* box. I learned afterwards that 25,000 England supporters – West Indian fans had been long since edged out – were going wild while West Indies, the world champions until five years before, were put to flight in the same sort of flurry in which England had been put to flight for the two previous decades. People were roaring and cheering as Lord's might never have roared and cheered before, or for Eton v Harrow perhaps, not an England game. But the media might as well have been watching in the Hampstead Odeon. Not a sound from the crowd was to be heard, not a scintilla of atmosphere to be felt. Reporting a Test match, I want all my senses – well, most of them – to be engaged, in order to feel which way the game is heading. This is what one gains from being outside the playing area, in the wood, not on the field among the trees: a feel for which side is on top.

Apart from the crowd noise, the sound of bat on ball is inaudible in a sealed, air-conditioned press box. Plenty can be deduced if we know how to listen. When the leading first-class wicket-taker of all time was blind, Wilfred Rhodes could still tell one of his successors as Yorkshire's left-arm spinner, Don Wilson, that he was bowling too short: 'Aye, I can tell where they've hit the ball when I hear the fieldsman's feet, especially when they've hit it in my direction, and they're hitting it in my direction too often. It means they're square-cutting and a slow bowler should never be square-cut or pulled.' In the Trent Bridge Test when George Gunn congratulated Everton Weekes, Rhodes had listened to Frank Worrell's bat on ball: on the second evening Worrell had finished on 239*, on the third morning he was dismissed for 261. 'Aye, I'm not surprised,' Rhodes said. 'His bat hasn't sounded today like it did yesterday.'

When West Indies collapsed for 61 in the fourth Test of this series at Headingley, the roars of the crowd could be heard. The Western Terrace has always been audible – but the view from the various media centres tried at Headingley has never been ideal. Of Test grounds in England, the old Edgbaston and new Trent Bridge have offered written media the best vantage point: behind the arm at one end; above, though not too far above, ground level, and NOT air-conditioned but having windows that opened. Worst is the Oval if you are inside the press box, seated and sealed darkly behind two plates of tinted glass. Outside, to either side, is fine, though not quite behind the bowler's arm at the Vauxhall End.

The bane of a cricket correspondent is not an officious media officer over-protective of players (well, not quite), or even a press box at deep midwicket about 200 yards from the action, like the overflow box at the MCG. It is air-conditioning, welcome though it is on sultry days in Colombo or Chennai. The most perverse element is that air-conditioning is virtually a self-fulfilling prophecy. Studies show that a city which installs air-conditioning is two degrees centigrade hotter than its equivalent which does not. Thus a just-about-tolerable 36°C, if tempered by fresh air through open windows and the shade of nearby trees, is man-made into an intolerable 38°C that demands air-conditioning.

Flying to Adelaide over the Simpson Desert in the 1990s, I saw a vast hole in the ground extending for miles; and two freight trains per day, each hauling a hundred wagons, would transport coal several hundred miles to the power stations of Adelaide, in order to cool down all the offices and hotels and houses which did not have windows to open. Press boxes too: every new stadium around the world that comes on stream has a media centre that is air-conditioned. Ahmedabad, before the stadium was renovated into the world's biggest, touched rock bottom during the England Test of 2012. The windows were so filthy on the outside of the air-conditioned box – beyond the reach of anyone without a cherry-picker – that neither ears nor eyes could detect what was happening in the middle. Just as well, you might say: England had selected three seamers for a slow and turning pitch, and only one spinner.

A walk to the ground can turn a day's Test cricket into perfect pleasure. In England, Headingley and Old Trafford are an hour's walk from the main train station, too far. Edgbaston is about 40 minutes, and Trent Bridge 20 minutes over the river, my ideal given a backpack containing a laptop and assorted – jumbled? – cables. The Oval is too close to underground stations for a constitutional. As for Lord's, all depends on where you can afford to stay. At the end of a day's play, I would rather avoid a scrummage for taxis or buses, and walk back to the hotel, maybe reading through my copy on the mobile one final time to spot a howler. Nothing worse than waking up in a sweat, which even air-conditioning cannot cure, after realising the error that one has earlier made: somehow it manages to surface in one's brain in the early hours. When younger, I would wonder whether I could hasten to my newspaper office with Tippex, and at least whiten out the mistake in copies that were going to be read by editors.

Australia's grounds often offer the chance of a constitutional, split in two parts, perhaps by stopping at a café along the river which offers fresh fruit, poached eggs and smashed avocado on sourdough, washed down with tea, on expenses. The founding fathers of an Australian city would establish the most important sites in the centre: the state parliament and law courts, a library, the cricket ground and the botanical gardens where they could find out which plants, imported and native, would fit into their plans for colonial expansion. Brisbane's botanical gardens, beside a river that flows, take the palm ahead of Adelaide where the Torrens is dammed. Most Australian press boxes, however, are execrable. Grounds are so big that from a press box at the back of an enormous stand 11 cricketers appear more like seven dwarves.

The old Adelaide Oval, therefore, used to be my favourite when the press box was square to the wicket and maybe only 80 yards distant. Behind it, Sir Donald Bradman might be sitting in state, at the front Bill O'Reilly having one last yarn with Clarrie Grimmett. Straight ahead, across the ground and above the Victor Richardson Gates (dedicated to the Chappells' grandfather) rose the Adelaide Hills, where German settlers planted their vineyards. To the left were St Peter's Cathedral, a solid reminder of the immaterial world, and the scoreboard constructed of wood for the Ashes Test of 1911–12, and the Hill where spectators could sit or stand where they wanted, without being boxed into a specific seat. This scoreboard, when the afternoon wind springs up and timbers creak, is the nearest I have come to being at sea in an old sailing ship – the same boards that bore the names of Hobbs and Rhodes, Barnes and Foster before the First World War, repainted to spell Smith and Cummins, Root and Stokes.

Australian scoreboards, and especially Adelaide's, spell it out: no hiding place for the underperformer, because the bowling analyses are displayed all day or until the whole innings ends: 0 for 117, 0 for 38, 2 for 143. The current value of a player is displayed constantly, up to date, before his very eyes. If you are out for a duck in England, your humiliation will only be displayed until the next man is out and 'Last Man 0' is removed from public sight, and even then your name is never attached. In Australia your offence is paraded, as in the public execution of a convict; more rarely, your success.

West Indian grounds had the folksiest press boxes, before the 2007 World Cup entailed – at the insistence of the ICC – purpose-built stadia with air-conditioned prisons to house the media. A comfortable prison, yes, in which one can live in shirt-sleeves, immune to wind and rain and excessive heat, where electric sockets are to hand, and the person at the other end of one's phone is audible, not drowned out by a passionate crowd – that is if spectators can be bothered to visit an out-of-town stadium. But more efficient is not more fun, so please give me a seat in the old press box in the George Headley Stand at Sabina Park, where I can see beyond the ground the Blue Mountains having a siesta in the afternoon haze. The press box at the Queen's Park Oval has its back to the Northern Range, but a walk round the ground – how about a goat roti from one of those stalls beneath the stands? – brings it into view: no house, no buildings, no afforested trees, just natural scrub and a grand view over Port-of-Spain, back in the day when England used to tour Trinidad.

The one country where I would settle for enclosed press boxes is New Zealand. A Dunedin Test can be as cold as they come. The wind from the Antarctic hits Christchurch too and the press tent at Hagley Park can hardly resist its clutches (Graeme Swann told me that in one game when he was the pro for a Christchurch club, at the fall of a wicket, every player would hit the ground to avoid the wind until the next man in had taken guard). The architect who designed the press box at the Basin Reserve, at the very top of a stand, had obviously not attended the ground on a windy Wellington day. No ground in world Test cricket has a shorter boundary than Auckland's Eden Park: the middle seems too close, as if the media were looking over the garden fence and interfering in proceedings. Are you a half-full or half-empty personality? At Mount Maunganui the optimist looks towards the Mount and its original flora (far too much of New Zealand's rainforest has been chopped down, if a Briton is in any position to say so); the pessimist towards the marshalling yards where the tree trunks are unchained and sawed before deportation.

Galle takes first prize for a backdrop, which inches ahead of any hill or mountain. Like anywhere else in Sri Lanka, the heat stuns if you step out of shade for even five minutes and are unfit, but if you stay in the media centre you can spend all day admiring the Fort built by Portuguese then Dutch to guard their entrepôt. Therein lies a World Heritage Site, where backstreet shops still sell the main reason why European merchants came to Serendip or Ceylon: cinnamon. It is nothing like the heavy, dusty powders which Americans spray on their apple pies; a stick of cinnamon is thin, light and slightly sweet. The factories in Galle Fort where it was stored – we would call them warehouses – are buildings of beautiful stone.

Does food, the lunch, play a part in making a day of Test cricket perfect? Australia and New Zealand offer ample, solid fare. The trouble with the rice lunches of India, Pakistan and Sri Lanka is their soporific effect, especially when a five-star local hotel has the catering contract (less tempting is when you see the staff handling pieces of chicken, as at Eden Gardens: my longest-ever throw was not on the cricket field but in the bathroom that evening). Goat rotis in the Caribbean, dribbling gravy, are the most tempting food outside a press box; inside I will go for Edgbaston. They feed photographers, who have to set up so early, a fine breakfast; it is followed by a three-course lunch, and tempting tea, rounded off by supper if it is a floodlit game.

To be professional, for a moment: the best view in Test cricket from a press box, behind the arm and under a covered roof which yet allows the sun and air and reactions of the crowd to circulate, is to be enjoyed at Centurion. Pretoria's outskirts are not tempting in themselves – England supporters are the only white people you see walking – but for absorbing a day's play, with all one's sensibilities, and getting the feel of a Test match, I would cite it as the best.

Cricket reporting used to be an outdoor activity in the main. John Woodcock turned nut-brown on tour. (At the opposite end of the spectrum was the *Telegraph* correspondent Michael Melford, who had to cover those tours which E.W. Swanton did not like. Mellers dived into a swimming pool, after removing his clothes to reveal a body which had turned pale during Second World War service. When diving in, his self-effacing humour evoked an early film of *Tarzan* as he called himself 'Johnny Weiz-Mellers.') I used to wear a hat, or put it in my bag for the cricket at any rate. I found it in Australia while travelling round the outback, writing a book called *Train to Julia Creek*. It was army surplus, a digger's hat against the sun. I don't need it now that cricket reporting takes place indoors.

Test No. 242
Faisalabad, November–December 2000

It was some shock when England won the third Test in Karachi and the dark. It was their first Test victory in Pakistan since 1961-2. England would never have got close if a) Mike Atherton had not drained Pakistan with his last monumental act of stubbornness: 579 minutes for 125 runs. He usually wrote his own column, but that evening I had to go to his hotel bedroom to ghostwrite it because he was so tired. Nasser was in the room too, but he showed no elation nor exuberance, just exhaustion, as much nervous as physical. Test cricketers hold it together while walking off at the end of a day; we never see them keel over in the dressing-room or hotel. Far fitter than the rest of us, yet still human. And England would never have got close if b) Steve Bucknor, the only neutral umpire, had not exerted his seniority and kept Pakistan bowling in the gloaming. Pakistan had never lost at the National Stadium, and they had been averaging one Test per year there since 1955, until England crept home in December 2000. The ground had been more impregnable than the Gabba in Australia or Kensington Oval in Barbados. Even Duncan Fletcher was seen briefly to smile.

Test No. 247
Colombo, March 2001

To beat Pakistan in Karachi, England had chased down – in the nick of time – 176 in 41.3 overs, Graham Thorpe leading them over the line with 64*. He did it again later that same winter in Sri Lanka. Such words though are even more inadequate than normal. Thorpe was immense. On a few occasions a player stands out so far from the rest of his teammates that he appears to be twice their stature. Rarely does he or she appear to be thrice their stature: thus James Anderson in the Trent Bridge Test of 2013 when he was left to take half of the wickets for England; or Ben Stokes in the Headingley Test of 2019. Quite often Nat Sciver-Brunt, arguably the best in the world at hitting pace-off bowling, has thrice the stature in an England Women's match. I think Thorpe, in the series-deciding third Test in Colombo, was about four times better than any other England batsman, given the opposing bowling, conditions and match situation.

Thermometers do not convey what the heat of Sri Lanka is like: they say 30°C or maybe as high as 34°C, but no mention of humidity. Leave your hotel or press box (I have to say the air-conditioning in Sri Lanka is balm), and you feel more than halfway to the sun. It is stunning in that it stuns your head. Five minutes without a hat, or 10 minutes with, and I'm dehydrating fast. Being surrounded by concrete in a city adds a few degrees; out on the field is not quite so bad, unless you are wearing a helmet.

This series – the first contests between England and Sri Lanka that were not one-off Tests – was more bad-tempered than any I have known, even including the Ashes. In an Ashes series there is always an Australian player or two – sometimes a handful – who are playing county cricket and therefore have ongoing relationships with some England players. No such comradeship in this series; no T20 franchises, either, with players of different countries in the same squad. This was more like gang warfare, the series standing at 1–1. The two gangs had entered a narrow alley, one from each end, neither side was going to back down and there was no escape, even if they had wanted one. With bats and balls they were going to slug it out.

In the opening Test in Galle, Marcus Trescothick had illustrated how relatively easier batting was for left-handers against Muttiah Muralitharan: these were the days when he still had only an off-break, with which I had no argument as so many of the revolutions on the ball were generated by his wrist (I have no idea how his doosra was ever allowed). Trescothick slog-swept and scored 122, next highest innings

33, as England lost. A left-hander could not be bowled – not clean bowled, he could drag on – by a Murali off-break that snaked like a cobra.

A fresher, bouncier pitch in Kandy allowed England's seamers to take 17 wickets and level the series. It was plain to see why Kumar Sangakkara succeeded outside Asia: up in the Kandyan hills the soil demanded that the schoolboy had to keep his wrists higher than in the plains, and Asgiriya College was Sangakkara's school ground. England under Nasser Hussain, who made a hundred, were not going to back down. They were not only in the Sri Lankans' face, they were in the umpires' faces too: not so much Rudi Koertzen, widely respected on the international circuit, as his Sri Lankan colleague B.C. Cooray (only one neutral umpire per Test then). Anarchy broke out as the fielders of both sides appealed for anything and everything. Cooray, a modest player and not a professional umpire, was overwhelmed, like most of us would have been in such a situation (he retired after this match). As for the ICC match referee, Hanumant Singh was sitting in the box next to the press. In a stadium nowadays the match referee and the TV umpire are sealed off but, like so much else, it was more informal then. I had a soft spot for Hanumant as I had watched him batting for the Indians at Bramall Lane in 1967: an old-school stroker of the ball through the covers who loved a late-cut. And he was dismayed at what was going on in the middle: Hanumant knew cricket as a gentleman's game, not gang warfare.

Sending the opposition in was soon to become the vogue elsewhere. In Sri Lanka, if a captain ever did that, he would be immediately given a concussion test: something had to be wrong with his marbles. England won this series even though Nasser lost every toss. But only in the opening Test did the customary pattern obtain, that of Sri Lanka ending day one on about 280 for two and every opponent exhausted.

The third Test at the Sinhalese Sports Club in Colombo was another result pitch i.e. a raging turner. This brought England's spinners into the equation, Robert Croft and Ashley Giles, and reduced the Murali effect because his off-break turned far too much to kiss an edge. And Thorpe was immense: he had virtually led England home in their run-chase in the second Test, scoring 46 with the next highest 21, and this time he went all the way. England scored 249 (Thorpe 113* and in hospital on a drip that night, next highest score 26) and 74 for six (Thorpe 32*, next highest 13). As the boat rocked and tossed in the stormiest sea, Thorpe again kept his hand on the tiller. No big aerial shots – only two fours second time round – and no bravado, no flamboyance, just working the spinners risklessly into gaps. It was the reverse of a Pietersen innings, with no disrespect to KP's style. In the traditions of English cricket, it was a Southerner playing the innings of a Northerner. Or a simple stat said it all: in the last three England innings at the climax of this series, in which Thorpe was dismissed once, the next highest score was 26. Had there been data about his interception points, I guess it would have shown that he played right forward or right back.

Test No. 268

Brisbane, November 2002

He can make fun of it more than 20 years later when the scars have healed. It was no laughing matter at the time. Nasser Hussain, on winning the toss at the Gabba, had decided to launch the Ashes series by sending Australia in to bat, and bat they did. At the close of day one, Australia were 364 for two. Their winning margin, after Matthew Hayden had puffed out his chest to hit a century in each innings, and the pitch had cracked, and England had been airbrushed out of the picture by Glenn McGrath and Shane Warne for 79, was 384 runs.

Few tensions in real life, let alone sport, are so great as those that an England captain feels at the start of an Ashes series in Australia. Not the whole world is looking at him, but most of the English-speaking world is, and not momentarily either. Such is cricket's fascination with its prolonged past that the England captain can rest assured he will be reminded of a wrong decision in Australia for the rest of his life.

It was a devilish decision to have to make. Early morning had been damp but the sub-tropical sun was drinking up this dampness fast. Would you bat first against McGrath, Warne and Jason Gillespie on a fresh pitch? Only with the wisdom of hindsight. When Nasser was walking off to tell his team they would be bowling, he was so absorbed that he walked up the tunnel to 'the rooms', as they call them in Australia, and straight past his best mate, Mike Atherton, retired from playing, who had just arrived in Australia to write columns and comments for *The Sunday Telegraph*. He and Nasser had been friends, not rivals, since school and their England Under-19s days; yet Nasser was so focused on the moment that he walked straight past.

Don't blame the messenger – or the ghostwriter. On the second evening, I had to ring Nasser, arrange a time, and sit down to record his version of events and write his column. Trepidation was not remote. But he was as good as gold. Straight up he admitted that he had got his decision wrong. Not the slightest hint of an attempt to blame his bowlers for not picking up three or four wickets in the opening session. He just played it straight – and this is what I have admired about most of England's official Test captains in my time. In press conferences the party line must be towed for public consumption: captains have to peddle the propaganda about how England are going to fight back from 4–0 down or whatever their plight might be. But one-on-one, in private, they tell it to you straight, they don't play politics. Machinations are left to administrators. It has often struck me what fine government ministers most England captains would make: they would take the decision they thought to be right, irrespective of considerations like their own popularity. But then they would not have the deviousness to be a politician in the first place.

Test No. 272
Sydney, January 2003

Here is the best part of being the cricket correspondent of a Sunday newspaper. At the start of the week we can get away from it all, hire a car and travel up-country to write a feature, going where we want, on expenses, and ideally transporting the reader with us. Sports and travel writing, work and pleasure, combined.

One difference on this occasion. We were heading for the outback of New South Wales for a profile of Glenn McGrath. On such expeditions I normally jumped in a hire car. But our destination of Narromine was almost 300 miles inland from Sydney: about six hours' drive from the city-centre hotel, given the faff of wading through Parramatta and out through Sydney's western suburbs. So it is the plane to Dubbo, about a 40-seater, designed for graziers and their kids at boarding school in Sydney.

You know those long-haul flights where somebody is a real nuisance, and the only one to keep the window-blind up, while everybody else is watching a film or sleeping? That could be me. I am fascinated by our Earth. The screen on the back of each seat, if not the in-flight magazine, will offer a map and I love looking out of the window to identify places. Flying over Anatolia, Iran and Afghanistan is a challenge – so few cities – but the outback comes a good second. Better than a plane, though, would be taking the train out west to Narromine – which takes at least six hours from Sydney – to absorb the scenery as described by 'Banjo' Paterson:

> And now beyond the Western Range, where sunset skies are red,
> And clouds of dust, and clouds of thirst, go drifting overhead,
> The railway train is taking back, along the Western Line,
> That narrow-minded person on his road to Narromine.

Pick up a hire car at Dubbo airport and it is less than an hour's drive to Narromine. The further west you go, the smaller the population of each settlement, so while Dubbo is a fair-sized town, Narromine has a few thousand inhabitants. Not much choice of accommodation: a motor inn will have to do beside the main road, but we can go to the old two-storey pub which has been the heart of town since 'the Banjo' last passed through. The first two lines of his poem keep revolving round my head, because the second is so neatly and tightly condensed:

The stranger came from Narromine and made his little joke —
'They say we folks in Narromine are narrow-minded folk.'

Start in the main street with the public library and tourist information centre. A bit of a downer here. McGrath's agent, they say, has told people in Narromine not to talk to the media. It is the first, and only, time I have come across this attitude. Usually everyone seems willing to talk about cricket and the local boy made good, wherever in the world. People aren't in it for money, or they weren't then.

Let's drive to the farmhouse a mile or two out of town where he grew up. The current owners are friendly enough and let me look around the paddock where he pitched his stumps and marked out his run. The next farmhouse is hundreds of yards down the road. I understand why McGrath can't bat: he didn't have anyone to bowl at him when young. We go to his secondary school in town. Old-time Australia: the classrooms are not air-conditioned, you learn to tolerate the heat and cold. No dedicated cricket ground, and the school played only the odd match, for the simple reason there was no opposition for miles and miles. Same for the local cricket club: a rough field was sufficient for the few annual games.

One pathway existed: the New South Wales Country XI. Get into that and you had a chance of following Don Bradman, Bill O'Reilly and Doug Walters and plenty more outback cricketers to Sydney and success. At the end of the summer term a very strong team, including former state or even international players, would arrive from Sydney in somewhere like Dubbo for a week of identifying, coaching and playing against budding outback talent. Once the tall gangly pace bowler had been spotted, it would be facile to say he was on his way. He would have good contacts if he made the move to Sydney, contacts who would introduce him to a grade club, where he would no doubt start in the fourth XI, no favours; but he had to get himself there first. So here comes an insight into the man and his success. As soon as he could legally drive one, the teenaged McGrath bought a motor-home, drove himself to Sydney, parked outside his club ground, lived there for months and months, alone, found a bit of part-time work and dedicated everything towards reaching the top.

Shane Warne, without much question the finest of all wrist-spinners, never took more than 12 wickets in a Test match. He did not have to. When Warne came on to bowl, Australia's opponents would be 70 for two at best. One batsman was new to the crease, if not both, and starting your innings against world-class spin must be even harder than facing Warne when you are 30*. McGrath opened the oysters for Warne to grab the pearls.

With respect to Paterson, McGrath was not one of Narromine's narrow-minded folk. He was utterly single-minded. He said he aimed to hit the top of off stump, but he was only going to do that in Bangladesh: on any other pitch his steep trajectory would make the ball bounce over off, fourth, or possibly fifth, stump. It was part of his propaganda that he was targeting the top of off stump: only 76 of his wickets were bowled. There was not much in addition to his stock ball, apart from a bouncer and a lot of back-chat. Having seen Narromine and his pathway, I could see McGrath for what he was: a lone wolf who devoured 563 sheep.

Subsequently, I have wondered how McGrath would have responded to batsmen attacking him in T20 style. He would not have been enamoured with ramps and scoops. Had a Harry Brook or Risabh Pant run down the pitch at McGrath, his length being so predictable, and driven him over extra cover for six, would he – after chuntering – have tried anything beyond a bouncer, like a slower ball or a knuckle ball, or a back-of-the-hander? The lone wolf now might not get away with conceding fewer than two and a half runs per Test over; Curtly Ambrose too. They were fortunate to have their careers before T20's full impact.

Bulawayo, December 2004

Although I have not visited an animal rescue centre, I imagine it was like going to one and espying a dog tied up in the corner – a healthy, good-looking dog that just wants to be loved. Let me explain.

For England's one-day tour of Namibia and Zimbabwe, Duncan Fletcher and his newish captain Michael Vaughan tried out a few new names. One, Kevin Pietersen, immediately took to the ODI format, scoring 27 and 77 in his first two internationals without being dismissed. But it was only against Zimbabwe's second XI in effect. Most of their white players had withdrawn their services, tired of never being paid properly or on time, or maybe not paid at all. The money from the ICC was going into a handful of kleptocrats strongly linked to the ZANU government.

Pietersen, desperate to make an impact for his adopted country (he had just qualified for England after four years of residence), did not bat in the third ODI: the gap between the two countries was growing to Great Rift Valley proportions. In the fourth international, in haste, he was out first ball to someone trying his hand at off-spin. When Zimbabwe replied, he buzzed around, energy to burn, no doubt trying to convey to Fletcher that he was as keen a fielder as any Zimbabwean. The home tailender Mluleki Nkala lofted a ball towards mid-off, where Simon Jones was fielding fairly deep, and as I recall Pietersen burst on the scene from extra cover to catch it athletically.

This ODI signalled the end of Pietersen's first tour with England. He was not wanted for the Test series in South Africa that immediately followed. Others were in the same boat: Vikram Solanki, Alex Wharf, Gareth Batty. But it was Pietersen who hung round the lobby of the Bulawayo hotel while the bags and suitcases were being loaded on a lorry. He so wanted to be wanted and called up. Obviously he thought, or knew, he was Test standard. But England's Test selectors had Trescothick, Strauss, Vaughan, Thorpe, Bell, Collingwood to choose from: no way in there, until Thorpe, 35, retired.

It was a brief flight from Bulawayo to Johannesburg. The cases revolved around the terminal's carousel. Almost everyone was going on to Potchefstroom for England's warm-up game before the Test series. Pietersen's suitcase had a sticker: Durban. It was home, but not the new home he craved. If he had been given the call-up, he would have leaped into the arms of his new owner.

Durban was where England had first come across this KP phenomenon. KwaZulu-Natal v England XI in December 1999 was an insightful game of its kind, a four-day first-class practice game in mid-tour, not something staged nowadays. Hashim Amla, aged 16, was one home player, his 20-year-old brother Ahmed another. Pietersen was already known to be railing against the new system, alleging that KwaZulu-Natal had not given him a contract because he was white and was therefore going to emigrate. Positive discrimination, I am afraid, is necessary at certain moments, otherwise imbalances will never be redressed. More than two decades on, South Africa are finally selecting from a large multiracial pool of players. Without positive discrimination there might not have been even one Test century scored by a Black African batsman before 2024.

Pietersen at this stage was known as much for his off-spin as his batting. At number nine for KwaZulu-Natal he hit 61*, mainly in a last-wicket partnership which *Wisden* called 'jolly', then he bowled 55.5 overs and dismissed four of England's top five. Ahmed Amla took two wickets and scored 53 in his second innings; Jon Kent, 20, made a hundred and went on to represent South Africa at ODI level. Plenty of youthful talent was competing for contracts in 'the new South Africa'.

I bowled a few balls at KP on England's 2010–11 tour of Australia. I guess it was Andrew Strauss's idea – a subtle way to get the media onside, and get players and journalists to know each other – in Hobart's indoor nets. Players just don't realise, until they retire and join the media, how keen journalists actually are, behind our impartial exterior, for England to succeed. Here the England players did the coaching and journalists had to do the drills.

At the end of this fun, KP still had energy to burn, as he was not interested in coaching us, and he might just have wanted to attract some attention. So he grabbed a bat – no pads or gloves – and went into a net while everyone else was packing up. I was still game for a bowl, even after Graham Gooch the batting coach had put journos through a stretching drill that made us hobble for days later (desperately though we tried to disguise our stiffness). I bowled my top-spinner and KP clothed it into the side-netting. I bowled my leg-break and he clothed that too to where a midwicket would have been fielding. Third ball – I still kick myself – I should have bowled a filthy little seamer, but he wasn't wearing any pads so I tried another top-spinner, and KP ran down the matting pitch and I swear that if it had been outdoors the ball would have soared over Hobart, crossed Bass Strait and landed somewhere in the state of Victoria.

KP found it difficult to put himself in the shoes of people. He would not have liked it if, while he had been England captain, a player in his team had been sending texts to the opposition of the pejorative kind he sent to the South Africans in 2012 about Strauss. Since retiring he has appeared to identify with wild animals: I have admired his efforts on social media to bring attention to the poaching of elephants and rhinos in South Africa, especially when done by syndicates in helicopters from Mozambique. Had he seen a Labrador tied up in a rescue centre, he would have been instinctively quick to sympathise, if not empathise.

Test No. 298
Cape Town, 2004

The *Mirror* had contracted Basil D'Oliveira to go back to South Africa during England's Test series. It would be his first visit since the official end of apartheid. Owing to cost-cutting, however, the *Mirror* wanted to pull out of this contract: would *The Sunday Telegraph*, as non-rivals, buy them out – to accompany D'Oliveira on his return to his native Cape Town? Two words sprang to my mind: 'lap' and 'plum'.

So it was, on a morning of pure and unpolluted sky, we took a taxi to Bo Kaap, the suburb of Cape Town that lies immediately beneath a piece of mountain shaped like a lion's head. I remembered seeing, on television, D'Oliveira walk out to bat on his Test debut at Lord's in 1966 and the reception that greeted him: not applause so much as a groundswell of popular approval that he had been given a chance. He was run out for 27: sufficient to bat another day. Running was not his forte by then, when he was officially 35, but he walked to the wicket, shoulders back, cloaked in majestic dignity. He could bowl too, medium-paced outswing (I tried to copy his action if I had a new ball) or off-spin, and he conceded fewer than two runs per over in his 44 Tests, in addition to all those crunching back-foot drives when up on his toes. He was one of few Test all-rounders who have averaged more with the bat than ball.

The taxi climbed the long haul, up from Green Point stadium, through Signal Hill's colourful two-storeyed streets, until Basil raised a hand. We stopped, and he got out. I waited, to give him time to compose his memories. Few people, let alone cricketers, have had to travel so far, from the very bottom of society (apartheid made sure of that) to reach the pinnacle. I had been digging out in Cape Town's library the local newspapers: the modest report of when he set off for England by ship to become Middleton's professional in the Central Lancashire League in 1960, aided by John Arlott; the effusion of delight, not confined to the Cape Coloured community, when he returned a hero (after struggling for weeks to make a run on English pitches) and he was greeted by a triumphal motorcade from the harbour through Cape Town's streets.

Soon, I could not wait much longer, got out and accompanied him. He showed me the street, following a contour of Signal Hill and therefore horizontal, where he and other children had played cricket. We looked across the city – above the centre in its bowl – to District Six, where he had grown up until all the non-whites were expelled. He had come to like Bo Kaap though, given its view across the Atlantic to the dazzling white of Robben Island and beyond. While Basil was abroad, cricketing in England, the freedom fighters of the African National Congress had their eyes dazzled for 27 years by and in the quarries of Robben Island. He laughed at the white folly of the apartheid era. 'Best view in Cape Town,' Basil said of Bo Kaap, where ejected Coloureds had been dumped.

Now the prize to be contested by England and South Africa was to be named the Basil D'Oliveira Trophy. He was staying – we were putting him up – in a hotel in Cape Town's central market square, nothing flash, not one of the multinational chain hotels springing up round the harbour amid the pizza restaurants and sports bars. Having written up and sent him my report, I called round to check that evening. 'I'm really sorry,' Basil said. 'I don't think the street we went to this morning was the right one. What shall we do – go back and try and find the right one?' My instant reaction: it was a detail that didn't matter. What mattered was that you, Basil, did not matter when you were growing up in Cape Town. Most South Africans would have admired you, had you been allowed to play sport on a level playing field, but you had not been considered a normal human being. He had been branded non-white for having a parent born in Madeira.

I asked him, more than once, about his actual age. Eventually he admitted that he had deducted 'several years' from his official age. I take several to mean three, four or five. If it was five, he would have been nearly 47 when he last played for England. I talked with Ian Botham about a Worcestershire game at Taunton when he had been bowling his fastest – and he was outright quick in the late 1970s – and a ball at D'Oliveira, static or statuesque, had zipped past his unhelmeted face: 'I thought I'd killed him,' Botham said. Officially D'Oliveira played county cricket until he was almost 49, or it might even have been 54.

After talking to Basil in his Cape Town hotel that evening – he was to be guest of honour next day at Newlands, where he had never been permitted to play – I did not stay for a drink. It was when Basil drank alcohol that all the pent-up feelings were liable to come out. Suppressed, for half his life. What must it be like to be suppressed, unable to do what you do best, until you are past your best?

Test No. 307

The Oval, September 2005

Never have I known the nation rally behind the England cricket team as in the Ashes of 2005. It must have been similar in the Ashes-regaining summers of 1926 and 1953?

While Duncan Fletcher was planning behind the scenes, preparations in front of them were the work of Michael Vaughan. I have seen England batsmen make double-hundreds in Australia and get on top of their bowlers, but not anyone who has shredded them, dismissed them, flogged them, as Vaughan had done in the 2002–03 Ashes. England lost 4-1 yet he made three big hundreds, and when he lifted his bat up in the crease before delivery you could almost see a flag billowing from the toe of his blade. When an Australian pace bowler dropped short, Vaughan was invariably pulling him into the stands. He had seen enough of defeatism in the face of Australia in the England dressing-room. The charge to regain the Ashes started here.

As he became a *Telegraph* columnist when he was forced to retire by his troublesome knees, I got the chance to know him better and talk more. I did not understand where all his positivity came from until we were having a coffee outside the Oval and I asked him what job his father did. A salesman, he said, and it clicked. Vaughan, the son, may not have sold things, but he persuaded you to buy into ideas, plans and strategies. I would ask him to rate a marginal England cricketer, and he would immediately reply that, yes, so-and-so is a Test player. Often this did not turn out to be the case, but this did not necessarily mean I was right. If Alex Hales or Chris Jordan had played under Vaughan's captaincy, they might well have become regular Test cricketers – or, at least, they would have been far more likely to become so.

The first signs that England could recapture the baton, after passing it to Australia during the Bicentennial Test of early 1988, were apparent in the opening Test at Lord's. Australia were still stronger, Glenn McGrath the boss, but England succeeded in taking all 20 wickets and Kevin Pietersen in making a pair of 50s on his Test debut. Next cometh the luck of great generals. The second Test was at Edgbaston – if I could sit through a Test again, this would be the one – and it kicked off with England batting in the same image as their captain had in the previous series, against an attack shorn of McGrath. His Achilles heel was exposed at last, when he stepped on a stray ball on the outfield while warming up.

It was the world heavyweight title now, England no longer welterweights. Their opening pair of Marcus Trescothick and Andrew Strauss were quick out of their starting blocks; all four fast bowlers fired; Ashley Giles, the media's butt as 'the wheelie-bin' after Lord's, took five wickets at Edgbaston, and we can safely assume that Vaughan had pumped up his tyres. No trace of defeatism: Simon Jones was intent on revenge for the barbaric reaction of the Australian crowd to his knee injury on the previous Ashes tour. This showed in his spikey batting at number 11: 19* in a last-wicket stand of 32, and 12* in a last-wicket stand of 51 with Andrew Flintoff. The second Test swung to and fro, but that last-wicket partnership between Flintoff and Jones was more than the difference between defeat and victory, such was their belligerence: it was the difference between psychological superiority and inferiority from that point on. At the close of the third evening Australia were 175 for eight, chasing 282.

I have placed two bets on cricket: once when a betting company gave the media a voucher of money to spend, and I lost. The other was on this third evening. An Australian colleague whom I much admired for his feel for the game – Robert Craddock – seemed to have all his senses attuned. He was walking round the ground after close of play on day three. He said he had just placed a bet on the highest run-scorer in Australia's second innings being Brett Lee. Nobody had so far gone beyond 31: Australia were eight down and Andrew Flintoff was working up towards the finest Test series any all-rounder has had and making his reverse-swing go. As a betting shop under the stands was still open, I went in and put £10 on Brett Lee at 20/1, if that is the correct phrasing.

On Sunday morning I wanted a quick finish at Edgbaston, not least because I was down to play at 2 p.m. that afternoon, a 90-minute drive away. Shane Warne and Lee twisted the knife instead, right into the guts of a capacity crowd. It was excruciating. Warne hit his wicket at 220 for nine, gone for 42. I wanted England to win, obviously, but stood to win £200 if Lee kept batting with Michael Kasprowicz. They both kept going, as Kasprowicz was a vastly better batsman than McGrath. Even Vaughan admitted later that the idea of England winning this series after going 2–0 down would have been a hard sell.

Lap of the gods: when nobody knows what the outcome of a drama is going to be, this has been the phrase to hand, ever since ancient Athens. When Steve Harmison pitched short yet again, and the crouching Kasprowicz took his glove off the bat before it was flicked by the ball – a slow-motion replay would have given him not out – Australia needed three to win. The Decision Review System had not been invented. To the naked eye it appeared that Kasprowicz was still holding the bat when it flicked his glove. England had won by two runs. Lee was left 43★.

Vaughan, with 166, reprised his form of the previous Ashes and England stayed psychologically on top after the draw at Old Trafford. Taking opponents down one by one is an essential part of winning a five-Test series. Jason Gillespie had been taken down by Vaughan's hook and pull in 2002–03, and Pietersen had continued that process. Kasprowicz was nearing the end, conceding runs at almost five per over, so Shaun Tait had to be given a debut in the fourth Test at Trent Bridge. When England chased 129, someone fast, wild and raw was exactly what they needed. Had Warne taken the new ball with Lee, I doubt whether England would have crossed the line.

At the Oval much of the country held its breath: England had last won the Ashes in 1986–87. Pietersen's 158 won him a newspaper contract and the nation's respect; and cricket was never so like a duel in the Wild West as it was on the final afternoon when Lee and Pietersen staged their shoot-out. Bowlers have long approached or even touched 100 mph; Pietersen's hooks were perhaps as near as any batsman had come to that point to hitting a ball at 100 mph, faster even than Ian Botham's hooks at Old Trafford in 1981, although straightish drives travel furthest.

One innings was the equal of Pietersen's in value. Because there was much less song and dance, Strauss's 129 on the opening day was almost forgotten, but I would rate it among the ten most important innings for England of all time. Without it, England would have been too far gone for Pietersen to rescue. Remember that even the outwardly phlegmatic Fletcher had been literally sick with apprehension on the first morning of the final Test. How did you do it, I asked Strauss, how did you go out and make a hundred when millions and millions were watching, the last Test cricket viewers on free-to-air television in the UK? Strauss had made his first Ashes hundred in the Old Trafford Test, after sorting out his troubles against Warne with advice from Uncle Duncan. 'Momentum,' he said.

I'm sure that Australia missed a trick at the Oval in 2005 and again in 2009, and consequently lost hold of the Ashes both times. Or, at any rate, they would have been far more likely to win the 2005 Test if they had selected Stuart MacGill instead of Tait: McGrath, Lee and two wrist-spinners, Warne and MacGill, to prey upon England's completely understandable anxieties.

Test No. 309
Faisalabad, November 2005

Earlier this year in London, after the 7/7 bombings, sport was seen to have all the more value as a means of escape from reality; and a cricket ground, especially if encircled by a wall, seals itself off from the real world. It has even crossed my mind whether the press box could be perceived as a womb, though not to the extent of swotting up on Freud.

An explosion was louder than audible during this Test in Pakistan. The players hit the ground as if to re-enact the famous photograph of the match at Lord's during the Second World War when a German flying bomb passed overhead. A gas canister appeared to have exploded: it had been cooling a soft drinks cart on the boundary's edge. No physical harm was done to the players, only to the pitch, when Pakistan's maverick Shahid Afridi in one of his madder moments twisted his heel into the pitch to assist his bowlers, oblivious to the game being televised.

It was a rare reminder that the outside world can intrude; that formal cricket matches, lasting several days, can only be staged in a stable society; that the sport is inherently conservative because law and order have to prevail first.

Test No. 313
Mumbai, March 2006

It was a gesture I had never seen before. Mahendra Singh Dhoni had lashed an off-break from Shaun Udal into the stratosphere above the Wankhede Stadium, so high that Monty Panesar at mid-on had all too much time to think. They are the worst chances, when you have time to think about catching it AND about the consequences of dropping it. Panesar had so much time, and nervous energy, as the ball descended, even though it gathered velocity, that he clapped his hands twice, as if to welcome the ball home. Only it never reached the destination of his enormous hands — he could hold five cricket balls in one hand — and spent itself in the turf.

It was an extraordinary gesture. More importantly, it was an extraordinary shot. India were 92 for six in pursuit of 313 on a pitch helping all sorts of bowlers, even England's spinners. And what immediately followed was even more extraordinary. Instead of putting his head down to bat out for a draw, with less than two sessions left, Dhoni unleashed the same shot, and almost reached the same altitude, before Panesar, to his immense relief, held this skyer.

The pitch had been at its best on the first day when India, most curiously, selected three seamers in addition to two spinners, which left their batting thin, and Rahul Dravid sent England in to bat. Alastair Cook admitted on the bus to the ground that he was too ill to play, and missed a Test for the one occasion in his career. Owais Shah, England's reserve batsman, had no time for nerves, used his feet, and shared a century stand with Andrew Strauss that took England to the heights of 230 for one, from which they could never fall to earth on a result pitch. India missed half a dozen chances as England racked up 400. This was England's first victory in India in 21 years, and it enabled Andrew Flintoff's side to share the series 1–1.

On an Indian radio station I heard Ajay Jadeja – the former Test batsman who had received one of the longer entries in the report by India's Central Bureau of Investigation – give his expert opinion that it was impossible for England to win, and this was after they had totalled 400 on a ground which had produced a definite result in seven of its last eight Tests (and Sri Lanka had just held on in the other). Mumbai's reddish soil wears, tears and turns.

Let me finally cite *Wisden*'s match report to illustrate how unexpected this result was – how most punters would never have dreamed of betting on something so improbable as an England win.

- 'Home supporters were mutinous' after India had lost by 212 runs
- 'A small section of the crowd had booed Tendulkar, Mumbai's most famous son, after a dismal first innings'
- 'The spectators' behaviour indicated how impossible India's defeat had seemed'
- 'Dravid ... strangely chose to forego the opportunity of bowling fourth, at a venue where no side had won a Test chasing more than 163 ... While India were sitting on a 1–0 lead, the strategy was simply foolhardy'
- When England made 400, 'India's catching grew indefensibly ragged as they put down at least six chances' then 'Flintoff was let off three times on his way to his second fifty of the match'
- 'The final day will linger in the memory as one of the most frenetic and dramatic bouts of Test cricket between these nations. From 75 for three at lunch, India crumbled to 100 all out in another 15 overs'
- 'Dravid later described the collapse as "a collective lapse of reasoning". That lapse was illustrated vividly when Dhoni made a madman's swipe off Udal to Panesar at mid-off – just three balls after Panesar had somehow failed to get his hands around an identical chance.'

Test No. 321
Brisbane, November 2006

It did not seem right at the time. England's captain Andrew Flintoff hurried over to Steve Harmison on the Gabba outfield, after Australia had won the toss and elected to bat. After a hurried chat, Flintoff went over to Matthew Hoggard. Television had cut to advertisements so these preparations were not being broadcast live. If I haven't misinterpreted, my observation was that Flintoff had told Harmison at the last moment that he would bowl the opening over of this Ashes series. Bowling the first ball of a match and series was what Hoggard routinely did, but not on this highly pressurised occasion.

England's team bus was reportedly silent en route to the Gabba that morning. Everything was set, all right, but set to unravel. Starting at the top, the appointment of the England captain for this tour was never so delayed while Duncan Fletcher mulled over which Andrew should take over from the injured Michael Vaughan. Strauss had led well as the fill-in Test captain; Flintoff, his senior, wanted the job and, at this stage of his life, might not have given it his best shot if he had been playing under Strauss. As it turned out on the tour, Flintoff tried plenty of shots of the wrong kind, trying to cope with the unique strains of captaining a losing England team in Australia.

Before a single ball had been bowled in the warm-ups, cracks emerged in the Ashes-holding side. As the national anthems were played in Canberra, Flintoff stood next to Marcus Trescothick and hugged him round the shoulders: within the week Trescothick could no longer face being away from home and was on the plane. Harmison, whom Australia feared, pulled out of the one first-class game before the series: England press conferences said that he would be fine on the night but the mechanics of delivery were askew. Ashley Giles, after a year out with a hip injury, went into the first Test without a game. The boat was rocking before England reached Brisbane, whereupon all the wives, girlfriends and children flew in. Dawn turns to bright sunlight by 5 a.m. in Brisbane. I would be surprised if many England players, before getting on the bus, had slept right through until their alarm.

Flintoff was trying to recreate the 2005 Ashes when Harmison had opened the bowling, but seldom otherwise. Even more tense, Harmison returned the compliment by immediately bowling the new ball straight to Flintoff at second slip. If asked, 'how long does momentum last when going into a series?' I would say about three-quarters of an hour: that was how long it took England's psychological advantage as the 2005 winners to evaporate. Australia were back on top by then. Ricky Ponting's USP as captain was to make a hundred in the first Test of a series, 196 in this case. Australia declared at 602 for nine. England had to fight hard to lose by only 277 runs.

Test No. 322
Adelaide, December 2006

Wisdom after the event used to be the cricket correspondent's best friend, in the days before newspapers were overtaken by websites. Now we have to pin colours to the mast online, instantly.

I thought, at the time, that the timing of Flintoff's declaration at 551 for seven was about right. That left nine overs with a new ball and England took a wicket. Obviously I was wrong in the end: England, in trying to win this second Test instead of batting on for a bore-draw, exposed their vulnerabilities and made themselves more liable to lose. Having lost their captain of 2005, Michael Vaughan, and the first Test, England were nervous when they had to bat out the last day in Adelaide, and who better to play upon nerves than Shane Warne?

With the wisdom of hindsight, Flintoff, had he not declared when 38*, could have gone on to a hundred against tired bowlers, and Ashley Giles from 27* to a fifty: two boosts to the overall morale. But I do not think England would have won if they had posted more.

Test No. 325
Sydney, January 2007

I tried asking Duncan Fletcher not to resign immediately after England had lost 5–0. They did commendably well to rally and win the one-day tri-series, against Australia and New Zealand, which followed, but much of the media was out for Fletcher's blood – anyone's blood. We were not going to be fobbed off with another review of English cricket, which would occupy months and change little. We were to make the same mistake – Somebody Had To Be Axed – after the next but one Ashes defeat in Australia in 2013–14, in this case Andy Flower. It was deemed secondary, if not irrelevant, that Mitchell Johnson had bowled as incisively as anyone in Ashes history. The media wanted heads, on a platter, and if it could not be the captain it had to be the coach. India handled a 4–0 drubbing in Australia in 2011–12 far more wisely: they carried on and did better next time.

When England were knocked out of the World Cup that followed all too soon afterwards, Fletcher still wanted to depart immediately. He told me that, if he had been taking over as the new coach, he would not have wanted his predecessor hanging around. But Peter Moores, England's new coach, had no experience of international cricket in any capacity. The media wanted an English coach of England again, and so did the ECB. Fletcher could have had a few wise words in Moores's ear: not to order the players around when they met before the opening Test of 2007, but to act like a consultant not a commander, and not to go off to the Lord's nets when the match started, but to see all and hear all. The ECB's knee-jerk appointment of Moores was never going to work in either his first tenure or his second – Test cricket is too far removed from county cricket, where his energies fitted well – but at least he could have set off on the right foot.

Kingston, February 2009

England have just been dismissed for 51, and I hadn't seen it. My colleague Steve James had the pleasure of writing up this England collapse against the clock for *The Sunday Telegraph*. I was immersed in proofs and papers at the temporary headquarters of *Wisden Cricketers' Almanack* in Norfolk. I had covered more than 200 England Tests in succession before missing this match.

Wisden was not an offer to be turned down, once my sports editor Jon Ryan had generously agreed to my missing England tours from the start of January to early February, for this is the critical month before delivery, as if it were a baby in the making. Every page of editorial copy has to be read in this month, thanks to the peculiarities of the computer system, and made to fit in the space available. As every page is small, the shape of a traditional brick, this month is challenging – especially if one of the many contributors thinks that an annual published in April must have a deadline around then. And the staff pray that someone famous will not die in the coming days so there is not a major omission in the Obituaries section.

Being the editor of *Wisden* is a seasonal job like farming. Summer is wonderful: all one has to do is occasionally ruminate about front-of-the-book articles. Would such-and-such famous writer be tempted to write for the most august of almanacks, for honour and prestige, for in truth the fees are not high? One is invited to a hospitality box at Lord's – and how about a speech in the Long Room, nothing lengthy? Oh, and a reception at 10 Downing St, for England's World Cup winners. RSVP.

In autumn the wind starts to stiffen. A review of every first-class county is filed, which will almost certainly require updating in January after the county in question has announced a big signing or release. The many tours and Test series; the review of every Test country's domestic season; and where has the Second XI Championship review gone? They all need proofreading and updating. Mercifully, Harriet Monkhouse will check all the numbers that go into *Wisden*, page after page of scorecards and stats, and most of the words too.

The Five Cricketers of the Year have to be selected. The members of *Wisden*'s permanent staff are integrity itself: they would not dream of profferring their candidates. If there was an exception, it was when we had to select Four Cricketers of the Year for the 2011 Almanack. Mohammad Amir (pronounced Aamir) would have been selected for his left-arm swing bowling, but for his spot-fixing in the Test at Lord's. I was at the hearing which the ICC staged in Qatar, and spent the day high up in a tower-block, perhaps the 12th floor with another 20 above, watching another tower-block being built a few yards away; the manual labourers, probably Baluchi, hauled in girders being raised up to their floor without any rail or barrier to stop them falling over the side, and no safety harness.

When Amir emerged, with a five-year ban, I accompanied him in the lift to the ground floor. A crowd of expatriate Pakistanis were protesting his innocence – only later did he admit to deliberately overstepping the crease and no-balling at the moments when he was paid to do so. He did not at all give me the impression of a naive and innocent teenager dragged kicking and screaming against his wishes into the underworld.

Winter can be bleak and the days long indoors: it was by far the hardest work I have done as a cricket journalist. The permanent staff retire to darkened rooms to recover. After the 2009 edition had gone to bed – the printers were in Bungay, not far from Beccles, where Gilbert Jessop went to school as a student/master for a summer and took a hundred wickets at an average of two! – I went to catch up on the England tour of the West Indies, and covered the fourth Test in Barbados. Andrew Strauss had asked me to ghostwrite his book about the forthcoming Ashes series of

2009 and we did several introductory chapters. I heard his version of one of the key meetings in England's cricket history that had recently occurred. After being dismissed for 51 in Jamaica, England were perceived to be in disarray, as they were. It was Strauss's first Test as the official captain, and the first result was no improvement on the unhappy regime of Kevin Pietersen as captain and Peter Moores as head coach. The media's disenchantment with the way England were playing was summed up by *The Sun*'s John Etheridge when criticising Pietersen's dismissal against a spinner in Jamaica: 'Dumb slog millionaire.'

When the England squad reached Antigua, Strauss called a meeting – and asked the assistant coach Andy Flower to chair it. Flower did it so well that his promotion from batting coach to head coach was an obvious piece of the jigsaw at the end of the tour. Everyone was asked to speak. The huge sums which Pietersen and Andrew Flintoff had just secured in the IPL auction, during the Jamaica Test, were complicating issues. One consequence was that Ian Bell was dropped, to return the stronger and more resilient towards the end of the summer's Ashes. Another was that Graeme Swann replaced Monty Panesar as the first-choice spinner. And Strauss set the tone, after the first attempt at a Test in Antigua had to be abandoned and the venue switched from the Sir Vivian Richards Stadium to the old Recreation Ground, by scoring 169. England did not win a Test in this series: they withdrew in good order but lost 1–0. Which made it all the more astonishing that they recaptured the Ashes five months later. Some leadership.

Spring, as the *Wisden* editor, is everything it is cracked up to be in cricket. The yellow beauty of daffodils is matched by the new Almanack's arrival in the post. It is one of the few cricket books nowadays that is reviewed in the newspapers. The editor goes on the *Today* programme to explain the views expressed in his Notes, rubbing shoulders in Radio Four's green room with the great and good, and with politicians. Fortunately, I was in the West Indies again, far from the madding crowd, when Claire Taylor was revealed as the first female Cricketer of the Year. A publicity agent had the task of fielding all the requests for interview, and her phone was red-hot from 6 a.m. until the close of play. Claire was calmness itself. I had met her at Reading, near where she worked (as she could not be a professional cricketer), to write her profile, and she was discretion itself from the moment I told her; for, of course, the identity of the Five must never be leaked.

Test No. 352
The Oval, August 2009

It was daylight robbery. England had the weaker team, yet they had just won the 2009 Ashes. The euphoria was not nationwide like 2005: there had been no long wait to regain the Ashes, and cricket was no longer on free-to-air. But this 2–1 victory under Andrew Strauss was no less of an achievement.

England scored two individual centuries in the entire Test series, Australia eight. England averaged 34 runs per wicket, Australia 40. Three bowlers took 20 wickets, all Australian. Sir Arthur Conan Doyle's brother-in-law, E.W. Hornung, had invented a gentleman burglar, who lived at the Albany in London, played cricket for the Gentlemen, and carried out sophisticated, non-violent burglaries when he was short of a spot of cash. The fictional burglar was Raffles, the factual burglar Strauss, and they shared the same initials of A.J.

Strauss had been asked by the eminent publisher Roddy Bloomfield to write a book about this Ashes series, which Strauss asked me to ghostwrite for him. I was doing *Wisden* as well as *The Sunday Telegraph*, but you don't reject the England captain, as much for the insights as the money. When we had done several chapters in the West Indies on England's preceding tour, Strauss was always punctual. We would meet at 3 p.m. in the captain's room or rooms – he would offer tea or coffee, and away he would go, dictating. The only time he was elusive was when he wanted to get away and play golf.

Pick a composite team out of the 2005 Ashes and they would be mostly England players, except Ricky Ponting for Ian Bell and Shane Warne for Ashley Giles (McGrath was injured for two Tests). Pick a composite team out of the 2009 Ashes and perhaps they would all be Australians, except Strauss for Shane Watson and Graeme Swann for Nathan Hauritz; and, if the pitch was a seamer, then Stuart Broad for the more erratic Mitchell Johnson. It was daylight robbery, the deftest of burglaries. While the rain-affected third Test was an even draw, Australia completely outplayed England in the first and fourth Tests, and England squeezed home after mighty tussles in the second and fifth. The scoreline, 2–1, was a travesty; or exemplary leadership if you prefer.

The last hour, or rather the last session, or indeed the last day in Cardiff, was as gut-wrenching as harakiri. When Paul Collingwood, the shepherd, was dismissed with about 12 overs left, and England still in arrears, several wolves could have savaged either James Anderson or Monty Panesar. Ponting should have unleashed Johnson or Ben Hilfenhaus, or both: one fast, straight ball from Johnson, regardless of length, would surely have sufficed, while a yorker from the Tasmanian outswing bowler would have targeted the left-handers' toes. England, i.e. Strauss, sent a physio on to the field, which perplexed Anderson, as he had no need for first aid after blocking the off-spin of Hauritz and Marcus North. Gamesmanship? Of course, and let no one pretend otherwise. Since England started playing Australia, both countries have done everything they can to win: W.G. Grace's blatant cheating gave the whole contest essential spice.

We can say these things now that Andrew Flintoff has emerged as a wiser, nicer and less egocentric person after his car accident while making a TV programme about motoring: he used to be a pain at times, not much of a team-player. This Ashes series was, as his knees gave way, the last hurrah: he would be set up for a career after cricket if he made himself famous. Strauss, when dictating his thoughts, never said anything explicit but one could read between the lines.

England had not beaten Australia at Lord's since 1934, and they had barely escaped from Cardiff. Yet they turned the series around at Lord's, led by Strauss taking his favourite old bat out of the cupboard and whacking 161 on the opening day. England bowled Australia out cheaply, batted again, declared, and set Australia 522. Flintoff fancied this occasion: Anderson, Broad, Graham Onions and Swann would have done the deed in time, but Flintoff, standing at second slip when Strauss was at first, announced: 'I'll bowl until we've won.' All Strauss could say was: 'Sounds like a plan.' Flintoff hurtled in for 27 overs. A wicket was celebrated with arms spread more flamboyantly than if he had been the statue overlooking Rio de Janeiro. It was his last 'five-for'. Indeed, he took only one more wicket for England in his career: he did not take one in the third Test, and had to be omitted from the fourth as he could not fulfil the all-rounder's role, in spite of much noise from his camp. A more sensible plan would have been to spread Flintoff's final overs through the rest of this series instead of concentrating them at Lord's in a game that England were always going to win. 'His apotheosis by the media might have been overdone,' remarked *Wisden* drily after Lord's. Before the series, when England were due to go on a bonding tour to visit First World War graves, Flintoff had emerged in no fit state. I seldom saw Strauss lose his cool but he did after being forced to explain Flintoff's behaviour at a press conference.

Australia had lost Shane Warne, Glenn McGrath and Adam Gilchrist since the previous Ashes of 2006–07, but they had time to rebuild. Strauss had inherited, from Kevin Pietersen and Peter Moores, a team at sixes and sevens with only half a year to go before the Ashes. After the second Test of 2009 he lost his best batsman, Pietersen, through injury, and Ravi Bopara was succumbing to fatalism: the belief that he would never succeed at Test level, in spite of three brilliant centuries in succession against West Indies earlier in the year. Bopara had supreme talent, his on-drive was one of my favourite shots, but he was short of self-esteem. I do not know of an England player since the Victorian era from a poorer background: when a child he loved visiting his aunt because she had a television and a sofa to sit on. By the end of this series Strauss and Flower had replaced him with a doughtier character, Jonathan Trott.

A team under different leadership could easily have disintegrated after the Headingley Test, which Australia won by an innings and plenty to level the series at 1–1. England were set off on the wrong foot when the fire alarm went off in their city-centre hotel in the early hours (the Australians were staying elsewhere) on the morning of the match. Standing around in a street at 4 a.m. is not the best preparation for going back to sleep. It can hardly have been a coincidence that Matt Prior's back seized up in the warm-ups and the start was delayed. England batted first, not completely focused. Strauss noted Jonathan Trott's disappointment when he was not asked to make his debut and replace Flintoff. The bottom seemed to be falling out of the England side, as so often happened towards the end of an Ashes in Australia. Even stalwarts like Alastair Cook and Paul Collingwood were no more than chipping in.

Strauss was seriously worried that his players' morale would be shredded by the innings defeat. But one of the very few departments in which England were superior was in the strength of their tail. Australia had seven batsmen who all weighed in, followed by four bowlers who contributed a few runs. England had no specialist batsmen who scored more than Collingwood's 250 runs except Strauss (his aggregate was 474), but Prior, Swann and Broad all chipped in with 200. It was a swashbuckling century stand for the eighth wicket off only 76 balls, between Broad and Swann, that allowed England to leave Leeds with some dignity. When the England squad re-congregated for a barbecue ahead of the Oval Test, Strauss found their morale was intact.

Home advantage was the card which Strauss played next. The Oval groundsman was asked not to water his pitch for at least a week before the game. Ponting made the amazing decision not to recall his spinner, Hauritz: rumours abounded that he was not fitting into their dressing-room. Strauss led from the front again, winning the toss for the fourth time and scoring 55 and 75. He coaxed a match-winning spell out of Broad from the Vauxhall End: he was like a colt, wind in its ears, sensing for the first time what it could achieve. The media want glorious individuals, so they went for Flintoff running out Ponting from mid-on with a direct hit. After one day's breather, Strauss calmly dictated his final chapter when I visited his home in Ealing, then I delivered it to Roddy. A week later the book was on the shelves. It was called *Testing Times: in Pursuit of the Ashes*. A more colloquial title, of which Raffles would not have approved, could have been: *How I Nicked 'em*.

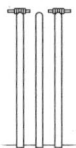

After his first series as England's stand-in captain, against Pakistan in 2006, Andrew Strauss talks with Sunday Telegraph columnists Michael Atherton and Steve James, and me.

Michael Vaughan sells his team the idea that the third Test at Old Trafford against Australia in 2005 has ended in a winning draw.

As one does after taking the wicket of Sachin Tendulkar on one's Test debut, Monty Panesar celebrates with his captain Andrew Flintoff at Nagpur in March 2006.

Ben Stokes, and no doubt half the country too, celebrates after he scores the winning runs against Australia in the Ashes Test of 2019. The finest innings for England I have seen.

2010s

Australia, 2010–11

Military historian I am not. But England's 2009 Ashes campaign might have contained traces of guerilla warfare: perhaps echoes of the Celts repulsing the invasion by Julius Caesar's war machine, completely out-gunned in equipment yet making use of superior numbers to intervene at the right moment.

In winning the 2010–11 series the roles were reversed: England invaded with the war machine. It was as if Strauss had heard Chappelli's dictum: to win the Ashes in Australia you have to beat the States. Winning from the outset creates doubt. No sign of English vulnerability or disunity can be permitted: if the England squad shows any sign of weakness, the Australian media will seize on it for ridicule and set the ball rolling. Invincibility is all. No players arriving injured as on some recent England tours of Australia. James Anderson suffered a rib injury while boxing on England's strenuous bonding trip to Germany, but bowled 33 overs in the first game against Western Australia. Unavoidable injuries will happen in any war of attrition yet before Stuart Broad had gone home, England's reserve pace bowlers were practising on the Adelaide Oval, moments after England had won the second Test – and strapping specimens like Chris Tremlett and Tim Bresnan. No sign of vulnerability.

This Ashes series of 2020–11 was therefore a completely different campaign, yet again the captain led it from the front. England batted awfully in their opening first-class match in Perth – 117 for seven in reply to WA's 242 for eight declared – but this was rock bottom: there was to be no resurrection of the old catchphrase ('can't bat, can't bowl, can't field'). Broad and Graeme Swann embarked on another of their swashbuckles, Strauss declared a bit behind, England bowled

WA out for 223 and had to score 243 off 52 overs. No wobbling, no Achilles heel: Strauss launched England's tour with 120* off 141 balls to steer England comfortably home. It was the first time England had won their opening first-class match on an Australian tour since 1965–66. Cause for Australian, if not doubt, then thought.

All the England batsmen inked in for this series were given three first-class games to attune to Australian conditions. Most made enough runs – Strauss two hundreds, Alastair Cook one and Ian Bell 192 against Australia A, which set a trend of 'daddy hundreds' – except Kevin Pietersen, who could not switch on until it mattered. All the first-choice bowlers had to play the first two games, then rest from the third, but with a difference. I saw their minibus setting off from Bellerive Oval to Hobart airport to fly to Brisbane: it was an astute move, to acclimatise them to sub-tropical Queensland ahead of the first Test, then give them a few days to rest before the battle. The reserve bowlers meanwhile had their game-time and rolled over Australia A for a 10-wicket win.

Equally impactful in winning this series was England's fielding. I was to despair on subsequent tours, before a ball had been bowled, to hear 'plans' which suggested that a warm-up game or two, perhaps of 14 per side, would be sufficient preparation. My observation is that English slip fielders need day after day of standing and concentrating in Australia's heat and bright light before they are catching as safely as they do in England. No short cuts can be taken. As for vulnerability, nothing gets an Australian crowd jeering on day one like a shelled slip catch, unless it is a Pommie opener gone first ball.

England's wicketkeeper Matt Prior took 23 catches, Brad Haddin (a very substantial counterpart) eight catches and one stumping. In the rest of the field England accepted 43 catches, Australia 25. I thought it was probably the best that England had ever fielded, at least since the late 1970s. Everywhere England's discipline was superior: 21 wides to Australia's 34; 13 no-balls to Australia's 21; 30 byes to the 46 conceded by Australia; and, most satisfying of all, four run-outs by England, none by Australia. Good housekeeping.

England won not only by three Tests — all of them innings victories — to one but by every main metric. England averaged an enormous 51 per wicket, Australia a mere 29. As for individual centuries, England scored nine, Australia three (almost the reverse of 2009, when England still won). Yet an element of magicianship was still required by Strauss in order to disguise the collective Achilles heel. England, as usual, were badly exposed by the pace and steep bounce of the WACA in Perth, historically their least successful ground in Australia: Mitchell Johnson clicked and added swing to his pace. England were thus pegged back to 1–1 after losing by 267 runs, wiped out for 187 and 123. On this occasion though, England did not panic: they did not replace old players with new, as Australia were busy doing. Strauss publicly stated that England were not departing from their campaign strategy. No sign of being scarred. The ancient Chinese war expert Sun Tzu would have been chuffed to see his stratagems reaffirmed.

Sleep. In our ivory towers we seldom make allowances, when a player shoulders arms to a straight one or drops a catch, for his being short of sleep. Had I been woken by that fire alarm in Leeds in 2009, I would have had time to go back to sleep before the 11 a.m. start; most England players were too full of natural nerves, the Ashes to be won, to go back to sleep at 5 a.m. In Brisbane, to sleep a wink after 5 a.m., I need curtains or blinds which completely exclude the sunshine: if one mote sneaks into my eyes, my brain tells me that dawn has come and it's time to rise and shine. Strauss went chronically short of sleep during the first Test of 2010–11. On the first day, he had cut the third ball of the series to gully. England were dismissed for 260. They appeared to have been caught with their trousers down, as Broad was: he was still getting dressed as he walked to the middle and could not prevent Peter Siddle's hat-trick. Worse, Australia totalled 481. In one of the finest wicketless spells, James Anderson kept passing the outside edges of Mike Hussey and Brad Haddin in their stand of 307. Yet another Brisbane disaster was shaping up. Or, put it this way, England would be grateful for holding the Ashes at the outset: a drawn series would be enough to retain them.

On the third evening, England had 15 overs to play out, 221 behind on first innings. Facing up to the first ball of his second innings, Strauss did not cut to gully, he shouldered arms and let it hit him on the front pad, directly in line with the stumps, trying to leave on length. It could be that the whole series turned on this one delivery. Bowler's umpire Aleem Dar gave Strauss not out. Australia reviewed; the ball was predicted to have been going over the bails – by an inch? England captain dismissed for a pair, gone third and first ball! That was almost the headline. It would have been the most unsuccessful Test in Australia that any England captain ever had personally. These were the days when the local newspaper would be shoved under your hotel-room door. The *Brisbane Courier-Mail*, which was to satirise Broad as an English medium-pacer, would have had Strauss wearing a rabbit's ears on their front page.

Blessed with the luck of better generals, Strauss needed no second escape. He lasted until the close of day three then tucked in on the fourth morning, cutting and working to leg, shadowed by Cook, who had not dominated an Australian attack before – survived but never dominated: 10 Ashes Tests for an average of 26. He needed an example to follow. Strauss set it by striding out across the tightrope. He had not made a Test hundred in Australia: on England's previous tour he had copped three poor decisions in a row and been ill during the last Test. Little landmarks accrued, bricks making the wall: Strauss 50 off 110 balls, England 100 off 35.1 overs, Cook 50 off 122 balls. For as long as an opening partnership lasts, a side looks invulnerable. By lunch on day four Strauss had reached 79 out of 135 without loss.

And he was exhausted. The effects of lack of sleep can be warded off for so long – he told me he used to drink 15 cups of coffee a day when captain – but they can suddenly strike. Nothing left in the tank. To refill it, in the dressing-room at lunch on day four, with England still more than 100 behind, Strauss tried an energy drink that was becoming well-known. When he went out to bat again, he was buzzing: frenticism was visible where there had been urgency. Strauss was now running across the tightrope to reach the other side. He just made it, his second 50 taking only 74 balls, before trying something rash against the occasional off-spin of Marcus North and being stumped for 110. This example-setting hundred was the biggest on-field contribution that Strauss could make: from this platform England's edifice rose. They did not lose another wicket in the rest of the game. Cook batted unbeaten for ten and a half hours, Jonathan Trott for six hours. It was as near to an overwhelming victory as any draw can be. England's psychological supremacy was established. After brushing aside the hiccough in Perth, Strauss's men stormed to the summit. Not since Len Hutton's 1954–55 success (1978–79 can't count because it was Australia's second XI) had England won Down Under by such a large margin as 3–1. A nice touch, I thought: Hutton's grandson Ben was Strauss's best man.

Test No. 370

Lord's, June 2011

It is the only time I have sung in a press box. I was forbidden to sing at school, for being tuneless, but I boldly decided to give this Abba number a go.

Even today very few right-arm Sri Lankan seamers have taken 100 Test wickets, but Dilhara Fernando is one. Taller than most

Sri Lankan bowlers, decent pace, he took a couple of wickets to make England wobble in their second innings. Another defeat beckoned at Lord's, where England were having a poor run.

'You're making us old and grey, Fernando!' I sang.

Yes, once was enough.

The Oval, June 2012

W.G. Grace used to bowl what was called 'a hanging ball', but I have never seen an exact description. I like to think that I bowled one in the nets at Jonathan Trott. It was a promotion by his sponsor in the Oval indoor nets. I tried a round-arm leg-break, which drew the batsman forward and landed around leg-stump, without much pace on it. Trott, after pushing it tentatively into the side-netting, generously said as he tossed it back: 'I bet you take lots of wickets with that ball.' If only... but I always thought he would become the finest coach of Afghanistan, and maybe other countries.

Rupertswood, December 2013

Only once have I been in exactly the same position as an England captain, as an Ashes-winning England captain in point of fact.

I was spending the night in what had been the chief guest's bedroom at Rupertswood, once the finest mansion in Australasia. I had visited before, to see where the Ashes legend had been turned into substance, but this was the first time I had stayed.

The Honourable Ivo Bligh first came here in November 1882 and immediately lost his heart. Ivo was 23, not simply fresh out of Eton and Cambridge but utterly innocent. He was a jolly good sport – he had scored a thousand first-class runs in the season of 1880 when that was a rare feat – and a dab hand at rackets and tennis, but women? Ivo's mother was famed in high society for her cold, nay frigid, demeanour. When, on the ship out to Australia in September 1882, he met a warm-hearted Australian woman called Janet, it was a revelation. When Ivo cut his hand in a game of tug-of-war on board, it was more than this wound that she bound up.

Sir William Clarke, Janet's husband, had made his wealth as a landowner and grazier, and he spent his money philanthropically after building Rupertswood. This 50-room Italianate pile would have adorned the Somerset countryside from where his father had emigrated. After his first wife had been killed in the nearby town of Sunbury, the horse having bolted and thrown her from the carriage, he married the nanny who had taken over the reins and saved his children. Janet was a bit of a brumbie, an outback Aussie girl, and this second marriage shocked Melbourne society, which was almost as snobbish as 'back home'. While a ballroom was being added to Rupertswood, the couple went to England, where Clarke endowed a music scholarship in London and received a baronetcy (the first Australian-born to be knighted). They toured Italy and the Swiss Lakes, where Janet purchased a little terracotta urn, which was to come in handy.

To feel the warmth of a woman – purely platonically – sent Ivo into raptures on the SS *Peshawur*. Janet would serve tea on deck at 4 p.m. for Ivo and the amateurs (eight in all, with four hardened pros to do most of the bowling). We know that tea was at 4 p.m. because Ivo wrote as much in a long poem which he composed on the voyage home after the tour. He had won the Ashes, two Tests to one, but it was winning the heart of another, much younger woman which stirred his muse.

The Clarkes had lots of estate-workers – a nice touch, the lake was designed to be the shape of mainland Australia – and a governess who also taught the piano: a girl of Irish descent, flame-haired, aged 19, called Florence Morphy. I suspect Janet had selected her for being a younger version of her spirited self, to give her a break. Florence's father had died the year after she was born, the youngest of seven children, and it was not a great job he had, issuing mining licences in the goldfields and breaking up fights between drunken miners and Chinese diggers.

On his visits to Rupertswood during this first Ashes tour, Bligh would have been able to reflect of a morning in bed, while the Clarkes slept in the main bedroom across the hallway on the first floor. They, and their chief guest, could look from their windows at the estate below, down to the paddock where cricket was sometimes played. Florence might have been giving the children their breakfast below stairs.

For Christmas Eve 1882 a plan was hatched: the England amateurs would come by train from Melbourne, stay a night or two (while the professionals enjoyed themselves in a city hotel under Dick Barlow, who had already 'flickered to and fro' with Hornby), and play a game against the estate-workers on the paddock. The ladies, meanwhile, were not idly fanning themselves under parasols. Janet and Florence, both familiar with the myth of the Ashes which had been conceived after Australia had beaten England in the Oval Test of 1882, decided to present the captain who won the game in the paddock with a prize.

After consulting the various sources, notably Florence and an estate-worker who played in this game, my interpretation of the evidence is that Janet and Florence decided to burn something to ashes. What did they have to hand that could burn quickly? For it was only an afternoon game on the paddock and a lot of festivities had to be enjoyed that evening, not only dinner, but a night of dancing in the ballroom, where Ivo had to be matched with a suitable partner. A veil! Every society woman had lots of chiffon scarves to keep her hair under control in Melbourne, where the wind made the seasons shift within a day. This has to be the likeliest interpretation. Coquettishly, even flirtatiously, they burned a veil to ashes and put them in – wait! That terracotta urn which Janet had bought in Italy for keeping mascara in: that would indeed be suitable. And once England had won the series 2–1, and Bligh had brought back two of the bails from Sydney, one formed part of a penholder at Rupertswood, and the other: well, it took a lot of time and heat to burn a hardwood bail to ashes, much longer than any old veil, but it was more appropriate for the man who was England's winning – in more ways than one – captain.

Bligh was able to drowse of a morning, on this country estate which reminded him of his home, Cobham Hall in Kent, to the sound of Australia's unique birdsong. It made a quiet break from the England cricket tour. Listen! Was that a knock upon the door? Morning tea? Or could it be she?

Lord's, May 2015
I had been appointed cricket correspondent of the *Daily* and *Sunday Telegraph* in November 2014. The accountants had been busy rationalising. To be a Sunday paper journalist is to be a lone wolf, to be a daily journalist is to hunt with the pack. Not sure the animal kingdom offers an analogy for seven days a week.

An admission here, not a confession. I watched every day of every England Test when I began, for a Scottish or English newspaper, because learning how to do my job well was the priority. I wanted to observe the patterns of professional cricket, for it is by observing patterns that we can understand human behaviours. So Yuval Harari observed in *Sapiens*.

Now I am the cricket correspondent of a Sunday and a daily paper, again I have to watch every day. In between whiles, I did not attend every single day of every England Test at home in person (I would have been burned out long ago). Tests would start on a Thursday and I would normally drive home on a Saturday night after filing for *The Sunday Telegraph* (I was not allowed to work for *The Scotsman* or *Glasgow Herald*). On Sunday morning, I would watch the Test on television, then play a club game in the afternoon, often with a television on in the pavilion. Back to the television coverage full time on Mondays.

Pros and cons. I have always found it instructive to play the game, even at bog-standard grassroots level. Occasionally, I have played against a top young player on the way up, like Marcus Trescothick playing for Keynsham and scoring 4000 runs in the season, aged 13, or batting against James Hildreth when he was bowling for England Under-15s. When I have played under the captaincy of Mark Alleyne and Andrew Caddick, or alongside Michael Vaughan and Graeme Swann, it has been fascinating to see how they go about their business in the dressing-room and on the field.

It is good to experience at first-hand a change in the Laws, whatever the standard, e.g. no more saliva after Covid. What are pitches doing around the country (getting flatter) and what are balls doing (getting shinier with more lacquer, favouring seamers even more)? What is the latest piece of equipment or kit? Above all, the feeling of being out there: of dropping a catch, at any level the worst feeling in cricket, or scoring a maiden hundred, the best. And the sheer hard work it can be, like a tug-of-war that lasts for hours, and the relief when wriggling over the line. It all makes me reluctant to use the word 'should': watching from the ivory tower of the press box, one is tempted to say that first slip should have caught it. But any experience of how hard it is to take a first-slip catch when the wicketkeeper is standing up and blocking your view?

I turned 60 at the start of the season before I was appointed *Daily* and *Sunday* correspondent, and thenceforth limited to weekday matches and the odd Sunday game, so I set myself a target of 61 wickets. In late August a top-spinner turned past an inside edge to brush off an off-stump bail. I was content as far as my playing career goes: no, that's untrue, one is never content playing cricket. I even managed 39 wickets the following year, not season. My 100th wicket, spread over two years, occurred in a media game against an ICC XI in Dubai. Appropriately, it might be said, it came from a full toss that a former Australia Under-19 captain, Tim Anderson, ran down the pitch to drill about head height to long-on. Swann, in that position, moved his position a pace or so to his right milliseconds after the ball had been hit. By reading the trajectory and making this adjustment so incredibly early in the ball's flight, he did not have to move an inch when it arrived at waist height. Here was a humbling reminder – and we all need humbling reminders – how far advanced, on a different planet, elite cricketers are.

Test No. 447
Melbourne, December 2017

While Christmas Day is the happiest day of the year for millions of children, it can pall every four years if you are captaining England on a losing tour of Australia. On every recent visit England have been blown away a week before Christmas and gone 3–0 down. Santa Claus is beaming, while the face of England's captain is deeply etched with worry lines. Neither the present nor the future will judge him kindly – and it was almost always thus. The diary of the first England captain to contest the Ashes, the Honourable Ivo Bligh in 1882–83, is riddled with doubts about his players and himself; and even when they had won the three-game series 2–1, Bligh was forced to agree to a fourth Test which Australia tacked on and England lost.

In this MCG Test, Joe Root's England managed to staunch the bleeding. Alastair Cook, as he still was, churned out 244 in ten and a half unvanquished hours to secure a painstaking draw. But something even duller took place: my speech at a Christmas Day lunch.

I have never had the gift of the gab; I barely spoke after I was sent (I did not voluntarily 'go') to boarding school. I had thought it was going to be a few informal words. After attending Root's press conference, helping to transcribe his quotes and writing up my piece and filing, I walked all round the MCG in search of this luncheon-room, found it as everyone sat down, and noted the attendance of several hundred England supporters. My speech was more indigestible than anything on the menu. I should have looked around and asked how many of them had just walked to the ground from the city centre, up the slope from the River Yarra. For this is what the free settlers did after they had founded Melbourne in the 1830s: they wanted to build a cricket ground, not quite at the heart of the new colony, but as its lungs. Thus the Melbourne Cricket Club was established, a conscious echo of MCC back home. This connection, and that between England and Australia ever since, is worth a moment's thought. What would it have felt like on Christmas Day, I should have asked, if we had been in a strange city, on the other side of the world, without this cricket to bring us together?

Hamilton, March 2018
He was only 26 and still had the hell-raising reputation which the ginger-haired have been known to cultivate. But there appeared to be more about Ben Stokes when he spent almost an hour walking once around the boundary at Hamilton during England's warm-up game before their two-Test series against New Zealand. His companion was Mark, or 'Rocky', Stoneman and, as Stokes did most of the talking, my binoculars suggested that he was going slowly and deliberately out of his way to pump up Stoneman's tyres.

Stoneman had won the right to be Alastair Cook's opening partner for England on the strength of being the leading run-scorer in Championship cricket. A Geordie lad, his cricket education was being ferried around the North East from one club game to the next by his parents: none of your Lions tours or training camps in the UAE or psychology courses in Loughborough. Stoneman had the game to be England's opener for more than 11 Tests: nobody who is not a Test-class batsman has scored a fluent 50 against Australia at the Gabba from what I know. He had no big forward stride, but that has not been the fashion in English batting, even for opening batsmen, for a generation. Instead he had balance, and the shots, and had often wintered in Australia so he could cope with the short ball, and he was less limited against spin than many an English opener.

What he lacked was self-esteem, or that arrogant streak which enables a batsman to stay at the top. Visibly, when batting or being interviewed, he would beat himself up. And that was why Stokes was shepherding him round the boundary and bolstering the morale of a teammate four years older. It worked too, temporarily. Stoneman was England's second-highest scorer in both innings of the subsequent Test in New Zealand. But as he made 11, and England collapsed to 27 for nine in one of Trent Boult's magic spells with the pink ball (it was a day/nighter in Auckland), and 55 second time round, before England lost by an innings, his Test career went unfulfilled. Stokes's career as a counsellor, mentor and motivator, on the other hand, was taking off.

Test No. 450
Christchurch, March–April 2018

It was kind of New Zealand's captain Kane Williamson to mark my 450th with a present. In Māori tradition the person who holds this stone is kept safe when voyaging overseas. He had already given me an interview lasting the best part of an hour. The world's leading quartet of batsmen at the time were agreed to be Virat Kohli, Steve Smith, Joe Root and himself.

When Williamson made this presentation, at Hagley Oval on the eve of the Test, I responded by saying thank you, adding that we had both represented Gloucestershire, and that I had taken a five for (for their Over-60s against Somerset Over-60s).

Test No. 456
The Oval, September 2018

Alastair Cook turned at the top of the steps, looked around for the final time as an England batsman, and appeared to be touched by the depth, as well as volume, of the unqualified applause. Before T20 — and, with the best will, Cook was not made for that format — cricketers were paid less than their counterparts in other sports; they might have the honour of representing England several days a week, but that did not pay many bills. In one way, however, England cricketers might be enriched provided they timed their retirement correctly: by a crowd of 20 to 30 thousand rising to their feet in approbation. Far too often, of course, they would take a weary sweater at the end of another thumping in Sydney, or be dropped during an English summer without ceremony or farewell. But Nasser Hussain set a happier trend when he bowed out at Lord's after a match-winning century in 2004, and Cook affirmed it here, to be followed by Stuart Broad and James Anderson, who would also be allowed to see where they stood in the nation's affections.

In the middle Cook was overtly calm (if, by his own admission, inwardly afraid of failure) and inscrutable, and stubborn in the long tradition of England's opening batsmen. And hair-shirted too, ready to limit himself to three scoring shots until the spinners came on, and that number descended to two after pace bowlers switched to round the wicket and denied him square-cuts. Off the field, outside the England changing-room at any rate, he was the same character: not to be pushed around but never confrontational either, simply prepared to absorb the blows, whether of opposing bowlers or media headlines, until he could patiently, stubbornly, resolutely turn the tide. I was 51 when Cook made his Test debut, aged 20, flown in from an A tour of the West Indies to Nagpur, his reputation preceding him because of a double-hundred for Essex against the Australians. Another hundred followed on his Test debut, although it is not uncharitable to recall that it occurred in England's second innings, when they were pressing for a declaration, and they could have done with longer than the fifth day to dismiss India a second time. And I was 64 when he made his 33rd Test century, and climbed those Oval steps, and had his moment to savour the ovation by spectators who, in all bar fact, were throwing palms before his feet.

As a teenager, in the absence of family and friends, I found solace in three cricket books, aside from Len Hutton's. Two were written by Dudley Carew, at times a schoolmaster in Sussex, at others a *Times* correspondent on county matches (and later their film critic). He was first to alert me to the connection between cricket and the passage of time. He spent the summer of 1926, when Britain was full of civil strife, travelling from game to game and writing a chapter on each. Though he had attended neither school, he went to Lord's for the grand occasion of Eton v Harrow, a two-day match, and watched the cricket less and less as it headed for a draw. More and more his attention turned to a female spectator, of middle age, who watched intently right up until the dreary close. At the close he dares to address her. They exchange nothing more than formal pleasantries – apart from her astute observation that one young batsman is skilful, and that Harrow do not look as if they are ever going to be sufficiently strong to win – before the thunderclap of his dreadful realisation: that her coming to Lord's every year for this fixture is an annual ritual, in order to revive the memories of her son, who went to Harrow, before being killed during the First World War; to revive and perpetuate them.

In addition to Carew's *England Over* and *To The Wicket*, I was soothed by another author who has been too little appreciated, Ronald Mason. In *Batsman's Paradise* he studies the interconnectedness of time and cricket as a human pastime that fills many a day of the calendar. For myself, I can hardly recall my mother's death without remembering the Lord's Test of 1967 between England and Pakistan: adults decided that, as grieving was unwholesome, I should not be allowed to visit the hospital and see her one last time. It was better if I continued the decorating of the bedroom which my mother had begun, before suffering a brain haemorrhage, while my father and I were in the Isle of Man. (Ostensibly this was a holiday but also a spell away from home, and my mother, to prepare me for boarding school, to which I had no wish to go.) So there I was, staring at and painting a wall, and listening to radio commentary on Hanif Mohammad's 187*, while the first Test of that series and my hitherto happy childhood petered out.

'Cricket has provided for me perhaps the most poignant symbols I have known of the passage of time,' Mason wrote. 'More than that ... it has lent to moments of emotional or nervous difficulty emblems of serenity that I could not, in those given circumstances, have done without.' As a schoolboy Mason had watched Jack Hobbs batting at the Oval, and, as Walter Hammond was passing his prime, he paid attention to 'a lad who walked with a distinctive roll of the shoulders, an utterly captivating swagger like a Cockney errand-boy delivering fish … and as he [Denis Compton] found his feet, he relaxed the sobriety and disclosed a beautiful unspoiled genius that infected his batsmanship with all the sparkle and scent of a May morning.' Following the Second World War, Compton was solider, less flexible, less liable to run down the pitch at pace bowlers or to sweep (behind square leg, Mason notes) like no one else then did. Compton carried on for England until Tom Graveney. Hobbs, Hammond, Compton, Graveney, Boycott, Gooch: each one represented England, and something more, alongside his successor. Afterwards Mike Atherton and Marcus Trescothick, or Alec Stewart and Michael Vaughan if you prefer, held aloft the banner until the appearance of Cook, who kept it raised and who finally doft it on that September morning, before handing it on to Joe Root. More than a century had passed since Hobbs began his England career in 1907; and you could go back to Wilfred Rhodes and W.G. Grace, to span the time from 1880 until the present, if you are searching for an illusion of immortality.

Lord's, July 2019
It is not hard or very skilled work — except, possibly, when a game ends right on deadline. The 50-over World Cup final had a delayed start because of overnight rain. This tranquillity did not last. Throughout the day the final between England

and New Zealand stayed on the edge of a knife, 50-50, until England's finest batsmen could not get the ball off the square and the required run-rate climbed. With a final lunge, Ben Stokes landed England on the line, but not over it. It was time to write up this tie, but the super over (or two of them) had yet to be played out. I cannot pretend that I knew how the match would be decided if the scores in the super over were equal. In the press box, never mind on the ground, it was seat-of-the-pants stuff, which demanded teamwork: every member knowing his or her role, all five of us in the *Telegraph* team, no rocking the boat, because that would add to the load on somebody else.

Test No. 464

Edgbaston, August 2019

Stuart Broad ensnared David Warner in this opening Ashes Test for 2 and 8. In the arm-wrestle that is a five-Test series, if an opening bowler gets on top of an opening batsman it is a major contribution (to be offset on this occasion by James Anderson limping out of the series and Steve Smith scoring a brace of 140s).

Not many of Australia's opening batsmen have failed to stand up to examination in England. Broad won this duel, for one particular reason. He went round the wicket to Warner and found a gap in his left-handed defences that had not been fully explored. Broad had dismissed Warner five times in the six years before this Edgbaston Test of 2019; he was to dismiss him, usually for single figures, 12 times in the next four years.

Only in the last decade has it become the convention for right-arm pace bowlers to go round the wicket to left-handers. It was okay for an open-chested bowler like Andrew Flintoff to do it against Adam Gilchrist in the 2005 Ashes – he could veer off the business part of the pitch when following through – but not for right-arm outswing bowlers. The alteration in the angle of run-up, delivery and follow-through throws them off course. But the overall benefits in switching to round the wicket to attack left-handed batsmen was worth the trouble for right-arm bowlers. About one-third of openers in Test cricket, not the old-time 10 per cent, had become left-handers.

In the process however, 'a thing of beauty' went out the window (to quote Keats, who was reportedly hit on the head by a cricket ball when young – but then he was always young). The off-side strokes of a gracefully balanced left-handed batsman have verged towards extinction. It is, as Duncan Fletcher said, a question of angles. The old-time right-arm bowler, delivering a ball that landed on the line of the stumps or outside them, had offered room for the left-hander to free his arms unless the ball cut back: thus the drives through the covers and the cuts could flow. Henceforth, as the ball was angled into them from round the wicket, no more Woolleys, no more Gowers, no more Saeed Anwars – or, more recently, no more Marcus Trescothick taking apart Brett Lee in the tide-turning Edgbaston Test of 2005.

This switch, this change of tack, had to be done, for the sake of efficiency, but cricket has become a less beautiful game – so when India's Yashasvi Jaiswal is given room to free his arms, all the more reason to enjoy it. Right-handed batsmen, in the mirror image, are never given much room by left-arm over-the-wicket bowlers: the latter are a rare breed in themselves, and tend to swing the ball into the right-hander's pads.

Test No. 463

July, Lord's 2019

I was amazed, not that Ireland were dismissed for 38 in their second innings, but that they had made a game of it until that point. A lot of England's players had not played any first-class cricket before this inaugural Test because they were engaged in winning the 50-over World Cup. But then not a lot of Ireland's cricketers had been playing first-class, ever. In one domestic season they had cobbled together four regional teams to play each other – and that was it.

What Ireland had, for resources, was one competitive 50-over league in Northern Ireland and a few cricket-playing schools in Dublin, totalling about 10,000 adult players, at the most. The equivalent of one of the smaller shires in England, or maybe Wales. Just as Dr Johnson wondered that a woman should be able to give a sermon, irrespective of its quality … no, let's not go down that path. Suffice that Ireland in their two Tests against England, both staged away from home at Lord's, have given them a game. Ireland have come second both times, but not third.

Ireland, in two passages of these two Tests, excelled to the point of playing to the standard of many an established Test country. In seam-friendly conditions on the first morning of their inaugural Test against England, they dismissed the hosts in only 23.4 overs, England's fourth shortest Test innings. You can only dismiss a Test side in so few overs if you have a decent hand of seamers, and Ireland did: in both games they have fielded sturdy seamers who could surpass 80 mph, with a bit of shape, and bowl only the odd bad ball.

In the second Test, in 2023, Ben Duckett and Ollie Pope enjoyed the rare opportunity to bat extravagantly and England posted 500. Ireland were sinking towards an innings defeat, when their seventh-wicket pair smacked 162 in only 27 overs. England's seamers and spinners went round the park. It was becoming embarrassing – and if Andy McBrine and Mark Adair had converted their 80s into hundreds, and if England had stumbled in their pursuit of a target, it would have been very embarrassing.

How do Ireland do it? From the minimum I know of other sports, they seem to excel at every one they try. Not a sedentary upbringing: kids try their hand at various physical activities. They have the priceless gift of making the most of what they have. I would say that, of established Test-playing countries, only Australia and New Zealand possess the same formula.

Test No. 465
Lord's, August 2019, the first Ruth Strauss Foundation Test

The finest human being I have met through cricket was Ruth Strauss. When Andrew Strauss became a *Sunday Telegraph* columnist in 2004, I went round to the team hotel in Nottingham to see if he needed help with his column, and he introduced me to her. Mr Strauss proved to be far quicker in working his laptop and filing his copy than I was, so I was free to talk to Mrs Strauss. Quickly we found we had the same sense of humour. I was immediately on the same wavelength, although only later did I appreciate that Ruth had the gift of being able to tune into anybody's wavelength.

On England's 2006–07 Ashes tour of Australia we were walking across a very windy terrace at the team hotel in Perth, along with our respective children and my wife, to find a café for coffee. She was pushing a pram containing her first-born son while contending with the Fremantle Doctor coming up the Swan River at full blast. I said: 'Right, Ruth, which would you prefer? I can push your pram while you hold down your skirt, or hold down your skirt while you push your pram.' For my impudence she did not smack me at all.

I asked Mr and Mrs Strauss, separately, how they had met in Sydney when he went to play grade cricket one winter. He had just graduated from Durham (a 2:1 after belated swotting, but he had exam-anxiety nightmares during his cricket career); and at this stage of his life, fresh out of university, he possessed the same self-assurance in dealing with women as his predecessor the Honourable Ivo Bligh had when leading the 1882-83 side to Australia i.e. none. Andrew and an English friend went to a pub in King's Cross. It was almost empty, except for a couple of women seated and having a drink: Ruth, then an actress, and her friend. The two young Englishmen were immediately attracted, but far too inhibited as they drank at the bar. So, Ruth said, she just turned her head, raised her eyebrows and smiled in their direction: nothing forward, yet sufficient encouragement for the pair to approach without embarrassment. How neat is that?

When Strauss asked me to ghostwrite his *Pursuit of the Ashes* in 2009, he drove up from Cornwall where he had been having a holiday with Ruth and their two boys. They could not have been more normal – except that he was about to lead, for the first time, England in the Ashes, while she had a rare radiance that combined the best of English and Australian qualities. She brought a loaf of olive bread, and played with her boys in the garden while her husband dictated a chapter. I showed her round our house afterwards and in the bathroom we discussed whether it was right to keep a tap running while brushing one's teeth. I said I turned it on and kept it running slowly while brushing teeth; and turned it on and off while shaving. She, being an Australian from Ballarat, where water is a precious resource, spoke in favour of turning it off while brushing one's teeth.

Some people are adept at throwing a spanner in the works; Ruth had the skill to make wheels go round. Perhaps her career in acting helped her attune to individuals as well as whole audiences. I know, from what I saw behind the scenes, she played a part in the Ashes of 2005. Before Strauss came into the England team, relationships between the various wives and girlfriends of the players could degenerate into rivalry: who was to be Queen Bee? Ruth brought them all together. If a new player was selected for England, and brought his wife or girlfriend along, Ruth was ready to help her settle in and enjoy some fun. In the footage of that Ashes-winning series, you can often see an England cricketer turn to where the WAGs were congregated with their children in an area of a stand reserved for them. Duncan Fletcher, and Ruth, had made everyone feel valued and included, no longer the mere estate-workers they had been six years before, and many more besides.

Couples have rows and arguments. On the evening before the second Test of the 2009 series, the Strausses did at their home in Ealing. He drove back to the team hotel near Lord's (England, you remember, had escaped from Cardiff by the skin of their teeth). Ruth, on the phone, made sure the row was resolved before bedtime. Next day Strauss was in the right frame of mind to score 161*. It was the innings which seized the psychological advantage after Cardiff. Alastair Cook, his opening partner, came the nearest he ever did to making a hundred against Australia in England. Mitchell Johnson became a figure of fun - as he bowled to the left and he bowled to the right, as the chant said - although not for long. The captain led from the front in setting up England's first victory over Australia at Lord's for 75 years, since 1934. Not even England's 2005 team had broken that hoo-doo: they had dismissed Australia twice, which was some feat in itself, but Glenn McGrath still ran through them.

When Ruth was informed she had a virulent form of lung cancer, even though she did not smoke, I occupied a few minutes of her precious time. She sent me several texts, which should not be repeated because they were private, though I have shown them to her husband. Her messages were radiant, life-affirming, witty and wise. She said she had learned to live in the moment and enjoy every minute.

And what do we do? We look at our phones and screens. Therefore we think about anything and everything except the reality of our current circumstances.

I recalled the high wind in Perth. She said she remembered my impudence (not her word, no criticism at all), and our debate about what to do with the tap while tooth-brushing. She was still in favour of turning it off. She then followed up with a self-deprecating message about preaching, which she hadn't.

We exchanged more texts and jests about our families: her husband and my son-in-law had gone to the same school. I told her about my family's visit to Indonesia to see Komodo dragons after one Australian tour. And still, almost every time I do my teeth, I think of her and switch the tap off.

Horribly soon Ruth knew she had less than a year to live. She just made it to the Christmas holidays, so the family could fly together back to her Australian home. She needed cocktails of drugs to survive the flight, and made it through Christmas Day with all her family, just. I can sense how her two sons must have felt. She died at the same age as my mother, 46.

Test No. 466

Headingley, July 2019

It was a diptych, two masterpieces in one. A masterpiece of defence, as Ben Stokes scored three runs off 73 balls, to be followed by a masterpiece of attack, as he accelerated when wickets tumbled at the other end to add 132 off 146 balls. He might have inside- or outside-edged a couple but let us not nitpick. It was perfection. Over the course of five and a half hours Stokes achieved human perfection, and not many of us in our whole lives attain that state for even a few seconds.

He crossed the finishing line with what might still be the hardest cover-drive ever smitten. Australia's extra cover, though the ball went near him, did not move hand or foot; and, the thing is, England wanted only a single to win. By then I was standing at the front of the Headingley press box, to the left-hand side so I was not blocking anyone's view, and I turned towards our serried ranks and said: 'Greatest innings ever played for England.' It is quite possible that nobody heard me amid the tumult, but I wonder, nevertheless, if it was arrogant to so much as say so, to prejudge their own assessments, to ram my opinion down others' throats. I had one qualification to speak up: I had seen Ian Botham in 1981 and Graham Gooch's 154* on this same ground in 1991, and Kevin Pietersen's several *tours de force*. Or is there a moment when somebody, anybody, has to stand up and say what needs to be said – and this was one of them? Would it not have been wrong if this occasion, this unparalleled occasion, had passed without any spoken recognition?

I do not want to write anything more about the innings itself. It was a something – a creation – that should not be unpicked. We do not need to measure the length of the forearms of Michelangelo's David. It was perfection. The longer I live in cricket, the more inadequate numbers seem, and now words are going the same way.

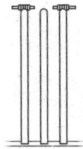

Andrew Strauss clips off his legs at Lord's during the England v India Test of 2011. Batting was the means to his end of leading and winning.

Never an ugly shot or gesture. Joe Root acknowledges the applause for his hundred against Australia at Lord's in 2013.

'When an old cricketer leaves the crease' by Roy Harper is a poignant song, even when the cricketer is not old. Alastair Cook, aged 33, and soon to be knighted, says farewell after the fifth Test against India at the Oval in 2018.

How times have changed: David Warner, as a left-handed opening batsman, might have got away with it in the days before data. But Stuart Broad, bowling full and round the wicket, pierced his defences – here at Sydney in 2022.

2020s

Test No. 474
Johannesburg, January 2020

It was time. I had always doubted whether the cricketer's adage – you just wake up one morning and know it is time to go – applied to cricket journalists as well. Maybe it was a slightly longer, more cumulative, process in my case; yet I knew when the moment had come to retire from touring.

On tour they are such long days and you are always on call: a WhatsApp from the ECB media manager will ping to announce a press conference, or the office will ring, or email, oblivious to the time difference (though, in my fortunate case, usually mindful). Let us not dramatise, though. More often than not, before start of play, one has time for a leisurely cooked breakfast – and let it not be a buffet, which brings out the worst in human nature, notably my own. Such indulgence is more justifiable after a virtuous visit to the gym. Then a walk to the ground – no, do not even think about finding a fake taxi receipt! – which includes stopping at a favourite café, like one in Regent's Park, pondering affairs of the world, so we come fresh to the cricket at 11 a.m. Truly, if the office did not pay me, I would do this job for free most days – on expenses, though.

Longest of days are floodlit games, whether Tests or white-ball internationals. You hang around all morning waiting for a game to start about 2 p.m., then about 6.30 p.m., when you are all ready to go home – a quiet dinner with that novel you keep meaning to finish? – the players come out for another session. If a Test, this session is always the longest because of the slow over-rate in the first two, to be followed by press conferences which finish around 10.30 p.m., so you might get back to the hotel by midnight, unwind by 1 a.m. and sleep by 2 a.m. The following morning, if it was a limited-overs international,

England's follow-up presser is probably scheduled for 9 a.m., and embargoed, to allow the coach or player to play golf in the afternoon; so you need to have packed and checked out in order to go to the airport after the presser. At such moments, if someone says 'I wish I had your job, can I carry your suitcase?' I would say 'Yes, please, let's meet at the airport check-in.'

The first day of my last tour was more prolonged. After a family Christmas lunch, I drove to Heathrow for the overnight flight to Johannesburg. My seat was in premium economy, in other words the size of an economy seat of a decade before, and I could not sleep: pins and needles in my elbows if I dozed off. Went straight by taxi to the hotel in Centurion, a short walk from the ground, where I was booked to stay. Booking cancelled. The Hennops River had flooded another hotel beside the lake, and hundreds of England supporters would otherwise have been left stranded for Christmas. No chance of a shower before going to the ground for the start of play, or of brushing my teeth, what remained of them: I had chipped off half a front tooth on Christmas Eve trying to open a tub of hummus.

Thanks to the perfect location of Centurion's press box – outside, open to the atmosphere yet covered – I could sense the play: some felt the Test was heading England's way, but James Anderson's wickets came too late in the day, after South Africa had cobbled a working total. Having filed my match report, I walked back to what was no longer my hotel, but where I had left my suitcase, and stopped en route at a cash-till in Centurion's shopping mall. A bit blurry by this stage after no sleep for 36 hours, aged 65, I was not alert to the scam after inserting my credit card. Some 'advice' offered by a friendly-seeming local resulted in the disappearance of my card and a couple of hundred pounds from my account, which the bank later refunded. I was rand-less and room-less, no space at the inn, but a hotel had been found on the outskirts of Pretoria which was not overcrowded, and better. After a couple of days a dentist in Centurion repaired my front tooth, only for the filling to fall out, without much prospect of getting it fixed over New Year in Cape Town. Nothing like illness or injury to make one feel a decade older.

Some days on this tour were happy as ever. The Barmy Army kindly allowed me to nip into their match in Soweto and enjoy a spell, on the same ground where England had played their opening first-class game on their inaugural tour after South Africa's readmission. The surrounding area was surprisingly lovely: you drove past the houses of two Nobel peace prize-winners, Nelson Mandela and Bishop Tutu, and the park was well-maintained, without any obvious budget, yet cared for. So too the surrounding houses: the ANC government had delivered basic housing, electricity and water to the majority. However, the cricket ground and its pavilion were in decline. The change, for the worse, had occurred when the South African board ceased to fund coaches to visit surrounding schools and bring kids to the ground. Temba Bavuma, and very occasionally Kagiso Rabada, represented the club in grade matches, but for the local populace cricket had reverted to being an alien sport. The Barmy Army now put back more than they take out: they had a whip-round of all their members on tour, not just their team, to help renovate the Soweto ground and pavilion. They are England's ambassadors on tour, while the England team are playing golf, and an institution all their own. Every other Test country has a different crowd of fans in each city; the Barmy Army is a cohort – sometimes a whole legion – that goes around together to all grounds.

The second Test in Cape Town ended in England overcoming old-fashioned South African obduracy when Ben Stokes took three wickets inside the final hour. Next morning, at 9 a.m., a media game started at Newlands, a few strips from the Test pitch. I didn't bowl well, and had a catch dropped that went straight to long-on, but held a couple of decent catches: I could prove that the pull shot to square leg went straight into the palm of my hand because the imprint stayed there for the rest of the day. We were using a locally manufactured ball that was much harder than traditional leather. England's head coach, Chris Silverwood, turned up to watch his young son bowling for the media XI, with the same flat-out run-up and hurling of everything into delivery as his father. As he was sitting on the boundary by himself, I asked him if he wanted to bat instead of me. He said he didn't have the right shoes or kit, so I lent him my trainers and he batted for half an hour, a bit rusty. It said so much about cricket: the morning after overseeing a titanic five-day tussle, the England coach was ready to play the sport himself. Maybe it said something about Yorkshiremen too: so many English coaches have come from and played for Yorkshire. I might have a bit in my blood.

Next day I went to Hermanus to catch up with Duncan Fletcher and his new love, ornithology. That evening I could not write up the interview, went to bed and slept for 12 hours, woke up, had an injection from the hotel doctor (there are a lot of viruses around Christmas in the townships where most staff had to live, he said) and went back to sleep for 24 hours. When I woke up, I got the embargo for a deadline wrong by several hours. Time to depart, I knew.

At the end of the fourth and final Test in Johannesburg, England having won 3–1, and at the end of the press conference held by the captain Joe Root, he said a few kind words: well, he actually said he hated me but it was in the nicest, politest way. I had long been urging him in print to give up the T20 format because he had all the tools and skills to become England's finest Test batsman. I tried to tell him how admirable his players had become, as human beings: nothing like the old days when each player was forced to look after himself first, and second. Root presented me with a copy of a painting of Newlands, signed by his players in pencil (if it is ink it must be a forgery). One does not write for the players, one writes for one's readers, but it was a nice gesture from the finest of ambassadors.

A fortnight after I returned from South Africa, Britain was shaken by Covid 19 and the world shut down. Many England players had been sick going into that first Test at Centurion, with what might have been some Covid prototype, as plenty of planes were then flying out of Wuhan. Four months passed before cricket resurfaced in England, and I was proud of what the ECB did to make cricket the first team sport to return to a semblance of normality (all places of worship shut in this hour of need).

Of course, they were driven by financial desperation – not mere necessity – to get Test cricket back on the road, to give broadcasters something to air live, but they still did it most efficiently. All the swab tests, all the face masks, all the gangways that had to be roped off, all the areas of Old Trafford and the Rose Bowl which had to be allocated to players, or media, or groundstaff, but never at once; and having to eat every meal at a table on one's own. I could sit back at home, safe in the knowledge that my colleague Nick Hoult had taken over as the *Telegraph*'s cricket correspondent.

After this England v West Indies series, when I watched Tests on television at home for the first time since 1976, I was privileged to cover the five rounds of county games that constituted the Bob Willis Trophy as a mini-Championship in 2020. Somerset came as close as they have ever done to winning their first such title, to be baulked by Sir Alastair Cook and Essex in the final at Lord's. Restrictions were such that, at Grace Road in Leicester, when a second XI player left his kit at the ground, the Covid regulations forbade him from collecting it until the next day. To watch county cricket when nobody else was permitted to do so, except a handful of media, and to convey to readers the pleasure of this escape from infected reality: here was the job boiled down to basics, and worthwhile.

Home, 4 March 2022
I can remember where I was on hearing the news that President Kennedy had been shot, and on hearing that Shane Warne had died.

I was walking home, about a hundred yards away, when my colleague Nick Hoult rang from the West Indies. Nick hears about what is going to happen as well as about what has happened, and the announcement of Warne's death, on holiday on the island of Koh Samui in Thailand, was about to be made public. A park bench was nearby, fortunately, so I could sit down to absorb this shock. Warne, dead, aged 52.

Normally, I back myself to write a thousand-word obituary about a major cricketer in an hour, but it was difficult on this occasion: no words could do Warne justice. He was peerless in his profession. Bill O'Reilly, and Abdul Qadir on an inspired day, are the only two wrist-spinners to have rivalled Warne, and neither was so complete a cricketer as he, a dangerous hitter and fine slip-fielder.

I played against him in 1989 when he was the overseas pro for Imperial CC in Bristol. He made a great reputation that season, for nocturnal rather than diurnal activities. When Imperial played a Sunday friendly at my club, Hinton Charterhouse, he bowled five overs for one wicket, then walked off for a fag and a pint in the pavilion. Imperial had several of their league players, we had barely a couple and were batting out for a draw, which was an option in those days before Sunday leagues. I was the non-striker, and all the fielders were clustered around the bat – Warne at slip where, he told me later, he was talking to another Imperial player about how to bowl a googly – when my partner, having blocked for several overs, latched on to a long hop and pulled it into the midriff of the short-leg fielder, a lad called Neil Thomson, who swallowed his tongue. He had about two, maybe three, minutes to live.

We rang 999 and an ambulance set out from Bath, about 15 minutes away if traffic was minimal. None of us knew the first aid required. By a miracle, one of our players had a sister who had just qualified as a doctor, and Dr Alice Tippetts had arrived at the Hinton ground a few minutes earlier. She ran out from the pavilion and pulled out Neil's tongue. What felt like a long while later the ambulance arrived, drove on to the square, and took him away. Nobody wanted to finish the game.

My mentor at *The Observer*, Michael Davie, was appointed editor of *The Age* in Melbourne (he should have been made *The Observer*'s editor much earlier), and in this capacity went to trace Warne's origins for an in-depth profile. Shane may have had larrikin tendencies, yet he was very middle class in birth, background and schooling, according to Davie's profile. Shane knew exactly what good manners were and how to behave in public. For years afterwards, so he told me, he would ask after Neil when he was in the West of England.

Fast forward to Grace Road, Leicester, in the following season. The Young Australians are practising there, because Leicestershire's nets have long been the best in England, ahead of their tour of the West Indies, and because Bobby Simpson was now Leicestershire's coach and had been asked to run his expert eye over the new players. Steve Bernard was the Australian Youth coach, and watched as Warne ran up to bowl his first ball at Jamie Cox, the tour captain. 'He rolled into his action and delivered a perfectly pitched spinning leggie,' Bernard recalls. 'I saw Simmo do a double-take and move across from one net to Warnie's net to watch the next ball. Upon him delivering another perfect leggie, Simmo looked at me and said: "This bloke has got something."'

'His behaviour was fine and on one of the last days of the tour he turned 21,' Bernard goes on. 'I remember it being a spirited but not outrageous celebration. Tabsy [Brian Taber the tour manager] and I gave a glowing report to the board about his behaviour and contribution to the tour, but the pygmies running the Academy decided he needed further punishment and refused to let him go on their next tour. Simmo obviously remembered how good he was and next year he was on a tour to Zimbabwe with Australia A, despite not being in the Victorian team.'

The trajectory of Warne's career was spectacularly steep. In 1989 his bowling figures in that game at Hinton had been 5–0–15–1 and he looked nothing remotely special. One year later, as Bernard noted, he was still 'over 15 stone, porky to look at, smoked like a green log, ate nothing but toast and wasn't scared of a drink,' but he was turning into a master craftsman. Three years on, at the Old Trafford Test of 1993, he delivered what Robin Marlar in *The Sunday Times* rightly hailed as 'the ball of the century'. I was too busy seething at the fact that if Warne had delivered it to a left-handed batsman – and David Gower should have been England's number three, not Mike Gatting, whose five-year ban for touring apartheid South Africa had been halved – the ball of the century would have spent itself harmlessly on Gower's front pad.

Series after series Warne dominated. Like Fred Trueman, he liked to fraternise with the opposition, perhaps too big a personality for some tastes in his own dressing-room. He might visit the England hotel and socialise with journalists before an Ashes series, telling them he had acquired a new type of mystery delivery. O'Reilly had been motivated by a hatred of all batsmen. Warne was the supreme choreographer, and a magician who made the batsman think that every ball was a mystery, even though, after a shoulder operation, it could only be a leg-spinner or flipper. He had the best supporting act too: David Boon, impassive as a wall at short leg, Mark Taylor at slip, Mark Waugh at second slip, or gully if you prefer, and Ricky Ponting, surely the sharpest of all silly points.

Warne's stamina would have stood out during an all-night lock-in at Valhalla. He had bowled all day in ferocious Cape Town heat. After a night on the town he could turn up at the pavilion in Southampton about 10 a.m., tell the 12th man to have a shower running and wake him up at 10.40, dress, light a fag and lead his Hampshire team out at 11. It was grievous news, but Warne was never one to grow old.

Test No. 491

Headingley, July 2023

Mark Wood's opening spell in this Test was the quickest I have seen by an England bowler. Nothing could gauge the speed of Patrick Patterson at Kingston in 1986 except the human eye, and the same with most of his antecedents. Brett Lee steaming in against England's tail in 2002–03 at the WACA was rapid. Jofra Archer cranked it up, firstly in an ODI against Pakistan at the Oval which clinched his place in England's World Cup squad of 2019, and shortly afterwards in the Lord's Test when he pummelled Steve Smith. But, simply on the evidence of my eyes, Wood's first spell here was the fastest.

I first took notice of Wood in St Kitts, when he had to cope with a strong crosswind which made him bowl inswingers: he looked barely big enough to stop being buffeted by the breeze. He was not complaining, either about the conditions or about having to bowl against, rather than for, England: fringe players in their squad had been farmed out to the opposition to flesh out the locals. Paul Collingwood, also from Durham, has been at the heart of England affairs for most of the time since 2010–11, when he stood in the slips near Strauss and was de facto vice-captain; Alastair Cook was nominally vice-captain, but they let him get on with scoring runs (766 in the series). I can imagine Colly reporting about Wood from Durham: 'he's only a slip of a lad but he's real rapid.'

A short run-up did not work. It was only when he could charge in, and find time to steady himself, that the rockets were ignited. St Lucia, venue of a 2019 Test, was the only pitch in the West Indies that bore any resemblance to the old-time surfaces of the Caribbean. Wood, warmed up, bowled with eight slips and a short leg. The slips were standing deeper than any I have seen. The West Indian batsmen, brought up on deadened pitches, were apprehensive. I would have been ducking if I had been short leg. I have never set much store by speed guns, ever since Shoaib Akhtar was timed at 100 mph in the 2003 World Cup: it was a half-volley to Nick Knight which, at the moment it was delivered, attracted no comment at all, let alone gasps of astonishment. The fuller the ball, the sooner it reaches the batsman – and the easier it is to hit. The searing bouncer which nearly takes your head off is routinely judged to be 5 or 10 km/h slower. Which would you rather face?

At Headingley, in this Test, it was now or never. With three games left, England were 2–0 down, after playing less sensible cricket than Australia. When Australia were chasing at Edgbaston, and taking on Moeen Ali (who had been called up from T20 after Jack Leach's injury), Ben Stokes refused to post a man back, so the Australians had only to pop the ball over Moeen's head to notch four. If Wilfred Rhodes had been at Edgbaston, blind and aged 145, he would have called it. But Stokes learned his lesson and devised his own novel solution: in future he would place a fielder on the boundary directly behind the bowler, which could cover 20 yards to either side, towards long-on and long-off.

At Lord's England's tactics were collectively senseless. From the moment that Nathan Lyon pulled a hamstring, England failed to add two plus two. A bowler who cannot walk to the dressing-room without leaning on someone's shoulder is not coming back later the same day, and probably the same game. For some unfathomable reason, when Australia resorted to bouncers, England's batsmen did not watch the three fast bowlers expend their energies fruitlessly and then cash in. Catching practice, instead, was the way they went.

Headingley was fast, true and fresh enough to be worth sticking the opposition in. Wood, it was rumoured later, had been so animated after his recall, following an elbow injury, that he was pretending to be a dog and barking at the heels of other England players in the dressing-room. He was soon at the throats of Usman Khawaja and Marnus Labuschagne, for the seventh over. The *Wisden* chronicler, Geoff Lemon, cleverly summarised that Wood's spell of 4–3–2–1 reflected the countdown to blast-off. He was so quick the batsmen had no time to get bat on ball except in self-defence – reflexes are quickest when survival is at stake. From his 24 deliveries only one scoring shot was played, a Khawaja cut for two, and that was off Wood's 23rd ball. But, for me, the most telling sign was Labuschagne's facial reaction: it was emphatically not a flinch, but something of a blench when one of the first rockets shot past. Imagine standing in the middle of a motorway and a car, going at well over 90 mph passes a foot from your face. He had been told about a ghost haunting England's house, and now he had seen it.

Wood shifted the pendulum towards England in this spell. Sun Tzu would have said that England were now on top, though 2–0 down. Chris Woakes was a noble yeoman with bat and ball, and Wood himself clubbed and carted 40 runs off only 16 balls in the game. Together they nursed England over the line, back to 2-1. And Australia caved in during the next two Tests, even though the series ended 2-2.

Test No. 492
Old Trafford, August 2023

Drainage has been one of the major developments of my time, not far behind helmets and DRS. It is amazing that a downpour at Lord's can be followed by play within the hour – a far cry, and lots of irate shouting, from the Centenary Test of 1980.

But nothing could stop the fifth day of this fourth Test of the series being washed out. England had to take only five more wickets – and Australia were still lagging behind, ever more shell-shocked by the speed of England's batting as much as their bowling – to level the series at 2–2 ahead of an Oval climax.

Whole days being rained off have become a rarity, but I still carry a reflex ball in my bag. At some grounds overseas you might be able to borrow some kit for an indoor net. At Christchurch one rainy day, at the old rugby-cum-cricket stadium, I tried and executed my first reverse-sweep against the left-arm spin of Steve Boock, no longer playing for New Zealand but their chairman of selectors. It was the ripest abuse I ever had directed at me. But I was incandescent too, the only red mist I have seen, when I was reverse-swept for the first time.

As it rained at Old Trafford, we tried England media v Australia media at reflex ball: its irregular shape makes for irregular bounce, so soft and swift hands are mandatory to catch it without fumbling. But even that palled after a few hours. My wife still says brightly, if heavy rain is forecast: 'You won't have to work today, will you?' It is not quite so simple, and never was: sports pages still have to be filled. I made do with feeding the *Telegraph*'s website. I actually stuck my neck out of the press-box door, and metaphorically too, by writing that England should have declared and should have been bowling when Jonny Bairstow was blazing away in his last-wicket stand. Cricket websites are, curiously, most popular during rain-breaks: when the viewer cannot follow what is happening on television, because it is showing old highlights.

Test No. 499
The Oval, September 2024

The best innings of this summer furnished an unexpected end to what had been two all-too-predictable series. West Indies, without Shai Hope or any middle-order batsman of experience, lost their three-Test series 3–0; Sri Lanka were 2–0 down, and 52 runs behind on first innings at the Oval. At this point four factors appeared to kick in a) some England complacency b) the wildest and most inexplicable batting I have seen, by Dan Lawrence, bizarrely installed as an opening batsman after Zak Crawley had broken a finger c) Sri Lanka's hunger to qualify for the World Test Championship final and d) the best batting of the summer, by Sri Lanka's opener Pathum Nissanka.

The World Test Championship is not enough of a good thing – as a single game between two qualifying finalists – but it is a very promising start to promoting Test cricket, by awarding points for every game in a league table. What I would like to see is the top four countries (the nation that is West Indies seem too far off their traditional pace) meeting in England in high summer: it could even be August, when the Hundred is appealing to new audiences. Most Test countries would feel they are in with a chance throughout the two-year cycle.

Each country would then play a Test against the three others in the course of the month: if they had to be four-day Tests, so be it, provided there was a fifth day in reserve, in case one was lost to English rain. I find in this age when every cricket match of note is broadcast or livestreamed, that it is possible to follow two games simultaneously, if not absolutely thoroughly: it adds to the entertainment and excitement indeed if the viewer can switch from one match, at the end of an over or an advertisement break, back to another. England's six main grounds would stage one Test each; each country would play once in the South (Lord's or the Oval), once in the Midlands

(Edgbaston or Trent Bridge), once in the North (Headingley or Old Trafford). The winner of this mini-league would be worthy Test champions.

What we saw in this Oval Test was the future of batsmanship. For the best part of a generation, batsmen of all countries found it next to impossible to switch their mindset and game plan from one format to the next then back again: especially to switch from T20, or even the Hundred as England players have to do, to Test cricket. But now the best young batsmen combine the best of both worlds: they have all the shots, along the turf and in the air, and can hit the ball 360° in order to manoeuvre fielders, yet they have the defence to play themselves in first. What does this ancient phrase, to play oneself in, mean? It means factoring in all the variables – the pace of the pitch, or it might have two paces, depending on the surface; the amount of seam movement and uneven bounce; the condition of the ball; the effect of any wind; and every individual bowler's particularities, both his customary methods, as supplied by the analyst, and what he is doing on the day. It also means allowing the brain, if not over-tense and flooded with adrenalin, to compute the right responses. It irks me when a batsman is said to play 'by instinct'. Take the finest athletes of the US, Russia and China and none would be able to middle a cricket ball; only highly conditioned reflexes can do that.

Two batsmen, one on each side, stood out in this match. One was Jamie Smith, whose second innings of 67 off 50 balls gave England something to bowl at. This Test was only his sixth, but he had already shown how to defend, problem-solve and attack. I was first struck by Smith when Ben Foakes was injured during Surrey's warm-up before a Championship game at Bristol, and Smith was brought into their team to keep wicket, and scored 234★. He played himself in on days one and two, kept the ball on the ground and acquired a hundred-plus both days. This experience took him back to his childhood, Smith told me later: 'In my first competitive game they didn't have a keeper and I put my hand up. It was for Sutton Under-12s and I was nine. It was the first time I'd put wicketkeeping gloves on. I'm not from a massive cricket family, more football, and I just fell into it. When Ben Foakes was injured [before that game against Gloucestershire], I felt I ought to take fewer risks than I do normally.' Smith played what was in front of him, a skill which will never be overtaken in cricket so long as it is played on turf pitches.

Nissanka, opening in this Oval Test after somehow being omitted earlier in the series, kept Sri Lanka afloat with 64 off 51 balls in his first innings, then set about their target of 219. Sri Lankan schoolboys by training, they would knock them off in 50 overs, I reckoned. Nissanka's forward defence was a credit to all those coaches and boys who had sweated over the MCC coaching book in Colombo. Drives, hooks and flicks were unfurled as his 127* from 124 balls took Sri Lanka to victory with eight wickets in hand. The demands of T20 – and Nissanka had played almost 10 times as many T20 matches as Tests to this point – can embellish, not destroy, Test batsmanship.

It was my 499th Test. When Hanif Mohammad had granted me an interview in Karachi in 1987, I had naturally asked about his 499, which had been the highest first-class innings to that point, and would still be so but for Brian Lara's plundering of Durham's bowling, including that of their wicketkeeper, in a very drawn match. Hanif, in fact, scored 499 run out, which did not strike me as the ideal way to go.

Hanif had already played the longest innings of all time, against West Indies in Bridgetown: he asked me to tell the editor of *Wisden* that he, Hanif, reckoned it lasted 999 minutes, but this cannot be proved so it remains as 970 minutes in the good book. During that series a bouncer from Roy Gilchrist whistled past his face, obviously unhelmeted: we were sitting on chairs in the shade on the outfield of the National Stadium in Karachi and Hanif swept his hand past his nose. Two months of facing taped tennis balls at short range were required before he regained his nerve.

It was the semi-final of the Quaid-e-Azam Trophy, Pakistan's first-class domestic competition, in January 1959: Karachi v Bahawalpur at the Karachi Parsi Institute. It was a delightful ground when I visited: near the city centre, yet you could hear kitehawks cawing in the surrounding trees, while an old man slept in his blazer on the verandah of the single-room pavilion. British regiments were playing cricket against each other in Karachi by 1847; Parsis, their loyalist henchmen, launched the KPI in 1883; and while most Parsis had emigrated from Pakistan (Jinnah, though he looked misanthropic, wanted a pluralist Pakistan, not least because he was Shi'i himself), one Parsi cricketer remained. The old man in the blazer turned out to be Rusi Dinshaw. He had represented Pakistan a couple of times, against Ceylon, before official Test status was granted, as a left-handed batsman. His mind then went; he kept hearing voices. All he said to me, more than once: 'I used to play cricket.'

In 1959, as when I visited, the KPI ground was sparsely grassed, so no need to loft the ball: it whizzed from bat to boundary. Hanif was intent on playing what he called 'copybook', and lofted the ball only once, over the bowler's head, and he was using a Gunn & Moore bat slightly heavier than usual at 2 lbs 2 oz, yet still hit 64 fours. Bahawalpur had been dismissed for 185. Karachi at the end of day one were 59 without loss. The pitch was matting: water and roll the ground underneath and it would be a belter; loosen the nails which pinned down the mat and the ball could jag and bounce or shoot. The home groundsman went to work dutifully and by the close of day two Hanif was 255*. 'Now you can go for the world record of 452 by Bradman,' his oldest brother Wazir announced at the family dinner table. Hanif turned in for his usual nine-hour sleep. 'I don't think I was a great player but my concentration was so good, and if you stay at the crease you make runs.

'When I got to 451 [on day three] I crossed the record of Don Bradman by hitting a two. I waved to Wazir and naturally everyone [a crowd about 1500] was clapping, including the fielders even though they were tired. I was relaxed and pleased and kept playing copybook, and when it came to the last over of the day the scoreboard said I'd made 496. One of the medium-pacers was bowling and I thought I needed four runs from the last two balls. So when I hit the fifth ball to extra cover, who was quite deep and misfielded, I thought I could get back for a second and score two more runs off the final ball. Then the next thing I saw was the ball going towards the keeper's end and into his gloves, and I was run out by four feet and I thought "bad luck!" But as I was walking off, the boys on the scoreboard put up 499. They said the score had been going so fast that the scorers hadn't been sure about what I'd made. Then I was very annoyed.'

Stuck on 499 after the Oval Test of 2024, I was not annoyed for long. My dear colleague Nick Hoult said that after covering England's first two Tests in Pakistan that autumn, he simply had to return for his wife's Significant Birthday – so would I care to come out of touring retirement and do the third Test in Rawalpindi for the *Telegraph*? 'Never go back' they say ... but this was a one-off. And it would make a neat symmetry: the first England match I had ever covered on tour had been in Rawalpindi in 1977. If I did go back, for one more game, the outcome could not be so bad as it was for Hanif's partner when he went for his 500th run. Abdul Aziz, Karachi's wicketkeeper-batsman, was known to have a heart condition and took around a bottle of medicine. In the final of the Quaid-e-Azam a few days later he forgot to bring his medicine to the KPI ground and, while batting, was hit over the heart by nothing more than an off-break. He fell down in his crease, foamed at the mouth, and died before reaching hospital. The scorebook read: 'Abdul Aziz retired hurt 0; absent dead 0.'

Anywhere in the cricket world, the present time
They don't know how lucky they are! Around much of our planet, and certainly where a professional cricket match is being played, your mobile phone will work and the connectivity will be such that within a minute of opening your laptop at a Test ground you can be ready to press send.

Actually, the technology was none too difficult when I started. In England, at every county or Test match, you had access to a phone: your newspaper would pay a fee for hire but those wheels were turned by the Sport Department's secretary (to whom very belated thanks). At a match abroad, wherever England played, there would be a Camp Telegraph Office, usually beside or near the press tent. Men, even if they knew no English, would type out the match report you had written on your portable typewriter, produce a long white tape punctured with holes, feed it through a machine after dialling the number you gave them, and a replica would appear in your newspaper office to be decoded: telex. You always carried a telex card, which guaranteed that the cost would be paid by your employer.

Trouble arose if you dawdled, or it was a bad day and you could not think of an intro. You might decide to return to your hotel room and write there: on most England tours you are ahead of GMT. A spot of dinner first perhaps? Oh all right, let's ring room service. But, after eating, that concise and witty intro remains remote as ever. Maybe a quick nap would help? And thus the evening drags on, by which time the CTO has long since packed up. Telephone? Well, you can try asking the hotel operator to book you a transfer-charge call to London – but maybe she has omitted to pass on the message to a colleague at the end of her shift and the call never comes or is put through to another room. In that case you have to leave your hotel, catch a taxi and find the central post office somewhere in the city, perhaps through the back door in an ill-lit alley. If you are conscientious, you will wait until the telex operator has completed the task – or, hang it, let's get back to the hotel because it will be another long day tomorrow. I remember a *Guardian* correspondent, a dear fellow, who let work expand to fill the time available, which is about 10 hours between England and Australia, and he would be seen leaving the hotel at midnight after perfecting his match report. After two consecutive tours of Australia (1978–79 followed by 1979–80), he retired from cricket.

Telephones did not always work. In St Vincent the population is less than six figures, and although it is a country in its own right, facilities are small-scale. On one tour we were invited to a reception at the prime minister's residence – not the players, just the media, whom he wanted to woo. Being English, and thirsty, we turned up in a couple of taxis at 6 p.m. sharp – although a few minutes passed while each of us sought from the driver a receipt, to be filled in anon. We knocked on the front door of a sizeable, though not luxurious, bungalow. Nobody there. We waited. We looked round the back, and thought it wiser not to try windows to break in. Soon the prime minister of St Vincent and the Grenadines turned up in a car, let us in and fussed round the kitchen to make drinks, in which task a lad soon joined him. It was a convivial evening, except for John Woodcock of *The Times*, on his last tour. He was waiting in his hotel room, and had been waiting in his hotel room for two (non-match) days, hoping for a call from his office so he could dictate his copy. He had never taken to the typewriter and telex. He still had a voice but no one could hear.

On the other hand, it would be most gratifying when an unlikely-looking telephone did work and the operator would transfer the charges. The only match England played in Guyana on their 1980–81 tour of the West Indies, owing to a muddy combination of rain and politics, was in Berbice in the northeast. Players were flown from Georgetown. Journalists rose before dawn, filled aged taxis with aged limbs and typewriters, and set forth in blurry pursuit. After several hours on the coastal road we arrived at the ferry station on the Berbice River. We still had a way to go on the other side through sugar estates, and the start of the one-day international was at hand. The chains of the ferry turned noisily, but exceeding slow, as it approached from the Albion side. A distant venue, but it was still a place on the cricket map: Tate & Lyle, who ran the sugar plantations, had decided to put something back by hiring Clyde (later Sir Clyde) Walcott as a cricket coach in the 1950s. Most of the sugar-planting community was Indo-Caribbean, sons of the bonded labourers whom Britain had shipped from India, and they took to cricket: Rohan Kanhai and Alvin Kallicharran were two sons of this soil.

Don Mosey, of the BBC, was striding towards us as we waited beside our taxis for the ferry. He was triumphant. He had found a telephone in the wheelhouse on a gantry, and it had worked, and he had been able to get a call through to London. Teams?

Toss? Pitch conditions? Not a clue. For a few precious minutes, though, he had a voice.

Tandy succeeded telex in the 1990s; and it was in this period between the landline telephone and present technology that vexations could creep in. Having typed out the match report on an up-market typewriter which contained some electricals (sorry not to be more specific), you dialled a number on a landline phone that you had to hire or borrow, waited for a high-pitched squeal and strapped two ear-muffs on to the phone, one at each end. Sometimes the report would emerge complete in the newspaper office, sometimes garbled.

Mobile telephones were a longer-term answer. The first cricket journalist I saw using one was Robin Marlar of *The Sunday Times* in the 1990s. It was like a briefcase filled with bricks and had to be charged frequently. Then came the internet, which was spasmodic, in England as much as anywhere. I came to dislike the cricketers' saying that you can only control the controllables. Yes, but if you are a journalist, you still have to file, even if the whole system of the internet and your laptop is uncontrollable. I remember looking at my Bangladeshi colleagues in Dhaka and Chittagong, and wondering why their connectivity was so much better than ours. But it has turned out to be a flawless means of transmitting copy. The strange thing is that, the more the means of transmission has changed, the more the copy itself – a report on Australia scoring 320 for three at the close of day one, or why England have collapsed against spin – stays the same.

Test No. 500

Rawalpindi, October 2024

I was nearly run-out while backing up, or strangled down the leg side. About a hundred England supporters had travelled to Pakistan for England's three-Test series, and a tour leader said about half of them fell ill, like me. Majority opinion was that they had picked up a virus on the plane.

On arrival at dawn on Monday morning at Islamabad airport, I was fine ahead of the third Test beginning on Thursday. Pakistan's capital had grown to resemble a poor man's Dubai. A six-lane highway ran from the new airport in Islamabad, which had replaced the old airbase I knew, then tapered into Rawalpindi. A metro-bus had been installed, and tickets cost 50 rupees (little more than 10p by the official exchange rate). This highway was not exclusively for civilian and military elites.

Other changes from the Pakistan of 1977–78 seemed superficial. Still many roadblocks. Roadblocks blossoming with barbed wire: they are a government's admission that it does not feel secure and does not connect with the people. Team buses needed their usual police escort to break through the rings of security surrounding the hotel, then to sweep through the traffic and reach the Rawalpindi stadium for a 10 a.m. start. But for lesser people, roadblocks were spread as extensively as a hurdle race. The British High Commission was a mile from the team hotel: roadblocks made a taxi describe 350° of a circle and take more than half an hour ro reach it. Rumours of a march by Imran Khan's supporters were in the air; and Pakistan's constitution had just been amended, so the new chief justice was no longer to be the most senior judge, but the one the government wanted: more bad news for the imprisoned Imran.

My impression, as before, was that for a Pakistani civilian living in Pakistan, it was like being in a room where the ceiling was six inches shorter than he was: he, let alone she, could never extend himself to full height. In addition were the self-imposed restrictions: even in the higher echelons of society, in international hotels, local men socialised together, and local women socialised separately. How sterile is that? No cross-fertilisation of attitudes and ideas. Civilian government, nominally, but the army and intelligence services were still in control. Imran Khan's party had won the most seats in the recent election, but that did not save him from being jailed on a never-ending list of charges. The consensus I gleaned at the British High Commission reception was that, Imran having tried to normalise relations with China and other neighbours hostile to the USA, Washington had approved of the military deposing him.

I felt fine on the Tuesday too, settling back into the swim. Made a reconnaissance visit to the stadium: it had an unusual entrance on the press-box side. After turning off the main road, sit blankly while security men look into the bonnet and put a metal detector under the car (a mild, bemused expression works best), before the security personnel inside the ground put you and your bag through x-ray machines; then drive past the Chicken Research Institute. I suppose poultry must be researched, given the widespread nature of avian flu, and it is understandable the chickens are shitting themselves when their time comes to be researched, but it was some stench for a cricket ground, as if the Wellington Hospital outside the North Gate at Lord's had become an abattoir. (Note to self: even if one of England's Bazballers plays an exceptionally stupid shot, do not compare him to a headless chicken in the Research Institute.)

On Tuesday afternoon I renewed what might be the second longest-running contest in the history of international sport, after the Ashes: tennis against Simon Wilde of *The Times* and *Sunday Times* (we might even have set a record for the most countries in which one particular sporting contest has been staged). At Wednesday lunch time Ben Stokes gave a press conference for the England media only, in the garden outside the hotel coffee shop – not so formal as the one the captain of each side has to give at the ground, more like a headmaster's chat with his sixth form. The ECB media manager, Danny Reuben, warned us that Stokes had not been himself on this tour and he did not know why. Later it emerged that Stokes had overextended himself training in rehab, after tearing his left hamstring while batting in the Hundred, and that during the second Test in Multan his house in Durham had been burgled while his family was inside. I asked him why Brydon Carse had been omitted after being hostile in the first two Tests: that left England with one pace bowler in Gus Atkinson, plus Stokes himself, who in the event did not bowl at all. Stokes said Carse was fit but tired. As it transpired, the third Test was decided by Pakistan's tailenders merrily clubbing England's three spinners without a bouncer or yorker in sight.

Wednesday afternoon. When the blood seems to drain out of your system, to be replaced by something less healthy, more toxic: you know the feeling? When I had got Covid in 2021, I was due to cover the T20 finals on the Saturday, and wandered round Birmingham in an increasing daze on the Friday evening in search of my hotel. Got through finals day, although I cannot recall who won, met the Somerset chairman Sir Michael Barber on the train home (I remember he talked about the enormous progress made in state education in Punjab over the course of his 48 visits to Pakistan) and played on Sunday afternoon. (I played the following Sunday, too, and feel that my figures of 0–100 over those two games should be expunged from the record.) This ailment felt worse than Covid. But I had never missed a Test through illness. Dosed with pills, I lurched down to the lobby at 8.35 next morning, apologised to my taxi-sharer, Lawrence Booth of the *Daily Mail*, for being late, and we headed round the roadblocks to the stadium.

It was another turner, like the second Test in Multan which had been staged on exactly the same pitch as the first. Pakistan had brought in a pair of stalwart spinners to do the needful. Nauman Ali had bowled as left-arm spinners have bowled since the dawn of Test cricket, using the width of the crease, now faster now slower, now higher now lower, now side-spin now under-cut: he had taken 8 for 46 as England were dismissed in 33.3 overs in their second innings in Multan when chasing 297 to win. Opposite him Sajid Khan fired his off-breaks through faster than most finger-spinners through the ages. I suspect that Pakistan's field placings, on those turning pitches of Multan and Rawalpindi, would sometimes have replicated those used in the first Test series of 1877. Stokes, by contrast, probably set a fielder in every place on the field except behind the wicketkeeper. I could not say whether the traditional or unorthodox field setting is better: it all depends on the batsman, and how he is playing in the game situation, and on the bowler and the pitch, and the state of the ball, an equation that could vary every ball.

What I could not fathom was England's batting at times in Rawalpindi. I could accept the way they played when chasing 297 in Multan: they were not going to win whether they defended or attacked. Both Pakistan spinners were, if not long in the tooth, thorough craftsmen. But I suppose there was an additional factor then which England could have considered. So disorganised was the Pakistan board — new chairman, new strategy, new cronies on the payroll, new coaches every year — that Nauman and Sajid had not played any first-class or red-ball cricket for almost a year. (It is why Pakistan do not produce any more star batsmen: their board does not stage enough competitive games at every level.) Their spinning fingers could have become sore and blistered if kept in the field for hours.

England won the toss in Rawalpindi. After one hour, drinks were taken on the field — and a presentation made in the room behind the press box. The Pakistan branch of the South Asian Sports Journalists Association presented me with a trophy to mark my 500th Test. If my colleagues muttered 'you take the cake', they were right: the Pakistan board's media officer had commissioned the team hotel to make a large chocolate cake, and most welcome a slice was. Sugar and pills kept me going until the lunch interval. Take each session as it comes.

Grinding it out on a turner in a Test in Asia was a far sterner test of survival before the era of neutral umpires. Remember Swaroop Kishen, and crowds of 50,000 roaring for lbw: research showed that an umpire is more likely to raise his finger for lbw when his pulse is racing. England's new mantra: put pressure on the bowlers. And, yes, please do so against bowlers striving to contain on a flat deck. But cricket retains some eternal verities, however much the sport has changed, and one is: do what the opposition likes least. Giving bowlers every chance, when conditions are in their favour, simply encourages them. Moreover, it gives opponents the heartening belief that England will lemming-rush again the next time they are in trouble. Jamie

Smith, with Atkinson his Surrey teammate, kept England in the game with a perfectly paced 89 in a near-par total of 267.

Friday's opening session lasted two and a half hours, followed by an hour for prayers or, in my case, a sleep in the back of our taxi. Take each session, play what is in front of you. The big change 'since my day' was not the match report but the *Telegraph*'s live blog which had to be fed with continual updates: things which the live blogger could not see on television but the correspondent on the ground could, like X is warming up, Y has been talking to the spin-bowling coach on the boundary, while an inventive field has been set with three boundary-riders on either side.

Pakistan's left-hander Saud Shakeel batted like the late Graham Thorpe would have done, taking every single offered without any risk. Nauman and Sajid clubbed England's spinners to take a lead of 77. England faced nine overs on the second evening, plenty enough time to lose three wickets. It would take a miracle, or an individual century, or both, to win this match and series. Pakistan must have known that they only had to keep doing what they had been doing since Multan to dismiss England again in fewer than 40 overs. A pattern of Bazball had emerged: taking their opponents by surprise, England had won the opening Test of a series, twice in Pakistan and once in India, as well as at home, but they kept losing the last Test. By then their opponents must have known that they had only to hang in to profit from some wild excesses by England's batsmen.

This script was not unfamiliar. I waited until the partnership between Joe Root and Harry Brook had been broken, and until Stokes had shouldered arms to a Nauman ball that was almost certain to turn into his pads – and, as chivalrous as any England captain of the amateur era, he stayed on bended knee to pick up the ball and return it to a Pakistan fielder before departing. Apart from a report, I had to do the player ratings of both sides for this series, and had done some of them (the England bowlers) before the start of day three. Then the deluge as England were brushed away for 112 in 37.2 overs. It is always easier to write up a defeat than victory, in sickness and in health, because there is more to say.

This is my match report for the *Telegraph* from the last day of that third Test, my 500th:

A pack of cards collapsed on the third morning in Pakistan. It went by the official title of the England Test team.

Batting was awkward on a turning pitch against Pakistan's two fine finger-spinners but the ball was only turning – at times lavishly, yes – it was not keeping low. England's response, in being dismissed for 112 and losing by nine wickets and the series 2-1, was, simply, inadequate.

It was inadequate to the extent that it calls into question the whole Bazball project. This England team, as a generalisation, have been encouraged to go out and play their 'natural game' and to 'express themselves', but in challenging circumstances like these, their approach smacks of mindless optimism. When the going gets tough for batting, they react artlessly.

Hard hands, not a lot of footwork, and the willingness to play a shot at almost every ball: this recipe works on flat pitches, and wins Test matches on them. The featherbed of Multan, in the opening Test of this series, saw one of the great chapters in England's annals when Joe Root and Harry Brook ran riot in posting 823 for seven, the fourth highest Test total.

Promptly, Pakistan changed their strategy – bring on turning pitches – and England did not. Their response remained as it was. They said they were happy to keep playing their natural games. Well, their opponents were even happier as England were dismissed in 33.3 overs in the second innings of the second Test, and in 37.2 overs in the second innings of the third.

The British army was reformed after the Charge of the Light Brigade. Will England's batting also be reformed? Will mindless optimism be replaced? This analogy extends to England's batsmen riding bravely towards danger behind Lord Cardigan in the search for glory; not for them a grubby fight for survival in defending the last ditch.

Put it another way. Other Test teams in England's history would have gone down for 144 and 112 in these same circumstances of the past two Tests, or for not much more. But the point is that they would have sold their wickets more dearly. This England team, under the current direction of Brendon McCullum and Ben Stokes, are more generous: take one wicket, get one free, or two, or three. Hurry, hurry, the sales are now on: all wickets to go cheaply.

And the knock-on effect of these sudden and seismic collapses, if they only could see it, is that England's batsmen encourage the opposition. The Australians can only be delighted at watching England's one-track naivety: they know that this England side is inherently brittle.

Pakistan had only to be patient and wait – this was the message of Pakistan's coach Jason Gillespie, an Australian himself, after the first Test – and an England batsman will try something completely inappropriate in the circumstances, a shot of excessively high risk. The last thing they will do is dig in and fight.

England needed much less than two hours on the third morning to be dismissed/to donate their last seven wickets. Resuming at 24-3, they lost three more merely in wiping out the first innings deficit of 77. Both of Pakistan's finger-spinners, the pugnacious Said Khan with his off-breaks, and the flightier, floatier Nauman Ali with his old-fashioned left-arm spin, enjoyed another field day.

In the second Test Pakistan's two finger-spinners took all 20 wickets, in the third 19. You would have to go back to Jim Laker and Tony Lock in 1956 running through Test opposition to this extent. The Australians then were naive in playing spin on wet turning pitches. Here England have been naive on pitches that have been dry to the point of arid. The difference is that the Australians were not full-time professionals; England are meant to be.

Harry Brook was adventurous while he lasted, when there did not seem to be so much need to hurry. He came down the pitch to off-drive Sajid's off-breaks, for which there was something to be said; and he tried to cut or force square on the off-side his sharply turning off-breaks, for which there was nothing to be said. A dab at Nauman and he was caught behind.

Stokes has suffered some dramatic dismissals in Asia — he will not be too distressed that England do not have to return there until 2027 — and this one was right up there. It must have been a brain-fade: he shouldered arms to a left-arm spinner that was destined to hit the stumps. He stayed on bended knee: ever chivalrous on the field, he even leaned forward from that kneeling position to toss the ball to a fielder. He did not care to discuss the possibility of a review with his partner Joe Root, which was worth a go.

It made for a poor match for England's captain, perhaps his poorest. His hands gripping the bat harder than most, Stokes has not played one of his great innings on a turning track in Asia. His first innings dismissal was artless, when lured into driving a wide off-break, and he did not bowl himself, when a yorker or two might have rounded up Pakistan's tail before they posted that relatively huge lead of 77.

Root in the middle of this latest debacle recalled the lines of the boy standing on the burning deck; he had no company. He played some reverse-sweeps at Nauman, which was sensible, when the ball was landing outside off stump and turning away, with only a backward point to stop him scoring. When a beautifully flighted and weighted left-arm spinner came along, he was good enough to edge it. Mohammad Rizwan has been dynamic in keeping to the spinners and further enhancing their value.

Rehan Ahmed had contributed four wickets with his zestful wrist-spin: with his low trajectory, as the ball skidded through, he was a good selection for his bowling. His batting is full of strokeplaying potential but it will drown if he interprets the Bazball project to be as cavalier as he likes. But then he was only copying Brook in sweeping — which the Pakistan batsmen have seldom done — in his first innings, and getting bowled behind his legs.

Calmness under fire, guts and resolution? Jamie Smith and Gus Atkinson had done it in their first innings and yet again Atkinson seemed to have more of a game plan than most of his top-order teammates. He radiated some assurance at the crease and had to be bowled out.

The big question is whether Smith's mistakes as a wicketkeeper are impacting on his batting. A missed stumping in the first Test did not matter. Dropping Salman Agha in the second was crucial, and so too the hard chance he dropped when Saud Shakeel had made 26 here, only to add more than a hundred runs off his own bat. Smith has the defence; he did not have to run down the pitch to cart Sajid over midwicket, such a high-risk shot. Was it the work of a frazzled mind when his decision-making until now has been near-faultless? The evidence is suggesting that he should give up the gloves and become number three, replacing Ollie Pope.

The rest of England's players obediently followed - obedient, that is, to the wishes of Pakistan's spinners. The home captain Shan Masood then knocked the runs off stylishly, even contemptuously. A target of 36 was no target. Reforming the approach of this England team is.

Lying there, I felt flat in more than one sense. It had not been a climactic, knife-edge series-decider. As soon as Shakil had blocked and Pakistan's spinners had bashed, England had crumbled. Stokes was so uncharacteristically muted, it was the opposite of a bang. The Pakistan players were fêted as they returned home, heroes for turning round the 1–0 deficit. Disconsolate England players had to hang around the hotel for their flight home. On 499 Tests, I had added a single; and that was it.

A friend, however, had suggested I should contact someone from the World Health Organisation who was visiting Islamabad: Hamid Jafri was going to watch a session or two of the third Test, when not finalising details of the WHO's polio eradication project in Pakistan. Afghanistan and Pakistan were two countries where poliomyelitis was spreading. It had threatened to spread in Gaza too, but Hamid had just supervised the vaccination of half a million children in south Gaza in spite of the ongoing war. The Israeli army did not want polio spreading to their own population.

Hamid had grown up in Karachi. His father had known Faiz Ahmed Faiz, one of my heroes. Faiz had been a colonel in Pakistan's army, became editor of the *Pakistan Times*, was forced to emigrate because of communist sympathies, and never became the wise leader that Pakistan needed. Exiled in Birmingham, Faiz composed songs, or *ghazals*, and poems on the theme of loss – loss, and yet there is hope. The male human voice is never so effective, in my ears, than when Faiz recites his Urdu verse, though I do not understand a word.

Soon polio-eradication volunteers were going from house to house in Pakistan. Hamid had negotiated in Kabul with the Taliban too. He said they were very prepared and straight-talking negotiators – if they did not agree with a proposal they said no – but were split between hardliners and those who wanted to liberalise, e.g. allow secondary education for girls. Hamid professed that he was 'an incurable optimist'. Even though he had soon to organise another half-million vaccinations in north Gaza amid the carnage, or *because* he was soon to organise another half-million vaccinations amid the carnage, he said he was optimistic about the world.

Ultimately, I reflect, this is the best of all things about cricket: the people you can meet, whether as a player or umpire or scorer or supporter or media person. There must be a billion people out there who follow cricket, pushing two billion as the population of India has exceeded China's. So you can go up to a quarter of the world's population, say hello, introduce yourself, and start a conversation on whether Virat Kohli is better than Steve Smith, or Yashasvi Jaiswal than Harry Brook. Within minutes you might well have identified a mutual acquaintance, and soon be exchanging email addresses. It is an inclusive social group: nobody is excluded. And as centrifugal forces seem to govern humankind as well as the universe, threatening to make the existing fabric unravel, including people is what we need.

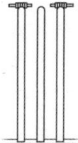

England's fourth Test in 2025 against India at Old Trafford was my 500th England Test, a landmark which nobody had reached before, not even Richie Benaud. A somewhat louder fanfare greeted Joe Root who, by scoring 150, shot up the table of the all-time highest Test run-scorers from fifth to second place, behind Sachin Tendulkar alone. Root's running of quick singles announced that he still had the appetite to reach this summit.

While savouring his innings I found myself comparing Root to Sir Jack Hobbs (from what I had read rather than seen), not in their differences but the similarities. Speed of foot, above all, so they played right forward or right back, not standing with static feet far apart like the power-hitters of today; and this footwork was translated into the quick singles for which Hobbs was the first to be famous. Root and Hobbs almost flowed into the ball's path and played strokes rather than shots, including the late cut, which had gone out of fashion in England before T20 arrived in 2003, and which has since been replaced by the reverse-slog or -sweep. Both are the most modest and self-effacing of Englishmen; knightable, too.

Nobody advocated four-day Tests during this England v India series, so slow were the pitches. Some blamed the extremely arid summer, and the balls going soft; others thought administrators were too intent on five-day matches and crowds. Either way, pitches in England were slowing down. So easily overlooked, they make every game individual.

More and more matches have to be staged at England's main grounds: new competitions for professional women players, to go with the Hundred for men and women, on top of previous schedules. The more matches staged on a pitch, the slower it becomes, unless the grass is grown longer, which encourages medium-pace, not the most skilful bowling. Homogenous hybrid pitches, part-natural grass and part-synthetic fibres, should be kept for limited-overs cricket; wearing-and-tearing has always been part of the five-day game. 'A new-ball pitch' was becoming the euphemism for one that went to sleep, or never had enough pace for the ball to carry to the keeper or slips. For all the excitements of Bazball batting, and they were numerous, tired pitches threatened the future health of Test cricket in England.

It was a pleasing landmark to reach – the first to cover 500 England Tests (to go with five neutral ones) – but I would not claim hard yards were involved. They must have added up to a total of at least 2000 days, or about six years; 24 Ashes series; more than 80 Tests at Lord's alone; thousands of taxis hailed, missed and shared, hundreds of dinners on expenses, dozens of witty colleagues, to whom much thanks for their companionship; hours of wrestling with telexes and Tandys, WiFi and connectivity; even a few press conferences; and memorable moments beyond counting. Those West Indian fast bowlers at full steam; Ian Botham pulling Australia all over Headingley and Old Trafford; Andrew Flintoff, English roast beef like Botham, and his double-wicket over at Edgbaston in the Ashes of 2005; the impresario supreme, Shane Warne; Kevin Pietersen running down the Headingley pitch to make Dale Steyn look medium-paced; Ben Stokes, for his 135★ of course, but also for run-outs of the utmost athleticism. It is the finest allrounders who mostly bestride this Valhalla of times recollected.

Great scenery too, like the Blue Mountains of Jamaica as seen from Sabina Park; Mount Maunganui; standing beneath, and even on top of, Table Mountain; a view from Old Trafford across to the sun-bathing Pennines. I know not about salvation. Yet, thanks to cricket, I have been able to lift up mine eyes to the hills.

Test players with the highest win percentage (over 100 Tests)

Name	Played	Won	Lost	Tied	Drawn	PercWon
ML Hayden	103	71	18	0	14	68.93
GD McGrath	124	84	20	0	20	67.74
JL Langer	105	70	17	0	18	66.66
RT Ponting	168	108	31	0	29	64.28
SK Warne	145	92	26	0	27	63.44
MA Starc	100	59	28	0	13	59.00
R Ashwin	106	61	28	0	17	57.54
NM Lyon	139	79	37	0	23	56.83
CA Pujara	103	58	27	0	18	56.31
SPD Smith	119	67	35	0	17	56.30
DA Warner	112	63	31	0	18	56.25
ME Waugh	128	72	27	0	29	56.25
MJ Clarke	115	64	32	0	19	55.65
CG Greenidge	108	57	14	0	37	52.77
IVA Richards	121	63	19	0	39	52.06
DL Haynes	116	60	15	0	41	51.72
HM Amla	124	64	34	0	26	51.61
GC Smith	117	60	30	0	27	51.28
SR Waugh	168	86	36	1	45	51.19
V Kohli	123	62	39	0	22	50.40
MV Boucher	147	74	37	0	36	50.34
MA Taylor	104	52	20	0	32	50.00
AB de Villiers	114	57	32	0	25	50.00
M Ntini	101	50	28	0	23	49.50
JH Kallis	166	82	42	0	42	49.39
G Kirsten	101	48	23	0	30	47.52
AJ Strauss	100	47	26	0	27	47.00
BA Stokes	114	53	49	0	12	46.49
IA Healy	119	55	29	0	35	46.21
JE Root	156	72	59	0	25	46.15

500 DECLARED

I Sharma	105	48	32	0	25	45.71
SCJ Broad	167	76	53	0	38	45.50
SM Pollock	108	49	27	0	32	45.37
JM Anderson	188	83	68	0	37	44.14
JM Bairstow	100	44	41	0	15	44.00
TG Southee	107	47	39	0	21	43.92
KS Williamson	105	44	38	0	23	41.90
AN Cook	161	67	55	0	39	41.61
Inzamam-ul-Haq	120	49	39	0	32	40.83
Harbhajan Singh	103	42	27	0	34	40.77
IR Bell	118	48	39	0	31	40.67
M Muralitharan	133	54	42	0	37	40.60
KP Pietersen	104	42	31	0	31	40.38
V Sehwag	104	42	28	0	34	40.38
KC Sangakkara	134	54	43	0	37	40.29
Wasim Akram	104	41	27	0	36	39.42
CA Walsh	132	52	43	0	37	39.39
LRPL Taylor	112	44	41	0	27	39.28
CH Lloyd	110	43	22	0	45	39.09
FDM Karunaratne	100	39	46	0	15	39.00
Younis Khan	118	46	45	0	27	38.98
DPMD Jayawardene	149	58	46	0	45	38.92
WPUJC Vaas	111	43	34	0	34	38.73
DC Boon	107	41	25	1	40	38.31
GP Thorpe	100	38	29	0	33	38.00
Salim Malik	103	39	14	0	50	37.86
MC Cowdrey	114	43	21	0	50	37.71
ST Jayasuriya	110	40	35	0	35	36.36
SR Tendulkar	200	72	56	0	72	36.00
VVS Laxman	134	47	41	0	46	35.07
RS Dravid	164	56	49	0	59	34.14
AD Mathews	119	39	54	0	26	32.77

SC Ganguly	113	37	35	0	41	32.74
A Kumble	132	43	33	0	56	32.57
G Boycott	108	35	20	0	53	32.40
IT Botham	102	33	32	0	37	32.35
CL Hooper	102	33	38	0	31	32.35
AR Border	156	50	46	1	59	32.05
Javed Miandad	124	39	23	0	62	31.45
DL Vettori	113	34	44	0	35	30.08
SP Fleming	111	33	42	0	36	29.72
BB McCullum	101	30	45	0	26	29.70
AJ Stewart	133	39	54	0	40	29.32
DI Gower	117	32	42	0	43	27.35
GA Gooch	118	32	42	0	44	27.11
MA Atherton	115	31	44	0	40	26.95
KC Brathwaite	100	26	57	0	17	26.00
BC Lara	131	32	63	0	36	24.42
CH Gayle	103	25	47	0	31	24.27
S Chanderpaul	164	39	77	0	48	23.78
SM Gavaskar	125	23	34	1	67	18.40
Kapil Dev	131	24	31	1	75	18.32
DB Vengsarkar	116	18	34	0	64	15.51

Selection of Test players (under 100 Tests)

50–99 Tests	Played	Won	Lost	Tied	Drawn	PercWon
AC Gilchrist	96	73	11	0	12	76.04
B Lee	76	54	11	0	11	71.05
DG Bradman	52	30	12	0	10	57.69
FS Trueman	67	34	11	0	22	50.74
Habibul Bashar	50	1	44	0	5	2.00

Tables courtesy of Benedict Bermange of Sky Sports. Figures correct up until July 2025.

Only the briefest mention of Brian Lara occurs in this text, which requires an explanation. On the one hand, as an individual, he comes first in my estimation for beauty of batsmanship; and the only time that we, as a family, have ever watched cricket all together was when Lara took West Indies to a one-wicket over Australia in Barbados in March 1999. On the other hand, cricket is also a team game. When Lara was first selected for West Indies in the early 1990s, they were still the world Test champions – and, when he finished, they had sunk to the bottom. Of course, West Indies ran out of fast bowlers, but my assertion remains: a side containing Lara ought to have won more than one-quarter of the Tests they played, and should not have lost 63 Tests, almost half. Individual record-breaking can be entertaining to watch but if it does not lead to victory, it is worthless in its effect; and if it prevents victory, it is even worse, e.g. Lara's 400* against England in Antigua in 2003–04, when he as captain batted on too long, so he could break the record of highest Test innings.

Acknowledgements

'Daddy! Why don't you write a book about your 500 Test matches?' Freya said. And where is the father who refuses his daughter?

I thank all the sports editors who have selected me for these Tests and tours. One retains a special affection for one's first captain in a cricket team, and so do I for my first sports editor, the late Geoffrey Nicholson. Since then I have been particularly grateful to Peter Corrigan, Colin Gibson, Jon Ryan, Peter Mitchell, Adam Sills and Julian Bennetts. I also thank the many sub-editors who have whipped my copy into shape and spotted mistakes: without them I might never have reached double figures, or even got off the mark. In addition to the thoroughly professional editing of Matt Lowing and Richard Whitehead, I must also thank a long-term friend Hugh Faulkner for his gimlet eye. Above all though, Megan Jones, for absorbing my late additions, like the best wicketkeepers take a wild throw-in.

PS The five non-England Tests I've covered:

1979–80 Brisbane: Australia v West Indies
1982–83 Faisalabad: Pakistan v Australia
1983–84 Delhi: India v West Indies
1983–84 Mumbai: India v West Indies
2010 Headingley: Pakistan v Australia

This is the way the world ends: Viv Richards climbs the Oval steps after his last Test innings in 1991.

When an old journalist leaves the box... My 500th Test at Rawalpindi in October 2024.